AN ORDINARY SOLDIER

AN ORDINARY SOLDIER

AFGHANISTAN: A FEROCIOUS ENEMY.
A BLOODY CONFLICT.
ONE MAN'S IMPOSSIBLE MISSION.

DOUG BEATTIE MC

with Philip Gomm

SIMON & SCHUSTER

London · New York · Sydney · Toronto

A CBS COMPANY

First published in Great Britain by Simon & Schuster UK Ltd, 2008
A CBS COMPANY

1 3 5 7 9 10 8 6 4 2

Simon & Schuster UK Ltd
1st Floor
222 Gray's Inn Road
London WC1X 8HB

www.simonsays.co.uk

Simon & Schuster Australia
Sydney

A CIP catalogue record for this book
is available from the British Library.

ISBN HB: 978-1-84737-376-2
ISBN TPB: 978-1-84737-377-9

Typeset in Bembo by M Rules
Printed in the UK by
CPI Mackays,Chatham ME5 8TD

The names of some serving soldiers and Afghans
have been changed to protect their identity.

To my dad, a proud man and a man to be proud of

CONTENTS

	Acknowledgements	ix
	Maps	xii–xvi
	Preface	xvii
1	Suicide Bomber	1
2	James Bond and Trying to Kill My Best Friend	17
3	Bully Boys, Rudolf Hess and Me	31
4	Big Blue Wing Commander	43
5	From Fun to Fighting	55
6	Old Enough to Know Better	69
7	Where Did It All Go Wrong?	85
8	Up Close and Personal	113
9	Taking Casualties	143
10	A Call to Prayer	167
11	A Question of Ethics	183
12	The Horrors of War	199
13	Out of Sight, Out of Mind	221
14	Ambush	235
15	That Was Close	253
16	Going Under	271

17	Pulling Out, Going Back	285
18	Going Home, Going to the Palace, Going Back Again	293
	Epilogue Citation	303
	Glossary	307
	Picture Credits	310
	Index	311

ACKNOWLEDGEMENTS

First and foremost I must express my deepest thanks to my wife Margaret, my children Leigh and Luke, and the rest of my family, for their unflinching love and support during all my years in military service. They are the ones who have kept me on the straight and narrow and given me a reason to do my duty – they have also wholeheartedly encouraged me in the writing of this book.

I am also very pleased to publicly acknowledge my colleagues at the Ministry of Defence – not least Colonel Ben Bathurst at the Directorate of Defence Public Relations (Army) and my commanding officer Lieutenant Colonel Ed Freely – for their backing of this project and their timely and appropriate advice when required. I owe co-writer and friend Philip Gomm a huge debt of gratitude for helping bring *An Ordinary Soldier* to fruition. Variously he nudged, cajoled and shoved me towards the finishing line.

Thanks too to Martin Pick, who helped us negotiate the path to publication. His enthusiasm and wisdom led us to our indomitable agent Andrew Lownie. He in turn introduced us to inspirational editor Kerri Sharp and the rest of her team at Simon & Schuster, amongst them Martin Soames who repeatedly offered wise counsel.

It would be remiss of me not to mention the names of some others who helped me achieve my goal: Kate, Iona, Finn, Raini, Tony Mewse – thank you all. Recognition should also go to Humfrey Hunter for his extreme good grace.

I must also acknowledge the tenacity and bravery of film-maker Sean Langan. His Channel 4 documentary about the Battle for Garmsir rightly won high praise.

An Ordinary Soldier would of course never have been written if not for the events in Afghanistan in the summer of 2006. I pay heartfelt tribute to the servicemen alongside whom I fought, and also to the Afghans, who have remained resolutely positive in the face of their country's troubles. Last of all I thank my other family, I R IRISH, with whom it has been a pleasure and honour to serve.

Faugh-A-Ballagh

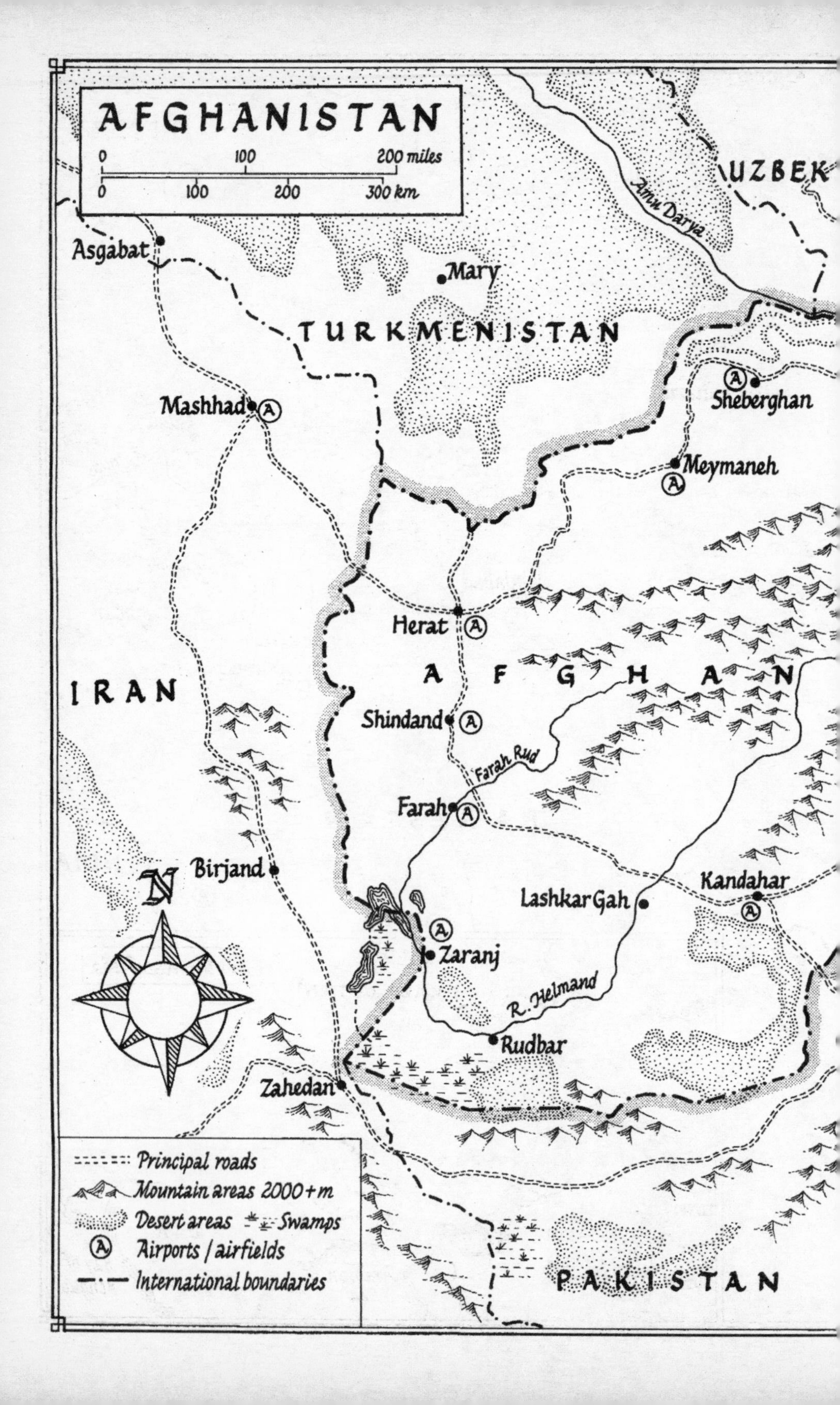
AFGHANISTAN
0
100
200 miles
0
100
200
300 km
UZBEK
Amu Darya
Asgabat
Mary
TURKMENISTAN
Mashhad
Sheberghan
Meymaneh
Herat
AFGHAN
IRAN
Shindand
Farah Rud
Farah
Birjand
Kandahar
Lashkar Gah
Zaranj
R. Helmand
Rudbar
Zahedan
N
Principal roads
Mountain areas 2000+m
Desert areas
Swamps
Airports / airfields
International boundaries
PAKISTAN

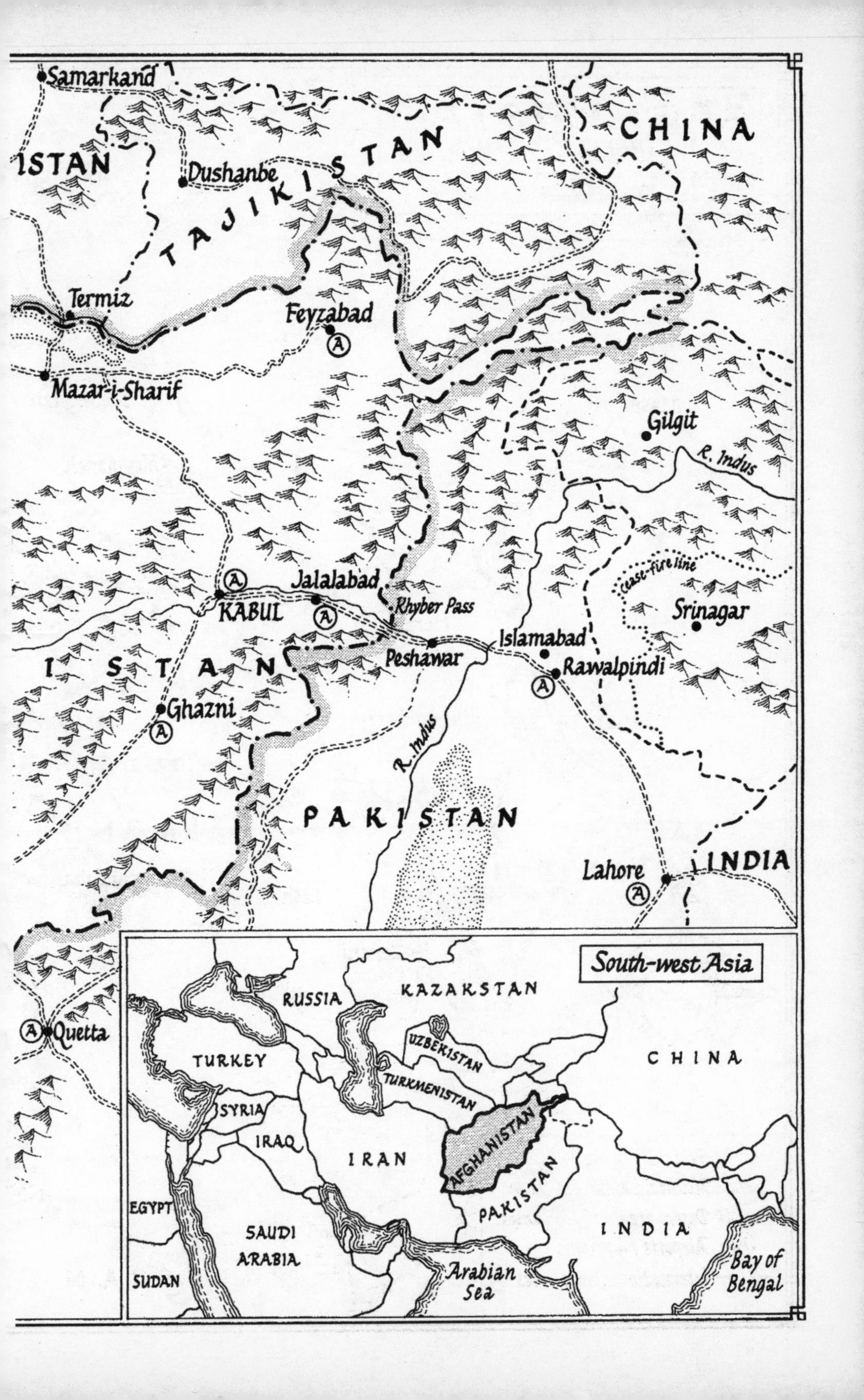
Samarkand
ISTAN
TAJIKISTAN
Dushanbe
CHINA
Termiz
Feyzabad
A
Mazar-i-Sharif
Gilgit
R. Indus
cease-fire line
Jalalabad
KABUL
Khyber Pass
Srinagar
Islamabad
Peshawar
Rawalpindi
ISTAN
Ghazni
R. Indus
PAKISTAN
INDIA
Lahore
Quetta
South-west Asia
RUSSIA
KAZAKSTAN
UZBEKISTAN
TURKEY
TURKMENISTAN
CHINA
SYRIA
AFGHANISTAN
IRAQ
IRAN
PAKISTAN
EGYPT
SAUDI ARABIA
INDIA
SUDAN
Arabian Sea
Bay of Bengal

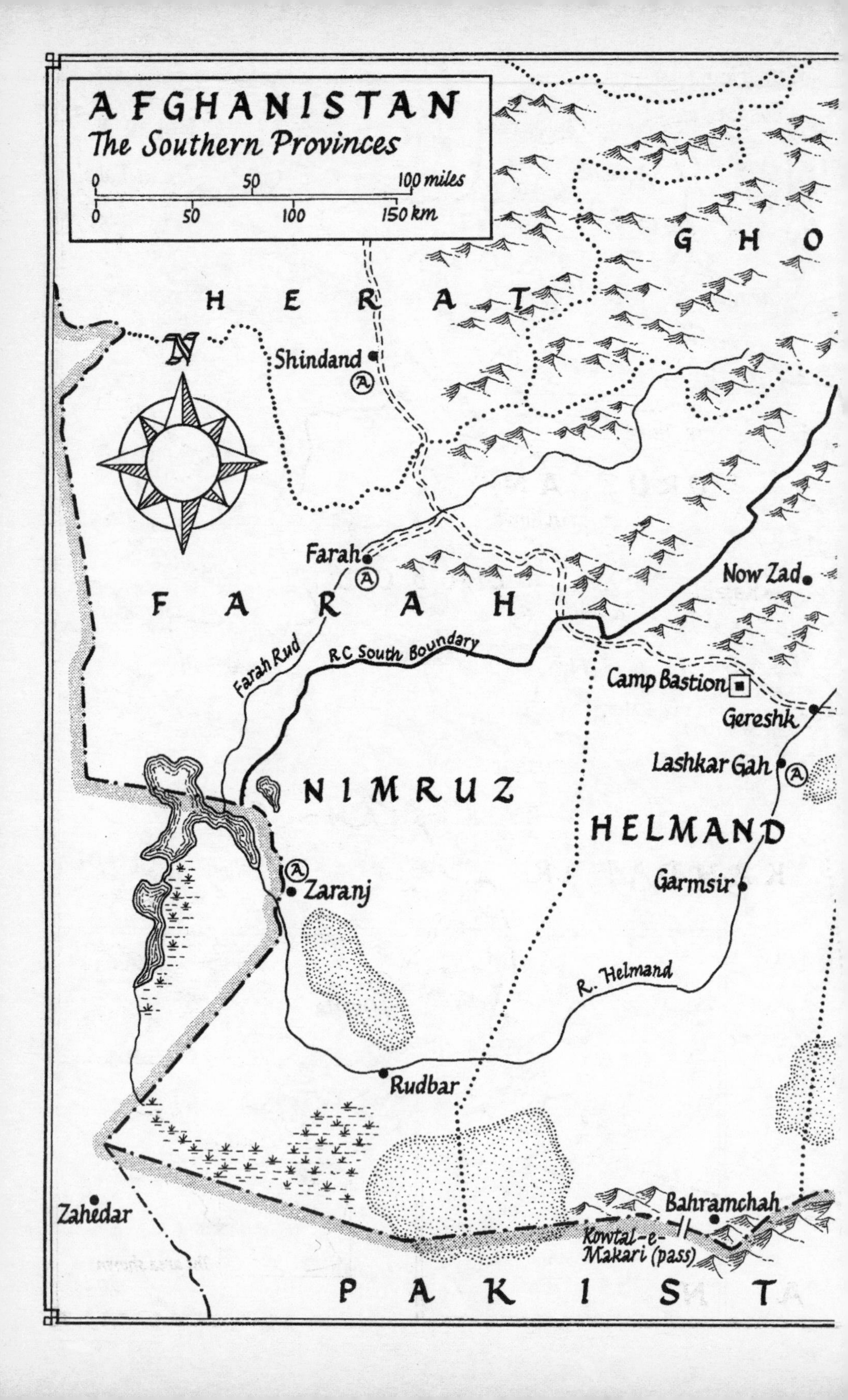

AFGHANISTAN
The Southern Provinces
0
50
100 miles
0
50
100
150 km
N
HERAT
GHO
Shindand
A
Farah
FARAH
Farah Rud
RC South Boundary
Now Zad
Camp Bastion
Gereshk
Lashkar Gah
NIMRUZ
HELMAND
Zaranj
Garmsir
R. Helmand
Rudbar
Zahedar
Bahramchah
Kowtal-e-Makari (pass)
PAKIST

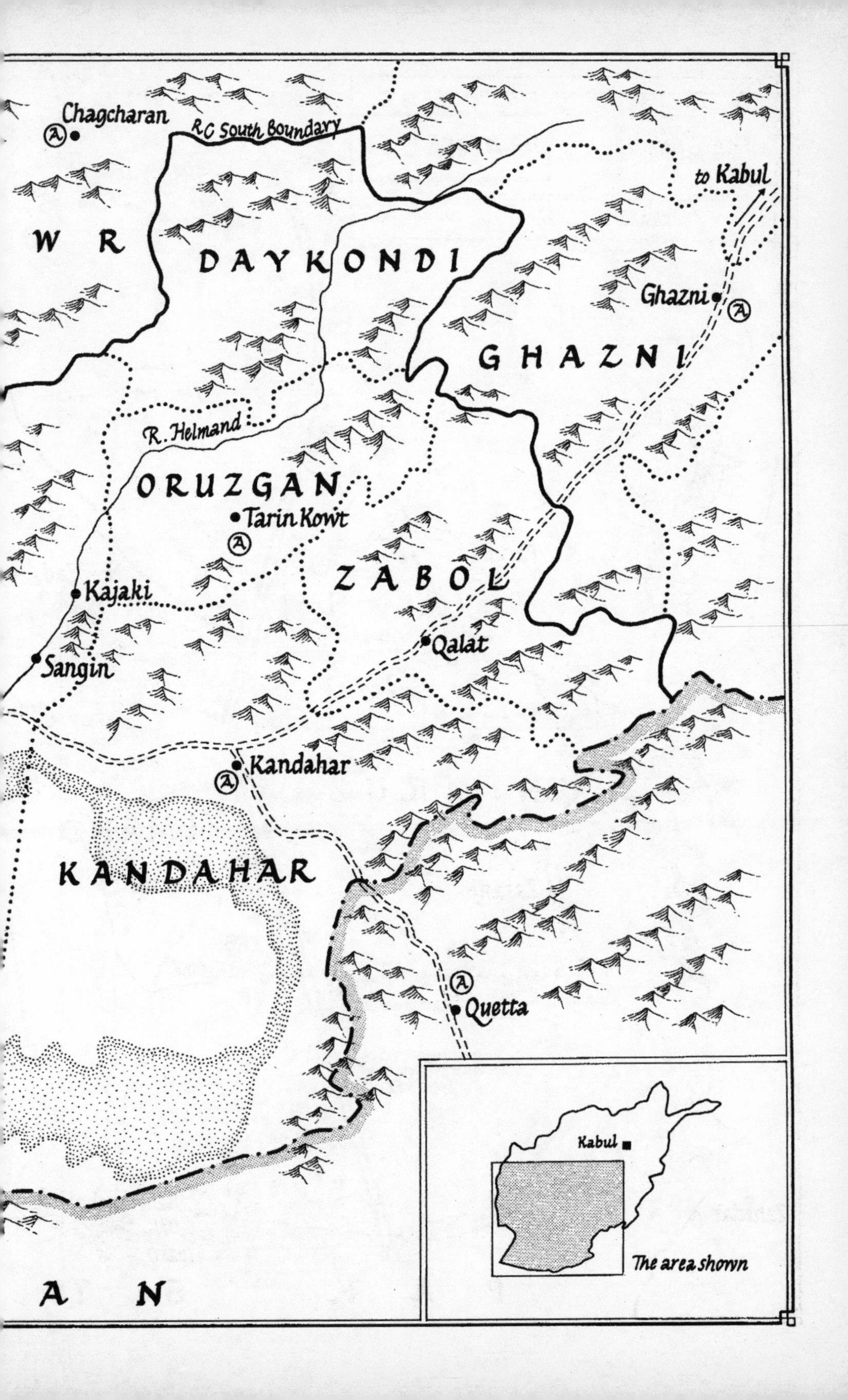

Chagcharan
RC South Boundary
to Kabul
W R
DAYKONDI
Ghazni
GHAZNI
R. Helmand
ORUZGAN
Tarin Kowt
ZABOL
Kajaki
Qalat
Sangin
Kandahar
KANDAHAR
Quetta
Kabul
The area shown
A N

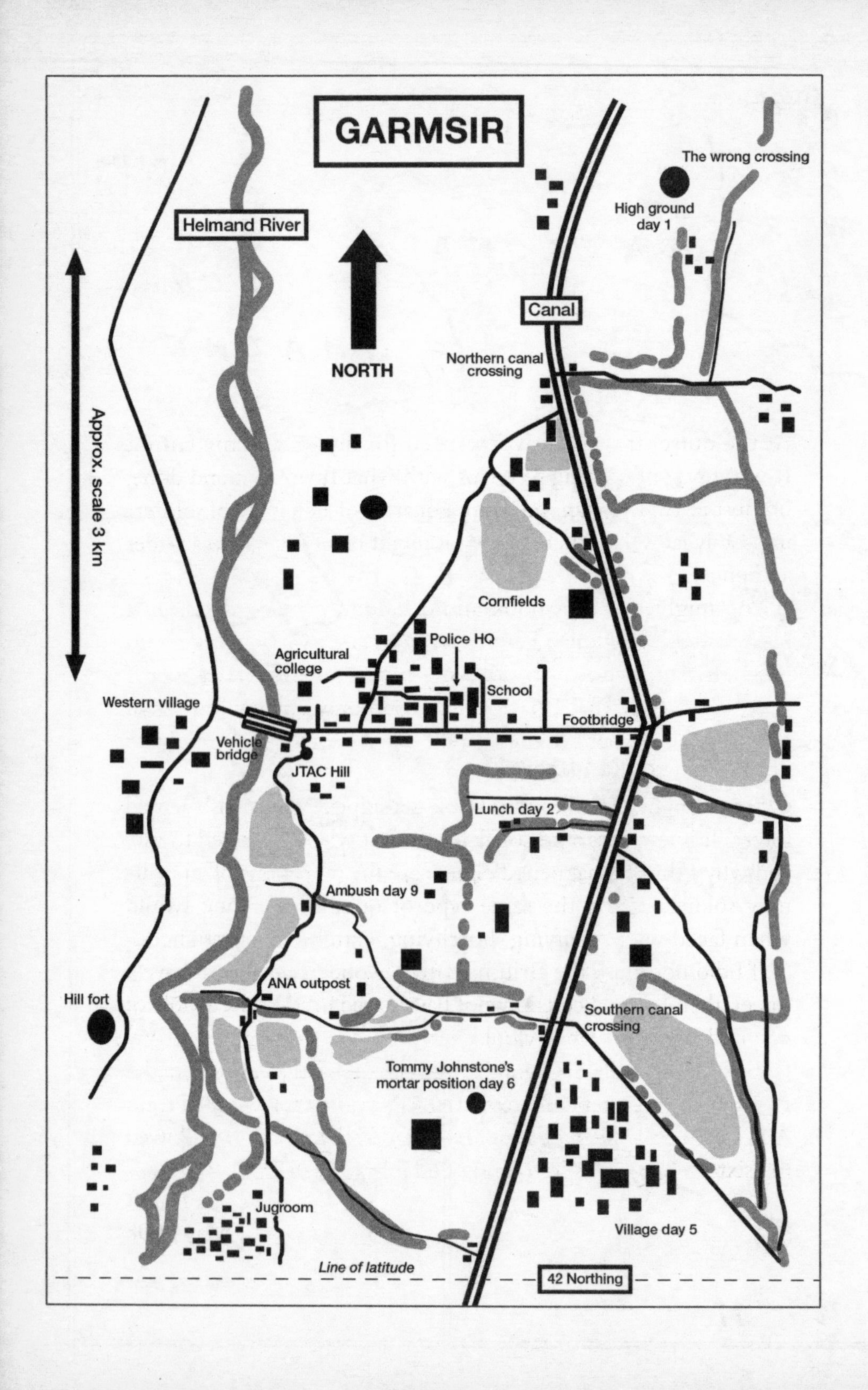
GARMSIR
Helmand River
NORTH
Canal
The wrong crossing
High ground day 1
Approx. scale 3 km
Northern canal crossing
Cornfields
Police HQ
Agricultural college
School
Western village
Footbridge
Vehicle bridge
JTAC Hill
Lunch day 2
Ambush day 9
ANA outpost
Hill fort
Southern canal crossing
Tommy Johnstone's mortar position day 6
Jugroom
Village day 5
Line of latitude
42 Northing

PREFACE

At the outset this book was written for myself and my family. It was a way of coming to terms with what I had seen and done, not just in Afghanistan, but over a quarter of a century of soldiering. Only later did others suggest it might be of interest to a wider audience.

You might read this book and decide to criticise decisions I have made and actions I have taken. You are very welcome to do so – it was my choice to open my life to scrutiny. However, I hope you accept that I have already endlessly analysed my own actions – please believe me when I say there is no greater critic of Doug Beattie than himself.

Some might also think this book is a snipe at the British armed forces. It is not. It is a personal account of what happened to me, and why I think it happened. These are the reflections of an ordinary soldier, asking the same type of questions anyone would when faced with terrifying, horrifying, extreme circumstances.

If I did not think the British Army a wonderful place to have a career, then I would certainly not have stayed in it for the whole of my adult life thus far. I would certainly not have agreed to my Commanding Officer's request to delay my departure from the Royal Irish Regiment and return to Afghanistan for a second tour. And I most certainly would not have signed the papers that allowed my sixteen-year-old son to enlist and follow in my footsteps.

Doug Beattie
May 2008

ONE
SUICIDE BOMBER

12 DECEMBER 2006

When it came, the explosion sounded rather insignificant. Muffled, rumbling, it could almost have been a roll of thunder. But there was nothing ordinary about its effects.

Shattered glass covered me as the windows blew in, drumming against my back, showering my hair, going down my neck.

The blast forced me towards the floor, bending me double.

Dust engulfed the room and everyone in it.

Everything happened so fast, chaos coming out of nowhere, scrambling my mind. I could see and feel what was going on, but couldn't make any immediate sense of it, my brain trying frantically to catch up with events.

An instant earlier and everything had been normal, as expected, routine even. I had been having lunch, sharing a meal with local members of the Afghan security forces, in the compound of the Governor of Helmand Province in Lashkar Gah, southern Afghanistan. I had already been feeling out of place, a long way from home, sitting there on a matted filthy carpet, next to men whose faces portrayed a lifetime of hardship and low expectation. Now it was as if a million miles separated me from my family and friends left behind in the UK.

With the others I had been digging into a communal pot of rice and meat – was it goat? lamb? – scooping out handfuls of food and piling it on the flat circles of bread balanced on my lap, adding fresh tomatoes from another bowl, talking as I ate.

Now the meal, like everything else, was strewn all around. Not that you could easily tell what was food and what wasn't; a layer of grey covered the contents of the room.

I fumbled about for the handset of the radio, all fingers and thumbs.

'Topaz Zero, this is Topaz 40. Contact explosion. Wait. Out.'

It was a struggle to keep the panic out of my voice, the words calm and coherent. I had to swallow back the fear.

The message flashed to the British base in the town. After five months serving in Afghanistan this was far from the first time I had made a contact report, but never before had the bland wording hidden such a catastrophic event.

I pushed the mic towards the signaller who was with me and shouted at him to get his helmet on and grab his rifle. He should have been the one who made the radio call, but he sat there stunned, rooted to the spot, his face painted with dirt, just his eyes visible behind the mask. I'd only worked with him on a couple of other occasions. I wasn't even sure of his real name. Everyone else called him Chilli. So I did, too. He never objected. Chilli was just nineteen years old, with a soft youthful face, yet his hair was already receding. This was going to do nothing to stop that.

I groped for my own gear, trying to steady my shaking hands, snatching hold of the SA80, struggling to pull on the body armour. Forcing my helmet down on my head, I stumbled upstairs to find the epicentre of the blast.

I didn't have far to go. Just ten small steps.

Emerging through the wooden door into the glare of daylight, the sight that met me was wretched.

I looked around the elongated courtyard trying to take in what I was seeing. An eerie silence hung over the scene as the dust cloud finally settled like a curtain falling on the last act of a hideous farce.

I stood there watching, a witness rather than a participant. To my left two men crawled – no, dragged themselves – slowly, pitifully into a flowerbed, seeking some shelter amongst the stunted shrubs. I couldn't make out any of their wounds, but there was little doubt they were fatally hurt, the blood that drenched their white robes telling its own story. With barely a murmur they both curled up amongst the withered plants to die.

Diagonally across the yard, perhaps twenty metres away, two more were already dead. Their contorted remains lay sprawled on the dirt, huge chunks of flesh missing from the bodies, fluids seeping into the Afghan earth.

Directly in front of me, by the main entrance to the compound, were parked a pair of open-backed pickup trucks, their bodywork peppered with holes, the windows smashed in by the blast. Hesitantly I walked over towards them, wanting to help if I could, but frightened of what I might find. In the first, behind the wheel, sat a young bearded man, as still as a statue, he too, far beyond help. His complexion gave it away; where it should have been dark, swarthy, it was pale, the life and colour sapped from it.

I turned my attention to the second vehicle. There were two people in it: one was propped up against the tailgate, facing away from me, seemingly unscathed; the other was on the floor of the truck squirming about in a crimson, sticky mess, seeking some sort of comfort from the metal beneath him, scratching and scraping, trying to dig his way out of pain, looking to ease the agony.

The silence had started to lift and screams, shouts and moans were beginning to fill the void. The movement of the second man slowed and stopped as he too succumbed to his injuries, his weak grip on life easily prised away, the blood already settling and congealing around his corpse.

I grabbed hold of the other Afghan by the arm and tried to

turn him towards me. As I twisted him round, I recoiled in shock, letting go. The majority of the front of his body was missing. Much of the skin on his face had been flayed away; what remained hung limply, looking as if it had been peeled back with a paring knife. The eye sockets were empty. I stared, mesmerised, at the vacant holes. His jaw had been wrenched from its anchors, resting now on his neck, forming a huge, ghastly, gaping grin. Innumerable fragments of the bomb had ripped through his smock and then into his torso, puncturing the chest and stomach, hacking away big swathes of skin, bone and tissue.

He must have borne the brunt of the explosion; been almost nose to nose with the suicide bomber when he blew himself to kingdom come.

The effects of the detonation assaulted all my senses. For a quarter of a century I had been a professional soldier. At various times I'd seen some horrible things, many of them in recent weeks. But here, laid out in front of me, all the possible horrors of war had come together in a nightmarish scene. It was as bad as you could imagine and then some.

The competing smells of burnt flesh, singed clothing, charred metal and flaming petrol mixed and swirled, contaminating the air. And there was something else – the unmistakable coppery odour of human blood. You could taste it on your tongue.

Other Afghans were now running about, trying to bring order to the aftermath, trying to help their friends, pouring out their anguish for the victims. Urgent voices came from all quarters of the compound but I couldn't understand anything of what was being said. The noise invaded my head and yet I felt completely alone and disengaged. Nothing of what was happening seemed to have form or direction. I was like an impotent speck caught up in a vortex of frantic activity. The noise was building to a crescendo; it was like the sea roaring in my ears. I managed to pick out some identifiable sounds, sirens in particular, probably from ambulances arriving from the nearby hospital, but the rest was just a jumbled mess.

Then a cry in English cut through the maelstrom: 'Captain, we have to go. Now!'

I turned to face Namir. My interpreter was just twenty-two but already married with two children. He was excellent at what he did – speaking Pashtu and Italian as well as English – and by Afghan standards he earned a good salary, but his job wasn't one to be envied. Many of his friends and neighbours hated that he worked for the British forces. Already he had received death threats because of his choice of employer. Namir was always nervous. Now there was a look of panic on his face. Or was it bewilderment?

With Namir close behind, I headed back to the main building and down the steps into the half-basement where we had been eating to send another sitrep (situation report), telling whoever was listening that at least eight people had died – including the bomber – and at least eight more were injured.

As I relayed my message it became clear that Namir, Chilli and I were on our own; the whole contingent from the Afghan Protection Force – whose job it was to guard the section of the Governor's compound where we worked – were long gone. The Governor remained upstairs in his second-floor office, shielded by his personal bodyguards, but we weren't going to feature on their list of priorities.

From outside came more shouting. Through the jagged shards of glass framing one of the broken windows I could see uniformed men frantically waving their arms.

'Namir, what's going on?' I demanded.

'They think there's another suicide bomber in the compound.'

This was not news I wanted to hear.

I got back on the radio. I could hardly believe what I was saying. 'Topaz Zero this is Topaz 40. Do not send the Quick Reaction Force. Repeat, do not send the QRF. Chance of another suicide attack.' My mouth was as dry as a desert, a result of nerves, and the dust I had ingested in the blast, and I struggled to get the words out.

The company commander in Lashkar Gah came on the radio network from our base at the HQ of the Provincial Reconstruction Team (PRT) four miles away. I confirmed with him that the QRF was to stay put. It's funny how things turn out. Just that morning he and I had had a conversation about how unsafe the town was. He urged me to call for help if we ever got into a tight corner and said he would come running. Very much in that corner, there I was trying to stop him carrying out his promise. But if I had allowed him to keep it, it would only have resulted in more men being endangered.

Reluctantly he accepted what I told him, before adding: 'If things get worse, if you change your mind, we'll get you out.'

If things got worse? How much worse could it be?

An insurgent had just got through two security checkpoints and blown himself to bits. Seven others were also dead. And now there was the very real possibility of another would-be martyr adding to the carnage. I was without Afghan backup and had just one British military colleague with me as support. How could the situation get any fucking worse?

I was terrified. My stomach churned and my heart raced.

What I really wanted, what I was desperate for, was to be overruled and for assistance to get on its way. I had an overwhelming sense of helplessness. This was now a game of chance, with the odds stacked against me, my fate out of my hands, my future left to the whim of some fanatical bomber who might or might not use the opportunity to meet his maker and take me with him. I could only imagine it was like being on a plane about to crash. You are alive, but know with utmost certainty that death will visit shortly and there is absolutely nothing in the world you can do to influence the outcome.

I want to say I felt a sense of paternalism and responsibility towards Chilli and Namir – God, I was old enough to be their dad – but most of all I was scared for me. I did not want to die.

There weren't many options open to us. Going back into the courtyard would only bring us face to face with any other bomber. Even going out through the shattered window would lead us to the same place. And anyway, where could we go from there? We had no transport and the environment outside the compound was probably as hostile as within it, with much of the local population not well disposed towards the British.

The only thing that stood between a second bomber and us was a glass door. I pointed my rifle at the entrance, double-checked that the safety was off and put my finger on the trigger, ready to shoot anyone who appeared through it.

Even before that moment, before my conversation earlier that day, the job of working in the compound and liaising with the Afghan National Police (ANP), the Afghan National Army (ANA) and the National Directorate of Security (NDS), the government's intelligence branch, had been recognised as important but high-risk.

All across Helmand Province, coalition commanders with the International Security and Assistance Force (ISAF) were nervous. Their men rarely travelled off-base unless in large groups with heavy weapons and medics.

In Lashkar Gah, the capital of Helmand, being somewhat out of sight and hence out of mind, the arrangements were a bit more flexible. They needed to be or else we would never have got anything done. But the bulk of the British contingent still wouldn't move without strength of numbers. However, I generally made my own ad hoc arrangements. If I had not then I would never have got to where I was supposed to be going. It was the reality of life on the ground.

When I first arrived in Lashkar Gah, transport was provided by the men of 21 Air Defence Battery Royal Artillery, who were based in the town. We also came to rely on assistance from foreign coalition colleagues serving with ISAF and this worked fine for two or three months. But ISAF became increasingly reluctant to help. The commanders were worried our movements were setting too regular a pattern and hence making us especially vulnerable to attack from the Taliban. So Chilli and I were forced to improvise by thumbing lifts. Luckily there were some people who were happy to oblige. The keenest was the man who ran the US-sponsored Poppy Eradication Programme (PEP) in Helmand, Charles Bennett. A jovial Irish Catholic from County Tyrone, he had served for many years in the Ulster Defence Regiment (UDR), leaving only when it disbanded. In his early life he had spent time living in Rhodesia. Charles was the epitome of the well-read, well-travelled adventurer. Some would say he was also well dressed, though in my view his sartorial style was more eccentric than fashionable. Certainly you could always see him coming. He insisted on wearing an old-style pith helmet that lent him a colonial air. This was no shrinking violet.

The PEP was a civilian organisation, protected by private security. The guards were mainly non-English-speaking Nepalese; not English or Indian Gurkhas, but soldiers from the Nepalese Army whose operational experience came from fighting the Maoist insurgency in their homeland. They were always extremely willing to help but, given the language barriers, communication was haphazard. However, we had no real choice but to grin and bear it. We needed them to get around.

Suicide attacks were not merely an academic threat. During each month of my Afghan tour, there had been at least one such incident in the region we operated in, the worst claiming the lives of twenty-six Afghan civilians.

And the Governor's compound had also been hit before, suffering collateral damage in a blast aimed at a Foreign and Commonwealth Office (FCO) representative being driven past at the time. Fifteen Afghans had died, though there were no British casualties – at least not physical ones. A woman called Rachel was amongst the FCO group. She was in her late twenties, slim, with long brown hair cascading down, framing her face. We used to meet most days. She lived with us at the PRT. On this, her first foreign assignment, she was the interface between the Governor and the FCO back in Whitehall. The attack left her completely overwhelmed; shaken to her roots. She would only emerge from the safety of the camp once more – on the day she left the province and then the country. For her it had been a stark introduction to the reality of our country's foreign policy.

But despite Rachel's lucky escape, there had been British fatalities in Lashkar Gah. In October a suicide bomber managed to kill Royal Marine Gary Wright whilst he was patrolling the outskirts of the town. A second commando was injured. Two Afghan children also died, their deaths barely mentioned, just another brief footnote in Afghanistan's desperate recent history.

Such was the threat background to our little operation in Lash, the Governor of Helmand's supposed stronghold, but despite it we needed to get out and about on a daily basis to meet with our counterparts in the Afghan police and army, and the NDS. Food was often the icebreaker with these people. Having a meal together, sitting cross-legged on threadbare carpets, was a key part of our diplomatic approach. It gave us a chance to talk about the future – security, patrolling, policing, intel – but also the past. Anything and everything came up: the Soviet occupation, the Taliban, previous jobs, home, family, the lot. The difficult part was trying not to eat too much, the unwillingness based not on a reluctance to increase our waistline, but rather an urge to preserve it. Diarrhoea and vomiting were common ailments amongst our troops who dealt with the locals. More than a few British soldiers could testify to just how debilitating the effects of D & V were. Not that I had ever envisaged these occasions might actually be the death of me; that a meal with Afghan colleagues might be my own last supper.

It seemed as if we sat there for an age, waiting for the next attack. But that day it did not come. Ten minutes passed. Then ten more. Finally after perhaps half an hour I decided to risk going back outside. Cautiously I re-climbed the steps, rifle gripped tight, leaving Chilli with the radio. Once again I emerged into the sunshine, the pleasant warmth on my face, the Afghan flag fluttering lightly over the compound against the bright blue of the sky, a gentle view completely at odds with the carnage below. The casualty figures continued to change. Two more of the injured were now dead. The number of fatalities was up to ten, amongst them, the Chief of the Vashir District, who had arrived for a meeting with the Governor.

With the situation coming under some sort of control and the likelihood of another attack decreasing, there was a chance to take in more of the chaos. Everywhere I turned my head there was another horror. I would see something new and for a second not be able to work out what I was looking at. Then the shapes became recognisable: a hand, a foot, a finger, all scattered carelessly about the place, incongruously separated from the bodies they once belonged to.

Amongst the cadavers was that of the bomber – in pieces. His head had been torn from his shoulders by the explosion. A large part of his brain lay on the ground, next to the broken skull, a grey mass quickly drying out. How old had he been? Twenty-five? Thirty? It was hard to tell.

What remained of his torso was up against a wall, naked and scorched, the clothes burnt off and blown away at the moment of detonation. Blood was everywhere; thick clots, smudges, specks sprayed on to innumerable surfaces.

I heard some shouting from behind me. The Governor and his security staff were leaving. For a moment he stopped, surveying the scene prime-ministerially, and then he was off, saying nothing to us.

Chilli and I remained in the compound for four hours. All that time, the Afghans were trying to clean up the mess, exhaustive in their efforts to recover each of the bodies, be they intact or in hundreds of pieces.

It wasn't the sort of environment in which to try and make conversation.

'Sorry your friends are dead,' was all I could think of saying to one of them as he tidied around me. Namir translated.

'Inshallah,' came the reply. 'God's will.'

'How did the bomber get past the guards?'

There were shrugs. 'Don't know.' Don't care.

To Afghans violence is routine. Life is cheap. They take a fatalistic approach to such matters.

Finally I decided things were secure enough for us to leave too, and head for the safety of the PRT building. We walked warily out of the front gate and into the bustling street to catch a ride, hopefully from Charles and his colleagues next door at the PEP. It was as if nothing had happened. There was no police cordon, no blue tape keeping back the curious. The road was teeming with bikes, cars and jingly lorries, not to mention people. Some were urgently forcing their way through the crowd to their destinations whilst others just stood around talking. More still sat in a line along the compound wall, waiting in vain to petition the Governor on some important issue or other. This was not to be their day.

Even as we went, there was a reminder of what had taken place. Part of a skull had been thrown over the wall into the road. It was lying there in the dust, perhaps thirty metres from the scene of the blast, passers-by barely bothering to afford it a second glance. Attached to the sliver of bone was hair – and an ear. As we paused to look at it an Afghan soldier came running after us. It seemed the authorities had managed to recover some bits of the bomb. He handed me a palmful of ball bearings. Then, in a most bizarre moment, he tried to give me a leg, half-wrapped in a piece of plastic. From the man responsible, I was told. I couldn't understand what on earth I was supposed to do with it. The soldier explained. After a previous suicide attack the hand of the bomber had been taken away for forensic analysis. I was doubtful about the whole exercise. 'Thank you,' I murmured. Then, rather uncomfortably, the four of us stood there as I dutifully tried to raise the Ammunition Technical Officer

(ATO) on the radio to ask whether he wanted what was on offer. He accepted the metal hardware, but passed on the limb. Apologetically I handed it back to the soldier.

In the days after the attack, I started to calm down, my nervousness disappearing as each successive hour passed without incident. It was now nearly Christmas and I even dared to look forward to the end of my tour in the middle of January. Then I received a call from a rather unexpected quarter. One morning whilst I was out of the office, someone rang the HQ in Lash and asked for me. He passed on his British mobile number when told I wasn't there and said I should ring him back.

Once at my desk I punched the keypad and heard the connection being made. It rang just a couple of times.

'Hello?' said a voice I thought I recognised.

'Doug Beattie here. You left me a message. Asked me to call.'

'Ah yes, Doug. Do you know who this is?'

'No, sorry, I haven't a clue,' I replied, still not quite placing the speaker.

'Brigadier Ed Butler.'

The commander of 16 Air Assault Brigade, whom I had been serving under in Afghanistan earlier that year.

What had I done to warrant a call from him? What trouble was Beattie in now?

'How are you doing, sir? Nice to talk to you.' Unconsciously I stood up from my chair.

'Why are you still in Afghanistan? You were supposed to leave.'

'I was kidnapped by 3 Commando Brigade in the same way 16 Air Assault Brigade kidnapped me. Not much longer now, though.'

'Doug, let me get to the point. You are going to get an MC.'

Me? A Military Cross? What on earth for?

'It's being awarded for your part in the capture and defence of Garmsir back in September. Congratulations.'

I didn't know how to respond.

'Thank you, sir.'

'Stay safe, keep your head down. Don't do anything stupid.'

I replaced the handset.

Perhaps some would have seen this coming. But to me it was a bolt from the blue. Garmsir, a town in the south of Helmand, the Taliban's gateway to the province . . . I had been trying hard to forget about my time there. It had been an awful two weeks, though in my view that was what came with the territory. I was just doing my job. A tough job, a dangerous job, yes. But the one I had signed up for. So why this unexpected honour? For a quarter of a century I had served my country. To be recognised in this way at such a late stage in my career was a humbling experience.

I sat back down and thought about what it all meant. Yes it was a tribute to me and, through their long sufferance and support, to my wife Margaret and our children. Yet it was also an honour to the Afghans who had worked with me over the past months. But as well as pride, I felt deep embarrassment, guilt even. The guilt of being singled out for praise when I knew I was only one of the many; the achievement that of the many, not of any individual – surely least of all me – and not just in Garmsir but across the whole of Helmand. And unlike me, several of my regimental colleagues would not be going home to speak of their experiences; would not be reunited with those who loved them. They were dead.

Weighed down by a tangle of thoughts and emotions I took myself away from the hustle and bustle of the busy HQ and cried.

I could not shake the news of the decoration from my mind. The perverseness of the situation stayed with me. Honoured for killing people. Decorated whilst others were not. Alive when so many had been killed. I carried a sense of shame.

Christmas 2006 arrived and I knew what I should do.

A lot of the men would put up decorations. Others allowed

themselves a furtive swig of the booze that had been smuggled in. But there was plenty to remind us this was not a normal Christmas. The patrols continued up and down Helmand Province, and so did the attacks.

On the morning of the 25th I caught the milk-run flight from Lash up to the main British base at Camp Bastion. I had made a promise to myself that I would go and pay my respects to the dead.

At both ends of the day there were religious services at Bastion. Even for those without a spiritual bone in their body, the ceremonies were seized on as chance for reflection. As ever, attendance was high. But I wasn't part of either congregation. I had my own pilgrimage to make.

In the middle of the camp lay the HQ compound. With armed guards at the entrance, and surrounded by razor wire, it was a camp within a camp. Standing discreetly, unassumingly, beside one of the sand-coloured command tents, was a memorial. A small cross had been moulded out of spent 30mm cannon cartridge cases. It sat atop a cairn. Set into the stones was a brass plaque full of names: the British war dead from the campaign in southern Afghanistan.

To me, four names stood out from the rest. They were men with whom I'd served.

Captain David Patten
Lance-Corporal Paul Muirhead
Lance-Corporal Luke McCulloch
Ranger Anare Draiva

They were all from my regiment, the best regiment in the world, the Royal Irish, 1st Battalion – 1 R IRISH. I'd known them as young men who had joined up full of life, optimism and hope. I said a silent prayer and took some photos to send to the men's families.

That evening I flew back down to Lashkar Gah, the helicopter skimming the bone-dry desert, mapping the contours of the earth as it went, me watching the myriad stones, rocks and pebbles below merging into a speeding blur.

It was only a short flight by Chinook, the double set of rotors whirring above my head, chopping through the thin Afghan air. But there was still enough time to ask the type of questions that exercise every soldier sooner or later, questions that were now constantly pushing their way to the front of my mind. Why did these others die and not me? Why were their cards marked? How do you account for the randomness of war? How in God's name had I, an average Protestant boy from Portadown, ended up in one of the most inhospitable countries imaginable, fighting an enemy whose ancestors had already seen off two British armies? How on earth had I found myself in such a desperate situation as that in Garmsir, and how had I got away with it? How did I survive Garmsir? How did any of us? Garmsir. Why were my actions there worthy of decoration? Garmsir. My thoughts kept coming back to Garmsir. Christ, Garmsir. How the hell did I ever end up there?

I suppose if you go back far enough it was all down to Raymond Best. God, that was a long time ago.

TWO

JAMES BOND AND TRYING TO KILL MY BEST FRIEND

When I was fifteen years old I shot my best mate in the head.

I didn't mean to.

Poor old Raymond. He didn't see it coming. Not surprising given the velocity of the bullet.

We were bored, my friends and I.

It was raining stair rods outside – again. There was nothing on TV – again. We had no money to go to the shops – again. What on earth could we do? I thought I had the answer. We'd play with guns. At the time my dad was serving in the UDR. He kept his personal-protection pistol under his pillow upstairs in my parents' bedroom. Appropriately for kids with imagination, it was a Walther PPK, as used by one 007, James Bond. I pushed my hand deep under the covers, feeling for the cold metal of the barrel and breech. It took me only a moment to find. The magazine was already locked in position. In the front room Raymond and John stood waiting, wondering what I had been doing.

As I reappeared and they turned their gaze to my right hand, it soon became apparent. I started to wave the gun about, having already pulled back the slide and cocked the weapon. Without warning and with barely a second thought I lifted my arm, raising the PPK to head height. The gun was pointed straight at Ray. I pulled the trigger. I was no more than a metre away from him. Maybe closer. He certainly wasn't smiling, but didn't seem scared either, just incredulous perhaps that he was staring down the barrel of a gun – not that he really had much time to react. It was all over so quickly. The trigger slipped past the point of no return and the hammer snapped back into place, striking the cartridge. I didn't feel any recoil, nor was there much noise from the .22-calibre weapon as the chain reaction continued.

Not that either of these things was of much interest to Ray. By this time he had been shot. By me.

The bullet went through the back of his mouth, the round tunnelling through his flesh, emerging from the right-hand side of his neck. It then – as I found out later – scored a path down his arm, causing a friction burn, before becoming lodged in his shirt. I couldn't see any sign of blood.

I hadn't shown the pistol the respect it deserved. I had been showing off, and this was the result.

Propped up on John's shoulder, Ray staggered out of the house, in a state of disbelief I suppose, not to mention pain. Who could blame him for his wonderment? Someone had just tried to kill him. Not that it was just Ray who was suddenly overcome by what had taken place.

Dumbly I stumbled upstairs and thrust the pistol back under the pillow, smoothing the bedspread as I left, as if this would throw my dad off the scent. Then I returned to the scene of the crime.

I sat down in my dad's favourite armchair. I had a frantic feeling. Complete panic. Was he going to die? What had I been thinking of? Of course I hadn't meant to shoot Ray. It was just bravado, a way of filling a few dull minutes. Who would believe that though? I tried desperately to block the whole thing out.

From then on the aftermath of the incident becomes a blur. Even now I can't remember much about what happened next.

Perhaps that's because I have never really wanted to. I am positive Dad would have been disciplined for not ensuring the weapon was correctly secured, but I don't know by whom or how. I was later questioned by the police, but that is a fog too. I was never charged. I suppose it was just the way things were in Northern Ireland at that time. To a greater or lesser extent firearms were part of everyday life. And there were plenty of people out there intent on, and capable of, more heinous acts than I had just managed.

As for Ray, he did survive and he was gracious in accepting my apology, delivered at his hospital bedside. Not that we had much to do with each other after that. Where exactly does a relationship go after one person has shot the other? Whatever the intent, it could only have bred a sense, probably a healthy one, of distrust. What is that bastard Beattie going to do next?

The thing is, that moment – almost killing Ray – was the moment that shaped my future. For most of my teenage years I had been listless, without direction. My family had never had much reason to be proud of me. I was going nowhere; not doing badly, but not doing particularly well either, just drifting along. But this changed everything. Now they had every reason to be thoroughly ashamed of me. I needed to take charge of my future and give my dad cause to smile when he thought of his son, not despair. So within a matter of months I had planned my escape route and was digging for freedom. In 1981 I joined the British Army. I took the first steps on the long, long road to Afghanistan; to Garmsir.

I suppose soldiering was in my blood.

My dad was a serviceman. My grandfathers had fought in World War Two, one with the Royal Artillery, the other with the Irish Fusiliers.

I entered the world in England, a result of the posting system of the army that Dad – then a colour sergeant in the Royal Ulster Rifles – was subject to.

Douglas Ricardo Beattie was born in Tidworth, Hampshire, on 13 October 1965.

I have no complaints about my first given name. Douglas is a good, solid provincial label. But I have never been so sure about my middle name. You will be hard pushed to find many Ricardos of Northern Irish extraction. Indeed you would need to head to Central America to find my namesake – one R. Montalban, a Mexican actor. *Hawaii Five-O*, *Star Trek II*, *The Man from U.N.C.L.E.* He was in them all. *Fantasy Island*, that was another. My mum liked him, hence her choice for me. Thank goodness she wasn't more besotted or else I don't suppose I would now be answering to Doug.

I was the sixth child and third son of William and Eve Beattie.

As is the military way, my early life passed in a repetitious whirl of moving house, adjusting to a new environment, getting to know new friends, and then, just as things settled down into some sort of normality, finding that the Beattie family was to be uprooted once more.

Nor was it the most glamorous cycle of tours: Gibraltar; Fort George, Inverness; Colchester. At each changeover I remember the whole lot of us standing by our beds, watching with a mixture of curiosity and trepidation as the housing officer marched in to inspect. Wearing white gloves he would carefully wipe his finger along the surfaces: door frames, picture frames, the top of the wall unit, along the skirting board behind the sofa. He checked them all for dust and dirt, any reason in fact to withhold some of our deposit.

As children do, I became used to this endless upheaval that in a way was a routine all of its own. To me this was normality, though it must have annoyed the hell out of my parents.

My dad was a strict, proud man. He wasn't tall, just five-foot six, but very stocky with a barrel chest. Topping it all off was a bald head, which had once been covered with sandy-coloured hair. His duties meant he was frequently away from home, working antisocial hours, so running the household fell more often than not to my mum. However much she loved us, controlling half a dozen children was an unenviable job. She was a lovely woman – taller than my dad, well built too, a native of Portadown, Northern Ireland – who made our childhood as fun as possible. As is ever the way with kids, we couldn't see the great strain she was under, trying to keep us in line. For if life was difficult for her, to me it was just carefree, a constant adventure, the strength and solidarity derived from having so many siblings helping to smooth out any insecurity caused by the steady round of moving.

Army pay has never been great and it was a struggle for Mum to make ends meet on my dad's monthly salary. The accommodation we found ourselves in was often shocking. If animals were housed the way we were, the RSPCA would have been outraged, yet when I was just six, all eight of us were crammed into a house built for four.

When I was eight, my dad's army career came to an end after twenty-two years of military service. Once again we packed our bags, this time to leave Cherry Tree Camp in Colchester and return to Northern Ireland to face the future as a civilian family. This last move should have been the easiest, going back home to Portadown. But returning to the Six Counties was to be the toughest of all.

Dad packed me and my brothers, Rab and Steve, into his battered Renault 12 and we boys took the ferry from Stranraer to Larne. Mum and my sisters followed on, a few days later.

If I was expecting a land of milk and honey, I was in for a shock. Our home was little better than what we had left behind. A terraced, three-storey council house on the Union Street estate, slap bang in the middle of a solidly working-class area. Solidly Protestant too. And that was the way it looked set to stay. For not every construction in the neighbourhood was a place to live. From the top of our house, peering out of the back window, you could just see the top of a huge wall, a five-metre-high barricade that stretched as far as the eye could see in each direction. It was probably built as a way of screening the estate from the main road, but in reality it was also a sectarian divide; made of concrete and topped with glass it kept Loyalist from Nationalist, Protestant from Catholic.

Wall or not, ours was a divided town. The funny thing, of course, was that anyone who wanted to see what was on the other side of the wall could just walk round it; one end of it melted away into the countryside, the other dissolved into nothing as it reached the middle of the town. If you had made the journey you would have found an estate similar to ours. The people looked the same as us, did the same sort of jobs and drove the same sort of cars, but there was one big difference. They were nationalists.

Beyond their estate was the Garvaghy Road, the site of an annual stand-off between the communities. Each July as members of the Protestant Orange Order attempted to make a pilgrimage from Drumcree church down the Garvaghy Road towards the town centre they were routinely confronted by nationalists. Invariably violence resulted.

It took place on the 12th, the Glorious Twelfth, the day on which unionists commemorate William of Orange, who defeated the Catholic King James II at the Battle of the Boyne in 1690. Orangemen regard 'King Billy' as the defender of their faith. And you couldn't accuse them of sending out mixed messages. As they processed towards trouble, they sang their songs. One was called 'Billy Boys': 'We're up to our knees in Fenian blood: Surrender or you'll die.'

For a young boy brought up outside of the province, all of this came as a bit of a shock. No one had ever bothered to take me to one side and explain 'The Troubles'. As with the Glorious Twelfth, my education came from events.

Take the evening of 16 April 1974. I was at home, squeezed on to our brown leather sofa in the front room with a selection of my siblings, *Nationwide* on the TV, Mum washing the dishes in the kitchen. Suddenly there was a huge explosion, not on the box but outside. The windows shook and the flowery curtains trembled. We fought our way off the sofa, scrambling to get to the window to see what had happened. More of my brothers and sisters ran in from the street, Mum arriving with a tea towel, trying to gather her brood to her breast, making sure we were all present and correct, that we had all our fingers and toes. Nobody was allowed back out; instead we were packed off to bed, with just the intermittent noise of police sirens outside to remind us something untoward had happened.

It was not till the next day that I found out exactly what. I walked down the street and followed a neat row of terraced houses. Number two, number four, number six, number eight, number ten. I stopped outside number twelve. Except there was no number twelve, only a big gap where it should have been; rubble and furniture strewn across the small front garden. Then normal service resumed. Number fourteen, number sixteen, number eighteen, and so on.

It was as if someone had taken a huge cake knife and cut the house out, the piles of bricks resembling the crumbs left on a plate. Damage to the neighbouring properties seemed to be all but nonexistent. I wasn't the only sightseer satiating his curiosity. Plenty of others had come to gawp, too. I strained to hear what they were saying. The word was this had been no gas explosion, but something more sinister, the result of blundering by a Loyalist bomb-maker. Joseph Neill had made a mistake and it was to be his last. Killed by his own hand. That evening when I was again sitting on the sofa watching TV it was confirmed on the news.

There was no real sense of surprise. Things like this took place in Northern Ireland. It was not common, but nor was it exceptional.

Take another example: I was playing outside, running about, not far from home, when I was brought to a halt by a massive bang. There was no doubting what it was. Following the sound I made my way to Burke's Bar. But like number twelve it had gone. A haunt of the Ulster Defence Association, it had been blown apart by the IRA. The headline casualty figures didn't sound bad: no fatalities, just one person injured. But try telling that to the woman whose leg was ripped off from below the knee, a cripple created by 'The Troubles'.

Not that humans were only hurt as part of collateral damage. More often than not they were the targets: flesh and blood rather than bricks and mortar.

Like my Uncle Sam.

We loved him and he loved us. Our mum's brother, he was slightly backward, but was warm-hearted with an infectious grin. He had a way of lightening our mood. He was a great football fan and rarely would a visit to our house pass without a kickabout in the street. One day in the early hours, we were woken by a ferocious hammering at the front door. At that time of night it could only be bad news. As we strained to hear, Mum went down the stairs and opened up. It was her other brother Tommy. We weren't allowed to go down but soon knew something was wrong as Mum started to cry.

Dad came up to tell us why.

He said Sam had been murdered. Walking across the Bann Bridge, he was on his way home from the pub. He didn't make it, gunned down before he could reach safety. Shot twice. Just like that he was gone. No one has ever worked out exactly why he was targeted or who was responsible, though the thought was he knew his assassin. One of the rounds passed straight through the middle of his hand, as if he had been shot as he raised an arm in recognition of his approaching killer. The suspicion has always been he was the victim of an internal Loyalist feud. He would not have been the first.

Mum took it terribly. Sam was her baby brother. It was especially tough for her at the funeral. Women weren't allowed on the processional march. It was men only. Aged twelve I took my turn to carry the coffin, heading to the church of St Columba for the service and then on to Seagoe cemetery for the burial.

Despite the provocations and constant low-level bitterness between the two communities I tried my best not to get sucked into the spiral of hatred and blame. And despite my family's own history, sectarianism was rarely a topic of discussion at our dinner table. To their eternal credit our parents made sure of it.

As my siblings and I got older we started to drift apart, forging our own lives. My eldest sister Edwina married a private in the Pioneer Corps, my second sister Tanya married a baker and part-time member of the UDR, whilst Rab, the elder of my brothers, joined the British Army. He moved to England to do his basic training with the Junior Leaders Battalion at Shorncliffe near Folkestone in Kent.

By this time my dad was back in the forces, like his son-in-law a member of the UDR, his experience of life in civvy street not to his taste. He hadn't liked his job as a welder and the money was certainly not enough to compensate for the tedium.

He was to do eight years in the UDR before the brutishness of some of those entering the regiment became too much for him to stomach and for a second time he quit the services.

Meanwhile my brother Steve had also enlisted in the army. But signing up wasn't such a straightforward decision for Steve to make as it had been for Rab. For two years Mum had been unwell, suffering miserably from a bad back. She had all manner of tests but doctors couldn't seem to find anything wrong. By the time they did it was too late. Shortly before Steve was due to head off for training we discovered Mum was going to die, terminally ill with lung cancer. Like my dad she smoked heavily. There was not much likelihood she would survive more than a few months.

Steve had to make the heartbreaking decision either to forgo joining up or risk never seeing Mum again. He talked it through with her and Dad. They backed his choice to leave for England. But the risk would turn to reality and she would die before he returned home again. The guilt of not being there at the end plagued him for years afterwards.

As Mum's condition deteriorated I watched helplessly, a mix of emotions battling it out inside me, love for her versus anger at the loss I knew was inevitable. Some people welcome time to prepare for the death of a close relative. For me it just piled on the agony.

Mostly Mum was at home, but stays in hospital became increasingly frequent. When she was with us, much of her time was spent in bed, where she would pass hours at a time absorbed in books, escaping the reality of her situation – she adored reading Mills & Boon.

Between chapters, when she needed something, she would summon us from below by banging on the floor with a heavy blackthorn stick. One of us would come scurrying.

My schooling had been going OK but the situation at home started to affect that too. Each morning I walked to Portadown Tech, some three miles away. During the lunch break I would walk on to the Craigavon Area Hospital. After a brief visit it was back to the classroom. At the end of the day it was a tramp home to start the fire before Dad got in from work at Banbridge Camp. This became the new routine. As the days became weeks I started to lose direction, tiredness and distraction taking their toll in equal measure.

I suppose it was assumed I too would join up. But I had no inclination to be a soldier; equally I had little inclination to do anything else either.

Mum's decline was shocking. She was regularly hallucinating, rambling on about her life, and there was nothing we could do to ease her pain. Or ours. Death might be a fact of life, something that everyone has to deal with, but does knowing that make it any easier? Not for us it didn't.

One day I arrived home to find Dad and my youngest sister Donna sitting in the living room. Our next-door neighbour Maureen – a chubby, jovial woman – was there too, the three of them chatting away happily. Dropping my bag I bounded up the stairs to say hello to Mum as I always did. The curtains were open, the sun was shining, light flooding into the room. It was September. She was lying there in her dressing gown, the garment buttoned up high to the neck. That was normal. Her breathing was not. It had become laboured; her eyes were only half open. I went back to the top of the stairs and shouted down.

'She's just sleeping,' said Donna, but Dad got out of his chair without a word. I passed him on the stairs as I went to join my sister. Minutes later there was a yell from the bedroom urging Donna to call a doctor. I rushed back upstairs and into my parents' room just in time to watch Mum die in Dad's arms. She was just forty-two. I was two weeks short of my fifteenth birthday.

I found myself helping to carry a coffin again. Me on the right-hand side; my dad on the left. Feet first we carried her, slowly, from the house to the church.

Like her brother she was buried in Seagoe cemetery, in the far corner beside a large stone wall, in the shade of a willow tree.

The wake was held at our house, relatives and friends packing the front room. All at once the conversations stopped. There was an even thump, thump, thump coming from Mum's room upstairs. The blackthorn stick was being banged on the floor above our heads. Everyone heard it. I put down my sandwich and made for the hall, but Dad beat me to it, and started up the stairs to see what Mum wanted. Only when he was halfway up did he check himself before turning and coming back down to join the guests. No one said a word about it. We just continued where we left off. It was the strangest thing.

Both Rab and Steve had been allowed leave to come to the funeral, but within a matter of hours had to return to base. I restarted school but was soon going backwards.

It was a difficult period for my dad. He was young, too. Only forty-five. He started to drink more than was good for him. Who could blame him? There was a huge hole in his life: his wife of a quarter of a century gone, and still so many years ahead of him. Whisky filled the gap – Bell's, Whyte and Mackay, whatever came to hand. Each and every night he would find some comfort in drink, listening to the songs and sounds of his youth – country-and-western music, Val Doonican, Millican and Nesbitt – reminding himself of his early days with Eve.

In the small hours he would often call for me, wanting me to come and join him and hear the story of his life. It wasn't a conversation. I was there to listen. I wasn't scared of him – this was the man I admired most in the world – but these were uncomfortable moments; an awkward teenager, already struggling to cope with the loss of his mum, now confronted with his dad's most intimate thoughts, the strongman façade falling away in front of his eyes. As I fought to stay awake he would slouch back in his chair, mesmerised by the coals glowing ever more faintly in the fireplace. I desperately wanted to help but what could I do?

During none of this did I talk to Dad about my future. In a way I felt guilty about burdening him with my worries. He had just lost his wife. There were money problems too. What were my insecurities compared to his woes? The army as a career for me wasn't mentioned. I wanted him to be proud of me, just as he was proud of Rab and Steve, but still I was not persuaded that becoming a serviceman was the answer.

That was until the day some six months after Mum's death that I shot Ray – and finally decided soldiering was the route to redemption.

Soon after, on a morning I should have been at school, I finally went to join up at the Charles Street recruitment centre, where I was met at the gate by the recruiting officer. Dressed in an immaculate uniform, he towered over me. Even then there was a chance of failure. They weren't going to accept all comers. Once. Twice. Three times I had to return to complete aptitude tests, but at last I was in. I had actually done quite well. It was suggested I join the Army Air Corps or the Royal Electrical and Mechanical Engineers. But these were never options for me. I was only going to join one regiment and that was my dad's. Not that I told him what I had been doing, even forging his signature on the necessary paperwork. I kept things secret for two reasons. One: I wanted to make sure I actually got in. Two: I was worried what he might say. Did he need me around? How would he cope with losing another family member? It was only on the day before my departure that I actually brought myself to reveal my plans.

He said very little as I explained, and kept any pleasure or pain he might be feeling about the news to himself. He wasn't there when I left the next morning, having already gone to work himself, to do his duty. He didn't see his youngest son walk out of the door and put Portadown behind him, following a well-trodden family path to begin basic training with the British Army.

[illegible]

[illegible] around me as he [illegible]

[illegible] the evil [illegible]

[illegible]

[illegible]

THREE

BULLY BOYS, RUDOLF HESS AND ME

It was only a short flight from Belfast to Bristol. From the small airport I took a bus to the railway station, and then finally a train on to Taunton in Somerset. I stepped down from the carriage, hauling my huge steamer suitcase behind me. I was not alone. Left and right of me were other new recruits.

Casting a shadow over the platform was a giant of an NCO, a chip off the same block as the soldier who had signed me up. He was wearing his dress uniform and looked immaculate. One by one he called out the names of those he had been expecting. Everyone else around me answered as he worked his way steadily down a list. I remained silent. I didn't seem to be on his piece of paper. He completed the roll call.

'Right, you lot. Grab your gear and follow me.'

The others traipsed off behind him and boarded the coach that would take them to Norton Manor Camp. Too nervous to say anything, I just tagged on at the back.

Drip. Drip. Drip. I squinted down my nose and watched as the blood trickled from the end of it, a tiny cascade of red falling to the ground. I couldn't wipe it away or staunch the flow because the bastard wouldn't let me. He was making me stand in a spread-eagled stress position, my palms flat to the wall. My arms were burning from the pressure. Let-up only came when my tormentor decided it would be amusing to kick away my legs and send me crashing to the floor of the barracks corridor that stretched away in either direction. Through the tears in my eyes I closely examined what I was lying on. But for the blood the floor would have been immaculate, buffed up perfectly, as smooth as glass – and so it should have been, for it was me who was made to clean and polish the damn thing morning and night. This was adding insult to injury. I was creating work for myself.

Renewed yelling from above focused my mind on other matters. 'Come on, you little fucker, back on your feet.'

I pushed myself up. Not for the first time that afternoon the instructor ordered me to stand to attention, the tips of my boots just touching the skirting board. Then he began pacing up and down. Every so often, as he passed by, he would come up close to my ear and shout and swear in his abrasive accent, covering me in spit. His breath smelled of stale smoke and he stank of sweat. Finally he grabbed a fistful of my hair and smashed my face into the wall. My eyes started to well up again and more blood and snot ran down my face. I was getting used to this.

My persecutor wasn't particularly tall or small, not particularly fat or thin; physically he was rather nondescript. But he stood out in a couple of ways. He was a poor excuse for a man. A poorer still excuse for a soldier. But he had the power and he was going to exercise it. He was not the sort of person to worry about how he might later explain his actions, though this time he felt there was a justification for my suffering; this was payback for an earlier misdemeanour. What had I done to deserve such treatment? During another punishment, which had seen me marking time – marching on the spot – I had caught his cup of coffee with my knee. Needless to say it spilled over him. It was all the excuse he needed. In his eyes he was more than entitled to mete out his own form of retribution. I closed my eyes and waited for the evil bastard to get bored.

To begin with, training at the Junior Soldiers Battalion had been pretty much as I had expected. Lots of shouting, lots of standing about, lots more shouting, endless lessons on the self-loading rifle (the precursor to the SA80), still more shouting, tuition on field-craft, and as much drill as a man could take.

But this other side of military life quickly started to emerge, something as depressing as it was disgusting. Bullying and, in my case and that of the only other Irish recruit in the camp, racism.

There were perhaps several hundred of us who had newly joined; perhaps several hundred more staff and instructors. Most of those charged with our care and development were great; however, a handful were just plain nasty.

They should have been people I looked up to, respected. Their professionalism should have reassured me that joining the army was the right decision. I should have wanted to emulate them. Instead I despised them with a vengeance.

Verbal abuse of those they were entrusted to protect and lead was standard but, increasingly, so too were demands for money and physical assault. Some of my colleagues took the easy way out, siding with the bullies, happy to do their bidding for them, intimidating the vulnerable who were finding it difficult to fit in and struggling to keep up with the course.

But it was the two of us from Northern Ireland who attracted most of the unwanted attention. We found ourselves repeatedly at odds with those around us. Our 'crime' was our background. It wasn't what we did, or didn't do, that made us targets; it was who we were. Irishmen. No matter that we were Protestants and not Catholics. No matter that we came from Ulster and not the Republic. No matter that we wore the same uniform as everyone else.

Most of those in my platoon took to calling me Paddy. It wasn't a term of endearment, but a slur on my heritage, a reference to the 'Irish boggies', 'murdering bastards', 'backward fuckwits' who dared join the British Army. On the mainland it seemed that anyone from the wrong side of the Irish Sea was viewed with something between suspicion and hatred. Perhaps we were the Muslims of our day – condemned by the broadest of labels; misunderstood by a wary public and a spiteful military.

The endless slights and ridicule cut to the heart of who I was and whenever another recruit called me Paddy it would lead to a scrap. It took a while but they eventually got the message – my name was Doug. DOUG. However there were some confrontations I had to turn away from. Despite the provocation I avoided the almost irresistible temptation to pick a fight with the NCOs who tried to make my life a misery. To them I remained Paddy.

In a way I was the fortunate one. The other Irish recruit got it even worse than I did. He was universally known as Mickrick and did little to stand up for himself. His abuse at the hands of those who were tasked with looking after him was awful. After one attack had rendered him half conscious, his humiliation was completed by the NCOs and some recruits urinating on him. Things culminated in a savage beating that left his head swollen to twice its normal size.

Not everyone was sadistic and malevolent. And certainly not all the times were bad. But enough of them were to make it an intensely difficult period for me. I had joined up at sixteen years old – a man in the eyes of the law perhaps, but in reality a callow youth. Over and over I contemplated leaving. The one thing that saw me through a literally torturous year was the thought of not wanting to let my dad down once again. I was proud of him and I desperately wanted him to be equally proud of me. Perhaps I also reasoned that my experiences were some form of rough justice, the penalty I had to pay for shooting Raymond.

When I look back at those twelve months it is with disappointment and regret. They should have left me wanting more, excited about a future in the army, keen to continue learning my trade. Instead I was scared, wary of authority and unable to communicate freely with the few friends I managed to make, my guard never dropping, my cynicism remaining sky-high.

If I had to come up with an excuse for these people it might be that they had the unenviable job of turning a bunch of raw recruits into fighting-fit soldiers, ready for battle at a moment's notice. This was still the height of the Cold War, and nobody knew just how soon it would be before any of us were called on to face the enemy. It might be that they had had bad tours in Ulster and had seen colleagues killed and injured. But I didn't have to come up with an excuse for them, nor should I have. These were bitter, small-minded men who were bullies in the army, and had probably been bullies outside the army.

Despite it all, I did make some progress with my soldiering, and with my training just about finished I even won my first award. On every course a best recruit was chosen from each regiment represented in the JSB. I came top of the class for the Royal Irish. No matter that there were only two of us – myself and Mickrick. Faint praise, I suppose, but better than coming second.

Almost a year to the day after I arrived in Somerset, I passed out as an Irish ranger, the regiment's equivalent of a private. I was looking forward to my passing-out parade, marching past my dad, looking him straight in the eye as a soldier in the same regiment as his other two sons. Except he wasn't there. Only Rab showed up. I never found out why Dad stayed away, never asked him. I put it down to the turmoil he was still struggling with following Mum's death. It was a great pity that he did not witness anther step on the road from boyhood to manhood, but then I suppose that is part of being an adult, too – learning to cope with disappointment. It was time to join my battalion.

I flew to Berlin on a civilian flight. There to meet me at the city's Tegel airport was Lance-Corporal Scone McWilliams from C Company the 2nd Battalion the Royal Irish Rangers. Through my brothers he was already well acquainted with the Beatties.

'You look like Steve,' was his welcoming remark as he helped me with my kit and dumped it in the back of the Land Rover. For a seventeen-year-old, it was all a great adventure. At that time Berlin was still divided by the wall keeping east from west. And unlike the wall in Portadown you couldn't walk round it. The city was split into four sectors: French, British, Russian and American, each segment influenced by the power occupying it.

For example, the US sector used dollars and was full of fast-food outlets you wouldn't see anywhere else in Germany. The French sector was the cultural hub, based around café society, a real little Paris. The British sphere of influence retained a Germanic flavour. Junk food came from roadside *Schnellimbiss* bars, and a local brew, called *Schultheiss*, quenched our thirst for beer. It was the Russian sector that remained pretty much of a mystery, our only glimpses coming when we crossed into it via Checkpoint Charlie, not as soldiers, but as tourists. From what I saw, East Berlin was a grey, dour, depressing place. I was always happy to leave it behind me at the end of a visit.

Scone dropped me at Wavell Barracks, my Berlin base, a series of four-storey accommodation and mess blocks surrounding the obligatory parade ground.

I was handed over to the company quartermaster, 'Legs' McConnell. He loaded me up with my equipment: 58-pattern webbing kit, large backpack, a sleeping bag wrapped in plastic.

That night I was on my own in the huge dorm. The rest of the company was out on exercise. I would be joining them the next day. I didn't sleep much, nerves and excitement competing for dominance.

It was Scone who took me out to join the rest of the guys. They were in the Grunewald Forest, a twenty-minute drive south of the base.

As excited as I was by being in Berlin I was also wary of meeting the men with whom I would be serving, and with whom I would face the invading Soviet hordes if the nuclear deterrents failed and the Cold War warmed up.

After the NCOs in Somerset, they were a blessed relief. They came from similar backgrounds to me. They seemed like family. Of course, some of them were.

I was in Nine Platoon. Steve was in Eight and Rab in Seven – he had already been promoted to lance-corporal. The pair of them were members of C Company. So was I. The Beattie boys were back together.

Monday to Friday was a constant round of training, testing and learning about the lives, tactics and strategies of our Russian counterparts. It was at this stage I found out all about Exercise Rocking Horse.

It had been calculated that, in Berlin, British forces would have a life expectancy measurable in hours if not minutes should an invasion take place. We got no mention on the order of battle, given our remoteness from the rest of the massed forces in West Germany. If attacked, no troops would be tasked to come to our relief and, as was made clear from the flash we wore, a red circle, we were surrounded by the enemy. Exercise Rocking Horse was supposed to test our response to such an attack.

The plan was as simple as it was basically futile. Before our inevitable destruction we had to give our colleagues hundreds of miles to the west an extra bit of preparation time to get ready for the onslaught. We needed to be a thorn in the Soviets' side, albeit one easily removed and tossed aside.

When the exercise was called, no matter where you were or what you were doing, you had one hour to get yourself into camp, get kitted up, and sign for your weapon, ammunition and other bits of equipment before being deployed into the city to man defensive positions.

This might have been a drill, but for some it was all too real and it hadn't been without its casualties. On an earlier occasion a number of German civilians had actually committed suicide by hanging themselves rather than suffer the fate of falling into the hands of the Soviets who they – wrongly – believed were banging at Berlin's door.

From then on, details of Rocking Horse were widely publicised before the event, with information appearing in the local press and broadcast on the city's radio stations. This did much to preserve the health of the city's population but little to create any sense of realism for us.

Most of my duties were fairly routine bits of soldiering, but some stood out. One of them gave me the rare chance to get out of Berlin and see more of Germany – well, after a fashion. Occasionally I was ordered to act as a guard on the train that ran from Charlottenburg in West Berlin through the East to Helmstedt in the Federal Republic. These services ran once a day. Once the train was loaded, before we set off, heavy chains were threaded through all of the door handles, then secured with padlocks, to make sure no one got out of the carriages as we trundled through the East. More importantly, I suppose, they were also there to stop people trying to get on. Quite what Health and Safety would say about such a system today, goodness only knows.

We made numerous stops along the way – not to change passengers; they were safely under lock and key – but to allow for documentation checks. At each halt I would come face to face with the enemy: Soviet-bloc soldiers dressed in greatcoats and wearing large fur hats – it was just like I'd seen in films. The troops would swarm around us, trying to swap their cap badges for anything we had on us that was of 'Western' origin. Some of my more seasoned colleagues came well prepared, carrying a good stock of West German porn magazines that our counterparts were happy to trade their insignia for. I wondered whether the chance to barter with the enemy was in fact the real reason for our laboured progress and all the talk of correct paperwork was just a cover story.

Back at camp our newly acquired trinkets were routinely traded with the others for 'beer tokens' – a euphemism for money, as almost all the cash we got our hands on ended up being spent on alcohol. Such was the demand for booze that some soldiers would even go to the local blood bank to sell their fluids for a fistful of Deutschmarks that they would unfailingly use to go out on the piss with.

Not everyone who attempted this proved to be a suitable donor, as their devotion to drinking often meant their blood-alcohol levels were too high.

There was one duty I had to do in Berlin where a stiff drink beforehand would have been a bloody good idea – guarding Hitler's henchman Rudolf Hess at Spandau Prison, a place as grim and forbidding as the man it held.

The jail was a redbrick building constructed in 1876. It had been designed to house hundreds of inmates, but in Allied hands, immediately after the Nazi defeat and the Nuremberg trials, there were just seven, and by the time I arrived there was only one.

The prison was falling into disrepair. What was the point of keeping it up to scratch for the benefit of a single man? There were two perimeter walls, one perhaps four metres high, the other about twice that. Then there was an electric fence and rolls of barbed wire. There was no chance of Hess getting out, and little of others getting in, either to help him escape or put an end to his life.

Although the prison was in the British sector, general guard duties were shared out amongst the four occupying nations. Each month the detail changed, responsibility for security of the site transferring from one power to another, although Hess's personal warders always remained the same. The transition was marked by the ceremonial handing-over of the keys at the gatehouse – an ominous structure with two castellated towers, one each side of the heavy wooden entrance, approached along a street of irregular cobbles.

I was about as ignorant of Hess and his past as it was possible to be. My education therefore came from colleagues and superiors. It was gripping stuff even for a teenager more interested in booze and girls than European history.

Hess first met Hitler when they served together in the Great War. Later they were both imprisoned following the failed beer-hall *putsch* in Munich. Hess is said to have helped Hitler pen *Mein Kampf* and develop the *Lebensraum* ('living space') policy that in large part led to the German invasion of the Soviet Union.

After Hitler came to power in 1933, Hess became deputy Führer. But by the start of the war he was falling out of favour. In 1941 he flew a Messerschmitt 110 to Scotland. After the 900-mile flight it crashed in a field in Renfrewshire. Hess had already bailed out, but was captured and imprisoned. His journey is usually explained as an attempt to reach the Duke of Hamilton, who he believed could help broker a peace deal between the Nazis and the British. At his trial Hess remained a staunch defender of Hitler. For his troubles he was sentenced to life imprisonment at Spandau – where our paths crossed.

Before starting our task we were given a list of things not to do. Not take any notes; not take any photos; certainly not talk to him. It only added to the enigma. What was it about this man?

By 1983 Hess was both old and frail. Yet he still had a presence about him and a macabre fascination for us. Not that we were even supposed to look at him. But how could you resist sneaking a glance at this gnarled remnant of the Nazi regime? Hess knew this and would bait his guards, trying to engage them in conversation, looking in their direction, smiling, occasionally staring up at the guard towers with his deep-set, keen eyes, framed by his trademark eyebrows, bushy and still jet black. Perhaps goading us was the only fun and mischief he had left in his life; the only small way of getting back at those he still regarded as the enemy. Anyone who succumbed to Hess's advances was immediately taken off duty and would face disciplinary action.

Hess had the run of the garden and spent much of his time wandering around it. What I did notice about this old man was that despite his age he still stood tall and proud. He set the pace, and if he decided he wanted to walk quickly then his guards would have to scurry along in his wake. Likewise if he wanted a quiet leisurely stroll in silence then his guards would keep their distance and slowly plod behind him.

Guarding Hess was not an enjoyable assignment. As well as the veil of evil shrouding the man, there was the oppressiveness of the prison. It was imposing enough when the sun was shining, but in bad weather it was full of foreboding, the lack of inmates and staff only adding to the menace. Night-time was worst of all. The mind ran riot. The stories of strange happenings were legion and only compounded the apprehension. Over the decades a number of soldiers were said to have taken their lives whilst on duty. Others had opened fire, engaging fleeting shadows and figments of their imaginations, and apparently on at least one occasion a comrade – a terrified French soldier supposedly shot his commanding officer, who came up on him unannounced.

Not surprisingly there were claims that Spandau was haunted and this frayed the nerves still further. I knew how those who had gone before must have felt. The place scared the shit out of me. I was happy when my short stint was over and I could leave. Of course Rudolf Hess never did. Allied prisoner number seven died in August 1987 aged 93. He committed suicide by hanging himself. The building itself was razed to the ground soon after.

FOUR

BIG BLUE WING COMMANDER

The company commander came striding over to where I was standing.

'Corporal,' said Major Robin Russell. 'You need to get this place in some sort of order. We've got a visitor coming. The Big Blue Wing Commander.'

I looked at him blankly. Big Blue Wing Commander? I had absolutely no idea what the hell he was talking about, so I asked him.

'The prime minister, Margaret Thatcher. She will be in the province in the middle of November and for some reason she wants to visit your checkpoint.'

Bloody hell, I thought. The PM. Coming to see me. Except she wasn't really coming to see me, or my colleagues. She would be in Northern Ireland because of something that had happened at our location the previous year.

Our particular vehicle checkpoint at Derryard near Rosslea on the border with the Republic was a symbol of the struggle against the IRA. In December 1989 two soldiers died in an attack by the Provisionals. The assault was eventually beaten back by their colleagues from the King's Own Scottish Borderers, two of whom were decorated for their courage. The intensity of the exchange was still evident almost twelve months on; pockmarks of varying sizes covered the concrete barriers. The PM was keen to demonstrate that as far as she was concerned this was a place where democracy stood up to terrorism. She wanted to show that for her there weren't any no-go areas. And, to make sure everyone knew that, she would be bringing the media with her to document the trip.

We were going to be under scrutiny and Major Russell was going to run the show like a military operation. We members of the other ranks were schooled in what to say and what not to. And anyone who looked like a trouble-maker was rooted out. Take for example Ranger Black. The major asked him what he would like to say to the PM if she came up to speak to him.

The answer was as hilarious as it was wrong.

'I'm going to tell Margaret bloody Thatcher that I won't be paying the bloody poll tax.'

That was it for Black. Off to do other duties. No way was the CO going to risk a confrontation, especially when Her Majesty's press were coming to capture every moment for posterity.

The big day came and as usually happens when VIPs visit soldiers Mrs Thatcher's time was stolen by the top brass. But she fought it all the way. She wanted to throw off her minders and talk to the ordinary man. And so she did, finally chatting to the ranks, and signing at least one autograph along the way. She also knew of course that the picture of the day was not going to be her mixing with the officers, despite their best intentions. She had other ideas for the photo-op and it involved a .50-calibre heavy machine gun. She eased us members of the armed forces to one side and assumed a position next to it. She stared defiantly into the middle distance and the cameras started to click. It was Margaret Thatcher as Boadicea. It was her as the Defender of the Isles.

And despite the politics she struck a chord with us soldiers. She managed to bestow on us a value. She gave us pride and justification in what we were doing. She was a friend of the armed forces. It is funny to think that within days of visiting us she had resigned.

By now there was another Margaret featuring pretty heavily in my life: my wife.

Though she would probably argue she wasn't featuring heavily enough. And she might be right.

At twenty-three minutes to midnight on 7 August 1988 my daughter Leigh was born. I know that because my mother-in-law told me so. You see, I missed what would have undoubtedly been the biggest moment of my life because I was off with the army.

As Margaret went into labour at the Cottage Hospital in Ballymena – her mum holding her hand – I was on exercise at the Magilligan training area on the northern Irish coast near Coleraine, blissfully unaware of what was going on until, that is, a message reached me saying the arrival of my first child was imminent. Whatever else I had been thinking shot out of my mind. Desperately I tried to hitch a ride back to camp, St Patrick's Barracks, but there was no one who would, or could, give me a lift. In the end the duty driver had to be sent out to pick me up and take me back.

Arriving at the base I charged in to the guardroom to hand in my weapon, a multitude of thoughts going through my mind. Would it be a girl? Or a boy? Would everything go all right? Could I still make it in time?

I soon found out the answer to that.

'Congratulations, lad. I understand you're a father.'

Good news travels fast. I looked at the NCO behind the desk, then at my watch, which said 3 a.m. I was not sure whether to shout with joy or yell with frustration. It was just brilliant that I had become a dad, overwhelming. But I was furious at myself for not having been there at the birth. Margaret and I had only been married for a year and already here I was, right from the very start, some sort of absent parent – it did not bode well for the future.

I walked the short distance to our married quarters. An upstairs light was on. I rang the door bell and waited. After a few moments a window on the first floor was pushed open. My mother-in-law looked down at me, a huge grin on her face. It was infectious. I couldn't help but smile.

'You've got a daughter, a beautiful daughter!'

A daughter. Wow. Fucking wow. Yes!

'No point in us going to the hospital now,' Susan said. 'Margaret is sleeping. We can head up there in the morning.'

She came down to let me in. I was totally knackered, but there was no way I would be sleeping that night. I was just so excited; and scared. What would she be like? How should I hold her? What would Margaret say about me being late? Could I provide for them both? What a responsibility. Up till this moment I had only been concerned about the pregnancy; I had viewed the birth as the ultimate goal. But now . . . now this was just the beginning. Perhaps the birth was the easy bit (it certainly had been for me). A lifetime of responsibility lay ahead.

A few hours later I went to see my wife and child. We had long ago decided the baby would be called Leigh if it was a girl, Lee if it was a boy.

I cradled my daughter in the palm of my hand. At just 4lb 4oz she fitted perfectly. To look at her it appeared as if she would break at the slightest touch, so delicate was she. I was spellbound, completely captivated. I stared and stared and stared; absolutely dumbfounded.

I realised I was neglecting someone. I turned to look at Margaret, but she was smiling, pleased for me, delighted to see how I was reacting to our baby. I should have been treating her like a princess after what she had just been through. I gave her a huge hug and thanked her for this amazing gift. We both started to cry, and there and then I made my apologies for letting her down. Between the tears I promised her – solemnly swore to her – that from that moment on I would always be there for her.

Except I broke my promise.

When our second child Luke was born I wasn't just a few hours late, I was four weeks late, having been sent away on exercise to North America. I had asked to stay behind but was refused as we were scheduled to be back before the due date. But things happened sooner than expected – I only found out something was up from a message left by the welfare office directing me to ring the UK. Stuffing a handful of coins into the phone box I managed to get through first to the hospital and then to Margaret.

'Doug, you have a son.'

I was speechless.

Not so the Canadian operator who was sitting in on the call. 'A son! Fantastic. Well done. What great news. That's fantastic.'

Once again the first person to congratulate me on becoming a father was a stranger.

'What are you going to call him?' the man asked.

The answer was easy. We had chosen Luke because it was a simple, biblical name. But I wouldn't get home to see him for another month.

For me the sacrifices had a trade-off. I continued steadily up the promotion ladder. It wasn't a meteoric rise, but I loved the job and heaven knows I put in the hours and effort. As my career progressed I found myself playing a role – to a lesser or greater extent – in some of the biggest historical events of the last quarter-century. Following my tours and deployments on an atlas was like plotting a course from one news event to another. Greenham Common. Cyprus. South Armagh. Kosovo.

In between there were exercises and postings in Germany, Canada, Kenya, Sandhurst, Dover, Catterick, Inverness. In twenty years of marriage I was to be away from home for more than a decade.

Every time I returned to Margaret I know she wondered whether I was back for good, whether Doug Beattie had finally got soldiering out of his blood. Time and again the answer was no. She was continually disappointed and, in effect, each homecoming was the first step on the road to the next enforced absence, the army life ensuring that our time together was, if not quite the exception to the rule, then certainly strictly limited, and always precious. Worse still, even the periods of apparently guaranteed stability were always under threat of disruption. A natural disaster here, a war there, a state of emergency somewhere else – events were always conspiring to wrench us apart. It was hard not to keep one eye on the front door, an ear open for the phone, anticipating the next sudden departure. It all added stress to the relationship, created an underlying strain. And the closer it got to going away, the closer that strain was to the surface.

As ever in such situations it seemed to be easier for me, the one leaving, than for Margaret, the one left behind. For her the countdown to my departures was routinely tough, knowing our finite time together was shrinking. Our moods would go in different directions. She would become more anxious. I would feel guilt at leaving my family, but that would be subsumed by excitement and anticipation; life was one big adventure. And anyway, I reasoned, it wasn't my fault I was going away. It was the army's. I just followed orders.

In Margaret's eyes I was married to her but owned by the military. Her view was that the army saw her and the children as an irritation, a distraction and burden to one of their soldiers that took his mind off the job.

She tried to take some comfort from the other wives and girlfriends around her. There was a regimental wives' club to provide support, the women looking out for each other, a reminder that while their nuclear family might have been rent apart they would always be part of a larger family – the Royal Irish family. And this was fine, but only up to a point. As with every aspect of army life there was a hierarchy. At the top of the tree was the CO's wife. Her 'right-hand man' was the wife of the regimental sergeant-major (RSM). And so it went on. It was never explicit but the unwritten rule was that the women assumed a standing equivalent to the rank of their husbands. It was not for Margaret.

The trouble was, she made it too easy for me. Quite rightly she would be upset about my going. Understandably she would want me to devote more time to my family and to my domestic responsibilities. Naturally she wanted us to be together. But she never set me an ultimatum. Never said she would leave me if I didn't leave the forces. Never called my bluff. She allowed me to get away with it. It is a wonderful reflection on her character that despite everything I put her through she managed to remain so selfless – and an appalling reflection on mine that I suppose I took advantage of it.

In my own mind I tried to justify my actions, my lifestyle. It wasn't as if I was such a bad husband: I didn't drink too much, when I was actually at home I did my share of the washing-up and the ironing, I loved the kids, I didn't have an affair. I was completely devoted to my wife. Except I wasn't. Yes, I was in love, head over heels, but not just with her. The army was my mistress. And she knew how to captivate me. Whenever things were going stale, whenever I thought of ending it, she offered up a new challenge, a new temptation, a new inspiration.

Colonel Tim Collins stormed the battalion in January 2001, invading our base at Howe Barracks in Canterbury with little resistance. Our new CO was one of us; a Belfast-born Ulsterman, forty years old, tall, confident, handsome with greying hair. The fact that he had served with the Special Forces only enhanced his reputation. It was as if we had struck gold. He was a breath of fresh air.

TC, as he came to be known, had strong views on most things, not least on the role of the infantryman and of the qualities soldiers under his command should possess. They had to be physically fit, mentally robust and a crack shot. He expected them to get on with the job as they found it – no whinging, no complaining. If you had these attributes, then you were welcome in his fiefdom. If not, you were out. He did not suffer fools gladly and wasn't slow to root out the deadwood.

His no-nonsense approach extended to the battlefield. He worked on the principle that you went to war with what you could carry on your back or in your pockets. Forget about a huge supply chain. Expect the worst and anything better will be a bonus. Quit the moaning and carping – whoever said life was fair?

When he arrived I was a company sergeant-major (CSM).

One of my first dealings with Colonel Collins came within days of his appointment. The door to my office burst open and there he was, flanked by the then RSM, Jim Pritchard. I jumped out of my seat and stood to attention; half in surprise at his sudden entrance, half out of respect for the new boss.

'Beattie, I want you to go back to Sandhurst. They want a CSM and I want it to be you. The Royal Irish have never supplied a CSM before.'

Bloody hell. This was a big privilege. It would be a great career boost for me and fantastic kudos for the regiment.

It only took a fraction of a second to make up my mind. 'No thank you, sir. I'm very happy serving with you in the battalion and am in no rush to leave.'

For the briefest of moments he looked at me, weighing up my reply.

'Fair enough, Doug,' was all he said, before he turned on his heels and left.

It was a strange exchange, but from his tone and body language it seemed it had not done me any harm. I hoped he was happy with my quick response and would value loyalty to him higher than the chance to take a job for what would essentially be career advancement. Not that my situation remained the same for long. I got shifted out of A Company to become the new assistant ops officer. I was also given the job of nurturing the junior NCOs.

On top of it all I was to oversee recruitment.

Manning-wise, we were in a woeful state. When Colonel Tim took over, the battalion was some 180 men under strength, about 20 per cent. As a stopgap we had been assigned a Gurkha company to make up the numbers, but we needed to bring in more of our own; more Irishmen. In desperation the regiment had been casting its net ever wider. In the previous four years, at least six recruiting offices had been opened in major cities across England, encouraging anyone with even the slightest trace of Emerald Isle ancestry to sign up.

Not that that was the end of it. We had got to the stage where we were happy to take English recruits without even a hint of green blood. The result had been startling. Now less than half of those in the battalion were men from the north or south of Ireland, the others coming from England and beyond. The essence of the regiment was being diluted. Not since the days of national service had the regiment comprised so few troops from those communities it had originally been set up to recruit from. Action needed to be taken.

The Colonel decided he would close all the offices on the mainland except for the one in Liverpool, a city that retained a strong Irish community.

In their place he opened five recruiting centres in Ulster. He was determined to maintain the Irish character of our regiment and not see it go the way of the Irish Guards, which had become Irish in name only. He was also prepared to consider any proposal that might get more people on to the books.

Soon after he arrived, the battalion had a visit from Air Vice-Marshal Niven, who at the time was head of Joint Helicopter Command (JHC). The pair must have been talking about the manning problems, because as Niven left he casually suggested to the Colonel that he get the regiment involved in an air show back in the province. That wasn't quite as strange as it sounds.

Such events drew huge crowds and despite being infantry we were part of 16 Air Assault Brigade.

Colonel Collins obviously liked the idea. He turned to me.

'Sergeant-Major,' he started. 'I want you to get us into a show over the summer, something big. I want something impressive. Come back to me in a week and tell me how we're doing.'

He didn't want to know the fine details, only the when, where and what.

Seven days later I gave him the answers. Late April. The Londonderry Air Show. One hundred soldiers, four Land Rovers, twenty Gurkhas, two helicopters and a couple of C-130 Hercules.

The plan – if our hastily concocted proposal was worthy of that name – was this. We would carry out a so-called TALO – a tactical air land operation – and rescue some 'kidnapped civilians'. The show organisers were billing it as the Raid on Entebbe, the operation launched by Israeli forces in 1976 to free hostages held by Palestinian terrorists in Uganda. That mission was a success. Fingers crossed, so would our pale imitation be.

The Colonel was pleased with the way things were going, but this was the proverbial back-of-a-fag-packet plan; no proper paperwork, no authorisation from above, no risk assessment. I explained my worries to the boss.

'Trivia. I will deal with all that later.'

So we ploughed on, myself and Captain Dave Middleton arriving in Londonderry a few days before the event. He had the job of narrating our part of the display. A bit of fine-tuning and we were ready. The big day arrived.

Right on cue the two Hercules approached. Thousands of necks craned skywards as they flew in, before at the last moment plunging towards the runway. But just as they were about to land my mobile phone rang. I picked it up.

'You are to stop your display right now, do you understand?' a voice screamed down the line. 'When you've done that, report to JHC at RAF Aldergrove. You don't have permission for this. Where are the aircraft now?'

Looking out of the window I could see them taxiing to a halt. 'Well, they've just landed and scores of troops are charging down the ramps, armed to the teeth.'

Before the caller could release another tirade I hung up.

Our display of strength certainly looked impressive and did wonders for our profile in the area.

At the end of the show I expected I would receive a rocket from the Colonel. It didn't come. He just shrugged his shoulders and said he would argue with JHC later. It was probably an encounter he would relish; telling a man whose job it was to shine the seat of his trousers on an office chair all day about the realities of running an infantry battalion and keeping it up to strength. I could just imagine the one-sided conversation. As the world was to later find out, Tim Collins had a way with words.

FIVE

FROM FUN TO FIGHTING

The ambulance came careering down the street towards me. It sent up a plume of dust as it passed by, but it didn't get much further. The driver slammed on the brakes, desperately trying to avoid the people who had emerged from God knows where, and were now blocking his path. As the vehicle came to a stop, the crowd surged towards it. How many people were there? Perhaps 100, maybe 200? It was difficult to tell. But there was no doubting the menace of the mob.

This was Al Medina in April 2003, the Iraq war all but over, the reprisals only just starting. Those who had been oppressed by Saddam Hussein were intent on wreaking their revenge on supporters of his regime. And in this southern Iraqi town they were starting with the occupants of the ambulance.

As the mob twisted and turned, I caught glimpses of the unfolding horror. Three patients were dragged through the buckled rear door, wrenched open by brute force. The men kept disappearing from view, submerged by the sheer weight of numbers.

As I watched, an old, old memory fought its way to the front of my brain.

I was taken back a decade and a half to Belfast in 1988 and something I had seen on television along with millions of others. Two British soldiers dressed in civilian clothes had taken a wrong turn and driven straight into the path of an IRA funeral cortège. Corporals Derek Howes and David Wood tried in vain to undo their mistake, attempting to reverse out of trouble, but there was nowhere for them to go, the mourners closing in on the men's silver Volkswagen Passat, sensing something wasn't right, suspecting perhaps that these were Loyalists intent on mayhem. As the furious and curious lurched forwards, one of the soldiers pulled his gun, leant out of the car window and fired a warning shot into the air. For a moment those in the crowd drew back and it seemed as if an escape route might be opening, but just as quickly as the hope was raised, it was dashed. The crowd had become a lynch mob, its members finding the courage and confidence to converge on the car once again. Not just to surround it, but also to clamber on top of it, one of the group kneeling on the bonnet, trying to smash the windscreen with a wheel brace. Another lashed out with a stepladder snatched from a photographer.

The driver and his passenger were pulled out and dumped in the road, then quickly swamped by bodies. The two men were kicked and punched. When they had been beaten senseless they were bundled into a black taxi and driven away. Stripped naked except for their underpants, the men were finally shot and left on waste ground near by.

What was shown on the TV was bad enough, but still only an edited version. Sometime later, when I became an instructor at the Northern Ireland Training Wing, I saw in horrible detail the whole uncut sequence of events, filmed mainly from an army helicopter which had been hovering overhead.

The viciousness of the attack stayed with me through the intervening years and now here in the heat and dirt of Iraq the whole macabre sickening act seemed about to be relived. And I wasn't going to stand for it.

No way.

We hadn't liberated the country to see one set of thugs replaced by another, no matter what the provocation.

'Get out of the way. Get out of the fucking way! Fucking move!' I screamed obscenities as I started to batter my way towards the injured.

Not that the words I used meant much to the mob, they would be doing well to understand anything I said. But there was no mistaking the tone. They would have recognised the venom in my voice and seen the blind fury on my face. The adrenalin was pumping, my heart pounding. I shouted at those who blocked my path, barging, shoving, elbowing them out of the way. I hesitated for a moment in a small gap I had created for myself. There were now Iraqis all around me and I was still some way from where the summary justice was being meted out.

I levelled my rifle and fixed my bayonet, trying to keep one eye on the crowd and the other on what I was doing. I pushed forward again. Yelling and spitting I used the butt to smash people out of the way. One of the men being attacked was already motionless on the ground. Another was writhing about, trying to free himself from those who were pinning him down. Above him stood a slim man with thin arms. He wore a mask of hatred, and looked ready to drop a big rock held high above his head.

I knew I was doing everything wrong. Here I was, one British serviceman out of reach of his colleagues, attempting to pacify a mob bent on retribution. If I had stopped to think I would have seen that there was every chance I was about to become the fourth victim. But I didn't stop to think.

Another Iraqi stepped in front of me, a second at his shoulder. As the first opened his mouth to remonstrate I struck him hard on the side of the head with my rifle. In the same movement I cracked his colleague square in the face just below his nose. Lucky for him it wasn't half an inch higher. Or lower.

As these two dipped to one side I was faced with yet another human obstacle, his back to me. This wasn't the time for politeness. I stabbed him in the calf with the point of the bayonet. There was a howl and he too ducked out of the way, clutching his leg. But it looked as if I was going to be too late. One of the injured had already been dragged away out of sight. The other two were lying moaning in the sand, the rock between them.

I raised the SA80 and fired. Not at anyone in particular but into the air. The sharp report caught the attention of everyone around me, including most importantly those intent on murder.

I reached the back of the ambulance. For the first time those carrying out the attack seemed to be in doubt. They stepped back metre by metre, leaving me standing over the two victims.

But now what? Everyone was shouting at me, pointing. I had become the focus for their wrath. To them I was the one who had prevented justice being done. Just as I started to curse my stupidity things improved. At the back of the crowd there was a commotion and more swearing. In English. Bursting through came Sergeant Jim 'Swayze' McNair, his nickname a reflection of his brooding good looks and way with women. And not just women – at that moment I would quite happily have kissed him. I had known Jim for an age, but never had I been more pleased to see him. And thankfully he was not alone. Other members of Mike Company started to appear behind him and between them they continued to push the Iraqis back.

I glanced down at the two bloodied figures at my feet, trying to catch my breath, sweat pouring off me. 'So what the fuck do we do now, Jim?'

'Let's get them to hospital. At least they should be secure there.'

The question was how? Our vehicles were in the wrong direction and the ambulance had been wrecked. We were going to have to manhandle them. In the blazing sun we hauled them 400 metres towards the hospital, yet again forcing a passage through a sea of bitter, questioning faces; scores of people kept at bay by the bloody-mindedness of a handful of Her Majesty's soldiers. Ten minutes later and we made it. Two of the three men – who we later found out were members of the previously ruling Baath Party – had reached some sort of safety. It hadn't been the easiest thing to do, but it was certainly the right thing to do. It was members of 1 R IRISH being magnanimous to the enemy, just as we had been ordered by our commanding officer before the invasion of Iraq had even begun.*

'*We go to liberate, not to conquer. We will not fly our flags in their country. We are entering Iraq to free a people and the only flag which will be flown in that ancient land is their own. Show respect for them.*'

Colonel Tim Collins began his address.

'*There are some who are alive at this moment who will not be alive shortly. Those who do not wish to go on that journey, we will not send. As for the others, I expect you to rock their world. Wipe them out if that is what they choose. But if you are ferocious in battle remember to be magnanimous in victory.*'

Bloody hell.

'*Iraq is steeped in history. It is the site of the Garden of Eden, of the Great Flood and the birthplace of Abraham. Tread lightly there. You will see things that no man could pay to see – and you will have to go a long way to find a more decent, generous and upright people than the Iraqis. You will be embarrassed by their hospitality even though they have nothing.*'

The CO was speaking at the centre of a hollow square, his men ranged around him on four sides, 500 members of 1 R IRISH. Myself and the other NCOs close by to the left, the commissioned officers to his right.

'*Don't treat them as refugees for they are in their own country. Their children will be poor, in years to come they will know that the light of liberation in their lives was brought by you. If there are casualties of war then remember that when they woke up and got dressed in the morning they did not plan to die this day. Allow them dignity in death. Bury them properly and mark their grave.*'

This was his 'eve of battle' speech, the last chance for the Colonel to address everyone before the invasion of Iraq. Here in the centre of the Kuwaiti desert, just a few miles from the

* For this act of foolishness I was awarded the Queen's Commendation for Bravery.

border, he laid on the line exactly what was expected of the regiment and left us under no illusion about what we faced. It was sobering stuff – and I had only myself to blame. The previous evening I was amongst those who suggested to the CO that the men needed to have an idea of the reality ahead.

'*It is my foremost intention to bring every single one of you out alive. But there may be people among us who will not see the end of this campaign. We will put them in their sleeping bags and send them back. There will be no time for sorrow.*'

But maybe this was all a little too much reality. I could see heads starting to go down, and it wasn't just a reaction to the sand swirling about in the stiff breeze.

'*The enemy should be in no doubt that we are his nemesis and that we are bringing about his rightful destruction. There are many regional commanders who have stains on their souls and they are stoking the fires of hell for Saddam. He and his forces will be destroyed by this coalition for what they have done. As they die they will know their deeds have brought them to this place. Show them no pity.*'

I don't know if Colonel Tim knew what he was going to say before he said it – he wasn't using notes – but it was exceptional stuff and it was being preserved for posterity by an embedded journalist called Sarah Oliver from the *Mail on Sunday*. She scribbled as he spoke, writing her pooled dispatch that would eventually wing its way back to London and on to the news wires. The words would become famous.

'*It is a big step to take another human life. It is not to be done lightly. I know of men who have taken life needlessly in other conflicts. I can assure you they live with the mark of Cain upon them. If someone surrenders to you then remember they have that right in international law and ensure that one day they go home to their family. The ones who wish to fight, well, we aim to please. If you harm the regiment or its history by over-enthusiasm in killing or in cowardice, know it is your family who will suffer. You will be shunned unless your conduct is of the highest – for your deeds will follow you down through history. We will bring shame on neither our uniform nor our nation.*'

I could see more and more frowns on men's faces.

'*It is not a question of if, it's a question of when. We know he has already devolved the decision to lower commanders, and that means he has already taken the decision himself. If we survive the first strike we will survive the attack. As for ourselves, let's bring everyone home and leave Iraq a better place for us having been there. Our business now is north.*'

Cheers, boss. Thanks a bloody lot.

As the Colonel strode off through a gap in the square, followed by the officers and Sarah Oliver, I knew I had a problem. He had left the men somewhere they shouldn't have been: thinking about home, wondering if they would ever return there again, fearful of the dangers that faced them in the hours, days and weeks ahead. The speech had been rousing, but also sobering – it pulled no punches, the message was stark. He had told the men they would not all be coming back, and now it seemed the majority of them were asking if they would be amongst the fallen.

They had to be snapped out of it.

Unlike the CO, I have never had a great way with words. I am no orator. Like most Ulstermen my language is straight out of the gutter. There would be no fancy phrases from me, no finely judged sentiments, just a string of barely separated profanities kicking these soldiers, my soldiers, back into life. They were going to stop thinking about Colonel Collins and start paying attention to their regimental sergeant-major. And woe betide any who didn't.

I began to bollock them.

I screamed at them about their lack of professionalism.

I yelled at them about the pitiful state of their weapons.

I laid into them over their poor state of dress, their abysmal personal hygiene, their failure to salute senior officers, their inability to get anywhere on time.

I told them they were a disgrace to their uniform and weren't fit to call themselves soldiers of 1 R IRISH.

I accused the warrant officers of running slack companies.

I blamed the sergeants for not properly advising the young second lieutenants and captains who depended on them.

Finally I embarrassed the section commanders for their lack of control over their men.

I left no one out.

At last I stopped.

Whatever the men had been contemplating five minutes earlier, they certainly weren't now. They must all have thought, 'That bastard Beattie.'

I called the CSMs to me. They sprung to attention as if on duty at Buckingham Palace and marched forward, coming to a halt in a perfectly straight line, shoulders back, chests out. Beyond earshot of the rest of the ranks I explained what I was trying to do.

'We've got to get the boys' minds back on the job in hand, not thinking about tomorrow and the day after, but on the here and now. We need to keep them busy. I want to see some action and discipline, and I want you lot to enforce it.'

It is true that battalions are commanded by their officers. If 1 R IRISH was a car then the driving would be done by them. But the engine that powers that car is to be found in the sergeants' mess, with the five men now standing bolt upright in front of me. Five good companies would make a great battalion and that is what we had. I watched as the CSMs returned to their men and continued where I had left off.

They pointed to imaginary rangers amongst the ranks, giving them hell for some fictitious misdemeanour. The CSMs then passed their companies on to the platoon sergeants, who barked out orders in a similar vein. And so it went on, the platoons breaking down into sections.

Within ten minutes of my initial merry hell I saw men furiously cleaning weapons, emptying and re-packing rucksacks, checking their kit.

I drifted off to find the Colonel.

'Sir, fantastic speech. The men are in no doubt about what

you want and what they have to do to live up to the reputation of the regiment.'

Colonel Tim looked up at me with a quizzical gaze. He seemed already to have forgotten what he had said, engrossed as he was in last-minute preparations, for as it turned out the clock was against us.

Training completed, rehearsals done, scenarios worked through, as many speeches made as you could shake a stick at, it was finally time to go to work. To go to war.

What did I think of it all? Was I scared of death and injury? Worried about the unknown that lay ahead? Yes, perhaps. But that apprehension was outweighed by other emotions. I was excited about finally getting the chance to do what I had been trained for, what the whole battalion had been trained for. Most of all, though, I was proud; immensely, overwhelmingly proud. Here was I, Doug Beattie, about to be the first regimental sergeant-major to take the battalion to war since Korea some fifty years previously. I relished the opportunity. What an honour. I couldn't wait.

At 06:00 hrs on 22 March 2003, after a night huddled in shell scrapes in our dispersal area, we crossed into Iraq.

At first glance one side of the border looked pretty much like the other, plenty of sand, a dearth of features. But something was odd. The sky was brightening as dawn gave way to day, but all across the distant horizon the blue was punctuated by huge pillars of thick black smoke rising from numerous fires. It seemed as if achieving our first objective – securing several gas and oil separation plants (GOSPs) before pro-Saddam supporters torched them – might already be beyond us.

In addition to this overall aim for 1 R IRISH, I was responsible for forming and running the prisoner holding pen. This was supposed to be a temporary facility used immediately (and briefly) prior to those who surrendered being passed back down the line to something more permanent.

We were due to take over a secure position about four kilometres into Iraq established by the Americans as they rolled in ahead of us. In the rehearsals I had been assured by my US counterpart that the camp would be up and running by the time we came to it, complete with wire, prefab watch-towers and the like.

What I actually found were 400 enemy soldiers standing around on a vast concrete pan previously used as a parking area for the heavy vehicles employed at a nearby GOSP. Their weapons had apparently, but by no means certainly, been removed; the doubt arising because they had yet to be individually searched. Amongst the detainees was a group of wounded – there was no sign they had received medical attention.

I walked over to an American officer.

'Ah, there you are, at last. It's all yours. We're off.'

And that was it. The total extent of the handover from the marines. With that, they mounted their vehicles and progressed into the desert heading north to form a bridgehead from which a breakout towards Baghdad could be launched.

I looked around me. Here I was, in charge of several hundred prisoners with only a defence platoon (men from various corps: chefs, mess waiters, stores guys, and provost staff, our own internal police) to contain them.

The first job was to try and get them under some sort of cover where they would have shelter from the elements and we could provide medical treatment. The answer came in the shape of a maintenance hangar on the same site.

It was pointed out to me that the building was full of tools and machinery that the Iraqis could use as weapons.

My reply was simple: 'If they try anything we will shoot them. If they riot we will shoot them.'

Not that I envisaged much chance of mischief. The prisoners already looked like members of a defeated nation and this was only day one.

But the willingness of our foe to surrender quickly presented its own problems. The number of captives was increasing rapidly; by day three we had almost 1,500 of them. They were all hungry. In the run-up to the allied invasion they had received little if anything in the way of physical sustenance from their own chain of command, and now I didn't have anything to give them either. I sent out a scavenging party to try and round up some rations. The best the men managed to come back with was a huge block of dried dates, though I suppose, given the fact that sand stretched in all directions, I was lucky to get this. But fortunate or not, the supplies were gone almost as soon as they arrived. Forget the feeding of the proverbial 5,000, I was struggling to sustain a third of that.

It was a tense period. I understood why my men's frustrations might so easily boil over: the heat, the physical exhaustion, the real danger, the imagined danger. But I was clear in my own head. There would be no lapses by the men under my watch. We would treat the prisoners correctly and with compassion. It was what I asked of them. It was what Colonel Tim asked of them. The response was fantastic. Not only did they do what was requested, but they often did more, giving up their own water and food so at least some of our charges could be satiated. I was and am extremely proud of them.

My responsibility wasn't only for the living, though – there were also the dead to deal with. We made sure the bodies were buried with dignity. Not for them a shallow trench and only enough soil to stop the dogs smelling the putrefying flesh and digging them up. My men did as they would want done. They went out with map and compass and dug the graves to face Mecca. Where possible they would ask a comrade of the dead to say a prayer. It took time and effort but it took place without complaint. They say that humanity is cast aside in war. I'm pleased that with my men it never was.

After seven days we were finally relieved of our prisoners and moved to a village built to house the oilfield workers, twenty kilometres away. We joined our colleagues guarding the GOSPs.

Another two weeks passed and I was beginning to think we had missed our share of the action and this was as far into Iraq as we were going to get.

But then we received orders to move north as the armoured battlegroup made huge gains in and around Basra. Colonel Tim told us we had been given the job of pushing forward to the town of Al Medina. His approach to the task was to form Mike Company, an ad hoc group of rangers from other sections, to make the charge.

A reconnaissance screen provided by armoured vehicles from the Household Cavalry headed the breakout. Mike Company followed behind them, and then it was the CO's group. The rest of the battalion came after that. Much to Tim Collins's frustration progress was painfully slow. The landscape was mostly flood plain with the only way ahead being along high-sided levees. This created bottlenecks as we kept stopping and checking for enemy ambush points and mines. It was driving the Colonel nuts. This was not the way he did business.

After two hours at a snail's pace, his vehicle – affectionately or otherwise known as the comms (communications) camel – dropped back to mine.

'RSM, I've had enough of this. Just follow me as quick as you can.' And with that we were off. We passed Mike Company and didn't stop. Then we passed the Household Cavalry and still didn't stop. In fact we didn't stop till we reached Al Medina. It took just twenty-five minutes.

(It was only later that I heard a story about how the cavalry reacted when we charged past them.

A message went out on the radio: 'All call signs, the American Tourist is trying to beat us to town. Get after him.'

And with that they began to pick up speed in a desperate attempt to overtake us. They didn't stand a chance.

I hadn't heard the term 'American Tourist' before. It referred to the Colonel's image. More often than not a cigar was firmly clamped in his mouth as he chewed and puffed away on it. A ready supply of others was stuffed into his desert-coloured fisherman's-style jacket. On his head were his Ray-Ban sunglasses. He looked the part, but he also acted the part – this was a serious fighting man who led from the front.)

Once in Al Medina we headed straight for the centre of town and, much to the apparent delight of the locals who saw us arrive, declared it liberated. The truth was the enemy had long gone. They had seen the battalion were on the move and had fled. The locals were already beginning reprisals against members of the local Baath Party who couldn't or didn't flee with the retreating soldiers.

Even so, despite the best efforts of the recce squadron and the so-far benign nature of the welcome we had received, we were still out on a limb, just our two Land Rovers miles ahead of any help.

A battered old saloon drove up to us. Slumped in the back was a wounded Iraqi soldier. We did what we could to dress his wounds, before getting the car to join us in a mini-convoy as we headed for the hospital.

On arrival we struggled to find anyone willing to deal with the casualty. Doctors and nurses stepped back from the patient. It wasn't really surprising. With recriminations and retributions already under way, no one wanted to have any association with the suddenly overturned former regime. As we walked through the corridors and wards we came upon scores of pictures of Saddam Hussein that had been wrenched from the walls and tossed on to the floor.

Eventually Colonel Tim made it clear to the medical staff that he wasn't going to take no for an answer. Everyone would be treated according to need, not political persuasion. Of course it was easy for us to say, but impossible to police. There was no way of knowing quite what would happen to the man we had brought in as soon as we were out of sight.

By now the rest of Mike Company had arrived in town. They parked up on a football pitch a few hundred metres away from the hospital. I headed off to brief them on what we had seen and done. The Colonel set off to look for the town elders.

Briefing over, I leant against my Land Rover, happy to let the warmth of the metal seep through my uniform.

It was then that an ambulance came careering down the street towards me. It sent up a plume of dust as it passed by. But it didn't get much further . . .

SIX

OLD ENOUGH TO KNOW BETTER

(GARMSIR, DAY 0)

> It is better to let them do it themselves imperfectly than to do it yourself perfectly. It is their country, their way and our time is short.
>
> *T. E. Lawrence*

10 SEPTEMBER 2006

Silhouetted against the rapidly rising orange disc of the sun, the ragtag convoy of vehicles had formed up, all set to move out, the British WMIK* Land Rovers towards the head of the column, that of Captain Paddy Williams right at the front. Joe, Sam and I, we were fourth. Behind us there followed a motley assortment of cars and pickups – Datsuns, Hondas, Subarus, they all seemed to be of Asian origin – containing our allies from the Afghan National Army and Afghan National Police. Bringing up the rear were the Estonians, amongst them a doctor and a bomb-disposal team. In total, thirty-three vehicles of various shapes, sizes and condition.

---

* A Land Rover with a Weapons Mount Installation Kit. The equipment allowed our Land Rovers to be fitted out with a range of machine guns.

Standing out from the crowd, shining brilliantly in the gaining light, was a large white Toyota Land Cruiser, surprisingly clean given the environment, complete with air-conditioning. It was fit for a king, though in this case its occupant was a mere general, the provincial chief of police, Durani.

Not that this was a fighting contingent through and through. Making up the numbers was Sean Langan, a film-maker, there to record the glorious progress of our slightly bizarre caravan. He had been denied access to our mission by the British top brass but had come up with an ingenious plan B, persuading the Afghans to take him along for the ride. Sean was an Afghan veteran, having already spent time with the Taliban, seeing their side of the conflict. How he did this, how he was brave enough to do it, I had no idea, but now he was ready to view the flip side of the coin. My view of Sean was one of indifference, really. To me, all journalists were merely after the big headline and the shocking stories, quite happy to leave out the detail and the context of what they saw. The truth? It was something they could take or leave. Sean would soon prove me wrong.

The order came to mount up.

I couldn't wait to get out of Lashkar Gah, to get on the road.

People jumped into their vehicles, an eagerness to move gripped the column: let's get on with it, let's stick it to the enemy.

There wasn't much room in the wagons for us soldiers, filled as they were to overflowing with ammunition, food and water. Whatever else lay ahead, we were determined not to die of thirst in the arid, hostile, bleak environment we would be travelling through.

I looked forward, squinting as the sun continued its sure climb to my left, and saw Colonel Charlie Knaggs, the head of the Provincial Reconstruction Team in Lash, and Major Al Stocker, his chief of staff, bidding farewell to Paddy. The formal goodbyes complete, we got the green light. Our twenty-first-century camel train was slowly snaking off, a cloud of dust rising quickly about us.

The man reading the map was Tim Illingworth, an acting captain in the Light Infantry. Tall and athletic, he had bright keen eyes. He was responsible for steering a course across 120 kilometres of featureless landscape to reach our overnight lie-up. As the crow flies, our destination was no more than half that distance, but we weren't about to make a beeline for it. One, because it would take us through enemy territory; and two, because any idiot would be able to extrapolate from our course where we were going to end up. From the lie-up we would launch our attack, an attempt to retake the strategically critical town of Garmsir, which had been overrun a few days before by the Taliban.

If Afghanistan's history since its creation in 1747 has more often than not been characterised by bloody turmoil, then the last three decades have proved no exception. There was the Soviet invasion of 1979, to prop up the Communist government, the USSR's withdrawal ten years later, and the subsequent series of civil wars. Then came the Taliban's seizure of power in 1996. After that the US led military action following the events of 11 September 2001, designed to punish the regime's support for Osama Bin Laden and al-Qaeda. For thirty years the country has lurched from one crisis to another.

The Taliban first emerged in 1994 around Kandahar. At its head was Mullah Omar, a village cleric who lost an eye fighting the Soviets. The speculation and suspicion has always been that the Taliban has benefited from secret backing from the Pakistani government. Certainly many of the group's followers were and are educated in religious schools known as *madrasahs* across the border with Pakistan, and support has been particularly forthcoming from the Pashtun community, which can be found in both countries. The Taliban's public goal was to bring to an end fighting between feuding warlords. Many people, weary of relentless bloodshed and hardship, welcomed the prospect of peace and stability, and the organisation rapidly grew in numbers and influence. But the curbs on lawlessness, the stamping-out of corruption and the reduction in the opium crop, all came at a price. Security and order were enforced using tough Islamic Sharia law. Executions and amputations were introduced as punishments. Television, cinema and music were banned. Men had to grow beards and women wear all-enveloping *burqas*.

In December 2001 international intervention saw the Taliban ousted from power but its leaders and ideals survived to fight another day. By later taking advantage of disillusionment with the government of Hamid Karzai, it steadily began cajoling the population into supporting it once again. Afghans are pragmatic rather than dogmatic. They are prepared to back whichever side they see as likely to gain the upper hand. Indeed often they will hedge their bets and quietly support more than one side. This trait has coined the saying that Afghans can be rented but never bought. Which is not to suggest Afghans are without loyalty. It is just that their long-term allegiances are more usually based on personal, familial and tribal connections rather than beliefs in institutions or political systems. Of course, the Taliban's willingness to use coercion, as well as polite persuasion, also helped recruitment, and the numbers of foreign fighters slipping over the country's porous frontiers only added to the Taliban's resurgent membership and menace. The situation in Helmand Province was as bad as anywhere.

Colonel Knaggs gave a nod and a wave to each of us as we swept by.

As I passed, he offered me a knowing look, something different to the genial smile he usually had planted across the lower part of his warm open face. It was brief, but unmistakable. The eyes held trepidation. Did he know what was out there awaiting us? Did he know what trials were in store for our cobbled-together contingent? If so, he did nothing to stop us. So on we went.

I was left feeling we were about to be confronted by something exceptional. Something that was, no matter how good our training and preparation, going to be one hell of a test. Inside me too was fear. Not so much of the enemy, but a fear of failure – of letting the side down, of not being up to the job; a job that had come my way by a rather convoluted route.

In the spring of the previous year, after twenty-two years of military service, I was commissioned as a late-entry officer (as opposed to a direct-entry officer who would have joined the army as a young man and been trained at Sandhurst). I was now Captain Doug Beattie of 1 R IRISH. It wasn't something I had always had the intention of doing, rather it was a means to an end. I had come to the point in my career where, as a man of the ranks, I would have been forced to retire, my useful life over at forty. Taking a commission meant the opportunity to stay in the army for the immediate future and well beyond. In fact for up to another fifteen years. But there proved to be a catch.

The army, probably for my own benefit, saw me best suited to a training and logistical role. In essence it was a comfortable number. And the forces got something out of the arrangement, too. They assumed (rightly) I had a wealth of experience, and also (perhaps more debatable) knowledge. What better for them than to give Beattie a post where he could pass on everything he knew to the next generation of soldiers? I could see the argument in that but it did little to give me any sense of real job satisfaction. Even after the initial training posting, when I was returned to my regiment, it was unlikely I would be back in the thick of things. Instead I would probably become a welfare officer, looking after the families of those going off to fight. It was not for me. My body might have been fast approaching middle age, yet in my head and my heart I was still twenty-one, and still craving adventure.

For twelve months I did my best to teach the young recruits the lessons I had learnt. But it didn't get any easier. I was not excited about entering civvy street, but being in the military and seeing others deployed to do what I wanted to, was like rubbing salt into the wound. I decided to resign my commission and broke the news to my boss that I would leave the following year.

Which was slightly ironic because a few weeks later he broke some news to me; before I left the army I was going to be sent to Afghanistan.

As I walked down the steps of the plane in Kabul I was struck by the intense July heat. The city is at an altitude of almost 2,000 metres, the population hemmed in by a wall of mountains. Not that I saw a great deal of the capital. Within hours I was on board another aircraft, a Hercules, heading south, bound for the sprawling airfield at Kandahar (KAF) and the multinational ISAF force stationed there. ISAF had been set up after the overthrow of the Taliban to help keep the peace. As the years passed NATO took control of ISAF and its role was steadily extended geographically away from Kabul. I was sent to Afghanistan as part of the third stage of expansion. Several thousand foreign troops were being sent to the south of the country to help reinforce the writ of the Karzai government there and create a secure environment within which humanitarian and reconstruction work could take place.

Eight nations were contributing manpower and machinery to the region: the UK, the US, Canada, the Netherlands, Denmark, Estonia, Australia and Romania. The British Helmand Task Force initially had its HQ at KAF, although most of the soldiers were based at Camp Bastion, a purpose-built facility in the middle of the desert. KAF was also home to the various national air forces on hand to provide air support across the south.

I had been told I would be doing a desk job at KAF, working with the Canadians as an intelligence liaison officer. I had no real idea of what it might entail and certainly no preparation for it, but this was a theatre of operations where the numbers of coalition troops were growing fast and there were gaps that had to be quickly filled. Hence the urgent trawl for staff back in the UK, which had netted me.

Except that when I arrived at KAF no one knew anything about Doug Beattie, or indeed much about the job. Not for the first time in my life, my name did not seem to be on anyone's list. I was directed towards a bed for the night in the transit tent and told to come back the next day.

The following morning there was still no news of the intelligence job, but it appeared there might be some other things I could do. I was given a choice. Either act as an operations watch keeper, another desk role also at KAF, or go down to Lashkar Gah to work at the embryonic Provincial Security and Co-ordination Centre (PSCC). In a heartbeat I reached a decision. Lashkar Gah it was. I didn't fully understand the function of the PSCC – in fact I did not have a clue – but it would get me out of the camp. I had not travelled all that way to push paper.

Arriving at my new home, the HQ of the PRT in Lashkar Gah, I was welcomed by Charlie Knaggs. I had met the Colonel before, in Northern Ireland. He had previously been the CO of the Irish Guards. He told me more about my role. I would work with the ANA, ANP and NDS at the PSCC, based at the provincial Governor's compound, trying to formulate some sort of common security plan for the province. Our attentions were to be focused on what was known as the Afghan Development Zone, a lozenge-shaped area which took in the towns of Lash and Gereshk. We were also to devote some effort to providing Afghan support to UK forces in Sangin, Kajaki and Now Zad, all of which had seen heavy fighting.

After the serious stuff Colonel Charlie took me up to the Crow's Nest, a sitting area on top of some of the huge freight containers at the PRT HQ. Out of a sock he magically produced a bottle of Jameson Irish whiskey. For the next hour we watched the sun go down, shared a glass or two and reminisced about past experiences and common friends. It wasn't the worst way of being introduced to Helmand.

Food at the camp was also a reminder of things left behind. We ate well. Eggs and bacon for breakfast, roast beef for dinner, and that army staple, chips. Sleeping accommodation was provided by a series of interlinked, air-conditioned pods, huge tubes, each big enough for fourteen camp beds. There was even hot running water in the shower units. But there was plenty enough going on to remind us of where we actually were, and as good as the accommodation might have been it was not going to stop us being exposed to the conflict beyond the perimeter. That we found out the hard way.

One night, our peaceful slumber was rudely disturbed by gunfire outside the PRT HQ. It was heavy enough for us all to tumble out of bed, drag on our body armour and reach for our rifles. As we were doing so there was a scream. It came from a young captain. He had been hit in the arse, or so it appeared from where I was now lying low trying to finish putting my kit on before I too was on the receiving end of a piece of lead. The round had come through the side of the tent and struck the unfortunate man as he was trying to pull up his trousers.

I am ashamed to say that as he fought to apply a field dressing to the wound, which was bleeding profusely, none of us rushed to his aid. Whether we were too busy struggling with our body armour or put off by the prospect of having intimate dealings with the casualty's rear I would not like to say. Eventually another officer crawled towards him. Someone was going to do the right thing. I breathed a sigh of relief. But it was to be short-lived. The Good Samaritan pulled out his mobile phone, pointed it at the hapless victim and proceeded to take a photo before scurrying away. Help finally arrived in the form of a medical team and the wounded man was treated. He would later be flown to Camp Bastion for further treatment and recuperation before returning to Lash. The final insult for him came when it was discovered that he had not been hurt as a result of enemy action but rather friendly fire; an ANA soldier had panicked and shot wildly at what he believed were members of the Taliban creeping away. I understood how our Afghan colleague might have got mixed up. It had happened to me.

For the first few weeks at the PSCC I was as nervous as hell. Each day there would be a constant stream of people coming to the compound to meet the province's Governor, Mohammed Daoud, known to everyone as Engineer Daoud. With my interpreter Namir I would often watch them file past. More than a few of those who turned up wore distinctive black turbans. Didn't our enemies wear this style of headdress? One day I articulated my curiosity.

'Talib?' I enquired warily.

'Not Talib, Captain Doug,' came the reply.

A little while later, 'Talib?' I enquired again, nodding towards a new arrival.

'Not Talib.'

And so it went on until I got bored of asking.

A bit later Namir tapped my shoulder, wrestling me away from my daydreaming. 'Talib!' he said triumphantly.

I looked at the eight men being escorted up the steps towards the Governor's office. 'How do you know?'

'Everyone knows who they are. And anyway they tie their turbans in a distinctive fashion.'

Namir explained. Our enemy wore their headgear large, tilted slightly to one side, and with a wide flap hanging down over the left shoulder. From then on I kept an eager lookout for Afghans with jaunty turbans.

As the weeks passed I settled into a routine, arriving at the Governor's compound each morning at about 07:00 hrs. There were two checkpoints to clear, both manned by the ANP. One was at the end of the road, the second at the main entrance to the front courtyard. Having passed security I would descend the steps to the PSCC's 'office' complex, a dingy half-basement divided into six rooms. It stank.

After mornings full of meetings, training sessions and time

spent playing out incident-response scenarios it would be time for lunch. As we all sat on the floor, the food would be served up by a young Afghan soldier. Whether I wanted it or not, he always ensured piles of it came my way. There wasn't much variation. Meat, generally goat, with rice. Every time a meal was laid out in front of me, I couldn't help but recall, with a smile on my face, a patrol I had been out on with the ANP into the desert to visit some of their checkpoints. When the time came to eat I asked the Afghans what we were having.

'Fish.'

Fish? In the middle of the desert? Where the hell had that come from? There was no water in any direction for at least forty kilometres.

I waited in eager anticipation to find out exactly what we would be having. A small boy finally appeared with a large bowl full of rice, tomatoes, peppers and cucumber. On top of it there was meat. Not fish. But meat. As usual. It looked like goat. As usual.

'That's not fish.'

'Of course it is,' replied the leader of the patrol, grinning. 'And tomorrow it will be chicken!'

Clearly the Afghans had their own little mechanisms for coping with the austerity of their lives.

At the compound, lunch normally coincided with about the time the Governor headed off. Once he went, so did we. Or at least we tried to, often having to wait for a couple of hours for our request for transport back to the PRT base to be sorted out.

The days rolled by and once again I was getting itchy feet. I wasn't stuck behind a desk in KAF but nor was I getting out and about as much as I wanted to, or as much as others seemed to be.

Garmsir would change all that.

The town had been under Taliban attack for weeks, a mixture of 107mm rockets, mortars and small-arms fire harassing the ANP force left there to try and thwart the insurgents. On 9 September they finally succumbed and the town fell. The

At home with my dad and brother Rab in Union Street.

Charge! A staged shot of the Royal Irish on the offensive circa 1980. My brother Rab is on the right.

Margaret and I outside St Columbus church in Portadown on our wedding day in August 1987.

Receiving the Accumulated Campaign Service Medal from Prince Andrew. Margaret is in the background.

St Patrick's Day 2003 before the invasion of Iraq.

Tim Collins addressing the men in Kuwait prior to 1 R IRISH crossing the border into Iraq.

Food for thought. Listening to a speech by General Sir Mike Jackson before the invasion of Iraq.

With RSM John D'Lacey from the Irish Defence Force on St Patrick's Day 2004 in Sarajevo during my time in the Balkans with SFOR.

Destructive and deadly. The aftermath of a suicide car bomb attack in Kandahar.

An RAF Regiment mortar team fires an illumination round to help pinpoint Taliban positions outside Kandahar Airfield.

A rooftop view of Lashkar Gah from the Governor's compound.

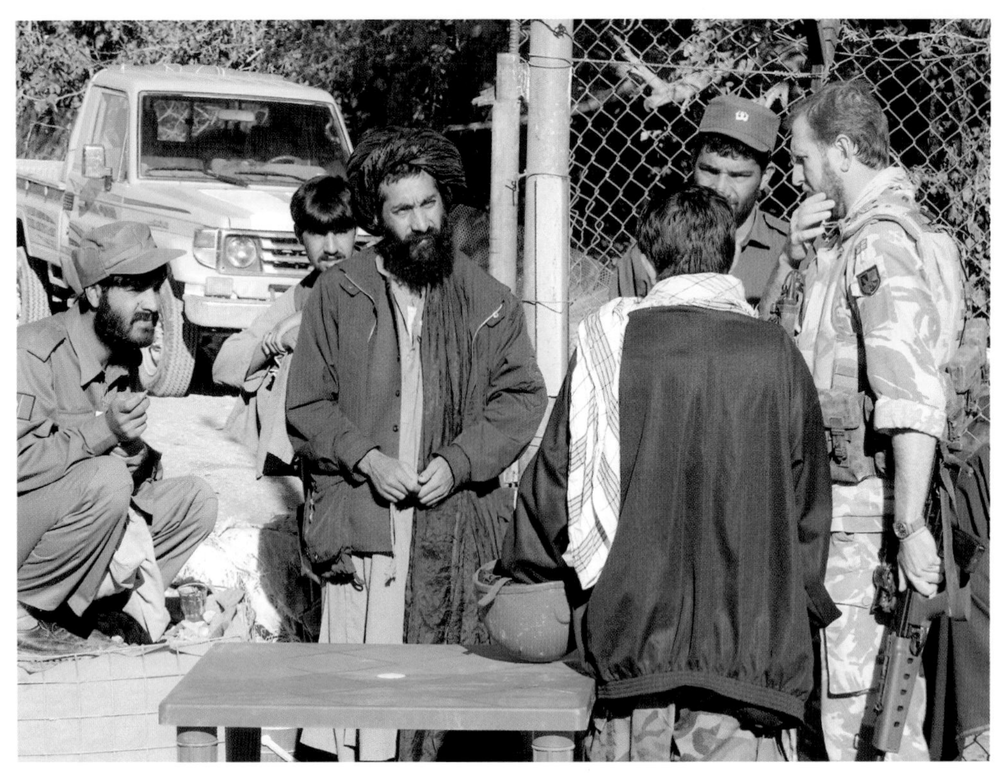

Chatting to members of the Afghan security forces.

The opposition. Taliban fighters.

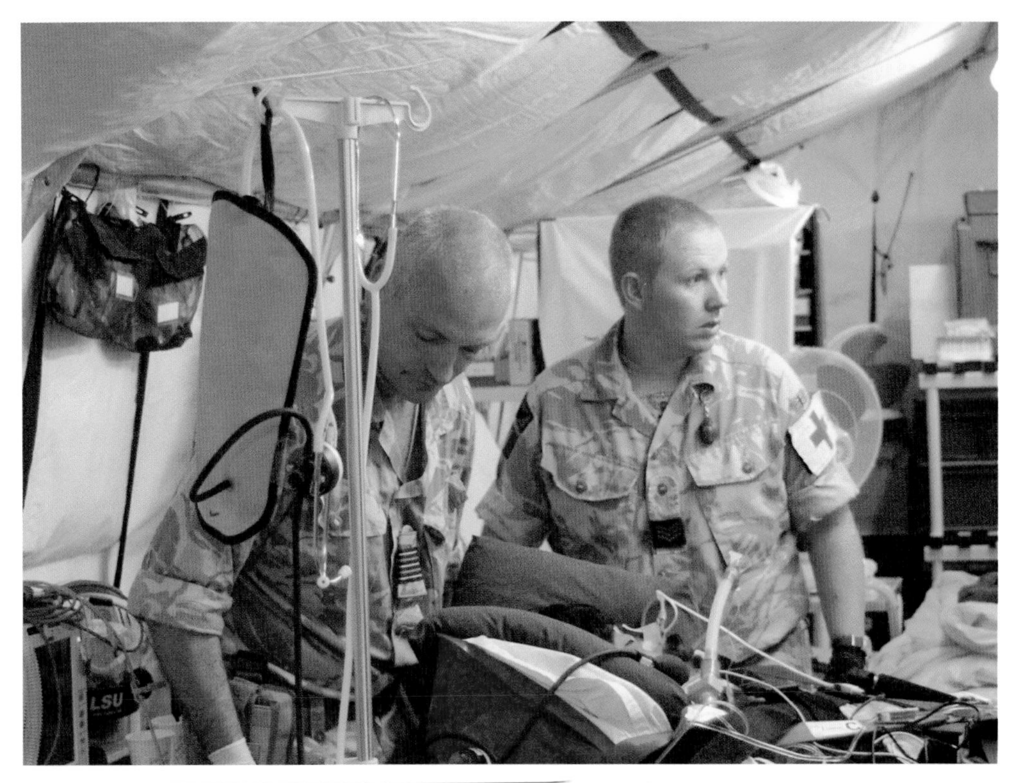

Medics at Camp Bastion prepare to casevac an injured Afghan soldier to Kandahar.

An Apache helicopter flies over Royal Artillery guns on the range outside Camp Bastion.

Chewing the fat. Afghans doing what Afghans do. Drinking tea in Garmsir.

Chipper's WMIK weighed down with men and equipment during a rare moment of calm in Garmsir.

situation had become critical and not just militarily. Under pressure from the Kabul government and the provincial tribal council in Helmand the Governor had been threatening to resign if just such a thing happened. Now it was all Charlie Knaggs could do to stop him going through with his pledge. The promise he made to Engineer Daoud to prevent him quitting his job was that despite ISAF having done little to prevent Garmsir falling into enemy hands it was going to do everything it could to get it back. It was a promise easier made than fulfilled.

Unfortunately there weren't enough men to go around, as 3 PARA, a large fighting part of 16 Air Assault Brigade, were fully committed to operations in the north of Helmand. It would be down to a thrown-together squad from Lashkar Gah to get the job done.

The contingent would be Afghan-led but with ISAF assistance. The ANA would be supported by an Operational Mentoring and Liaison Team (OMLT) – twelve men under Tim Illingworth's command – whilst I would head the ANP side of things, along with Sergeant-Major Joe Cummings from the Intelligence Corps, and Bombardier Sam New of the Royal Horse Artillery, a well-tanned and fit-looking soldier with an easy-going manner, who had been in the military for some eight years. For good measure a clutch of Estonians were coming, too. The unenviable task of trying to keep this disparate group working together fell to Paddy Williams. The plan had been that he would report directly to Lashkar Gah but command politics instead meant he was under the control of HQ at KAF.

After Colonel Charlie had outlined the details he turned to me. He wanted to know more about the readiness of the ANP.

'Are they up to the job? Can they muster a large enough force?'

'Yes, I would say they're up to it. All they need is a bit of strong leadership and someone to give them a good kick up the backside.'

I didn't really have much choice in my answer. For a couple of months I'd been giving the ANP the benefit of my wisdom and they'd come to trust what I said. Now it had come the point where I had to at least back my own abilities, if not necessarily theirs.

What I did think increasingly certain was that this was not going to be crash, bang, wallop and then home.

Forty-eight hours. That was the time the planners believed it would take us to complete the operation, their view being we would quickly overwhelm the Taliban in and around the town, before being relieved by more Afghan security forces. But I was preparing myself to stay in Garmsir for a while longer. I knew we would be out on a limb, way down south, beyond easy reach of our support units.

But hadn't I said I would prefer to be in the thick of things rather than office-bound? I wanted to see as much as I could of what Afghanistan was like, what it had to offer, the problems people were encountering; I wanted an insight into the conflict.

I should have remembered the old adage: be careful what you wish for, it might just come true – and in the shape of the mission to retake Garmsir, it did. I would get more of an insight than I ever wanted.

We soon cleared Lashkar Gah and entered the open country typical of southern Afghanistan – the huge mountains and sharp peaks of the Hindu Kush in the north, and the knife-edged ridges of high ground in the centre of the country, having given way to vast tracts of flat desert plains, an unwelcoming mixture of sand and rock. With the Land Rovers spread out in line abreast we rattled along at a steady twenty-five miles per hour. Not Lewis Hamilton speeds, but quite fast enough over the rutted, rocky terrain to keep us shaken up. No chance here of dozing off at the wheel. The ANA followed in single file, each driver keeping to the tracks of the man in front; the ANP, more ill-disciplined, going wherever they liked, weaving this way and that, like something from the old cartoon *Wacky Races*.

There is a romantic notion that comes over soldiers as they set off on the prelude to confrontation: the notion of a just war, of fighting not just for your colleagues but also for Queen and country in a legitimate cause. I was older than most and should have known better than most, should have controlled my exuberance, but I too had a Lawrence of Arabia moment. Or perhaps it was more a Blair Mayne moment, images of the WWII leader taking the fight to the Germans in North Africa seeping into my mind.

We were now making steady progress, although we'd already taken casualties. Two ANP cars had been defeated by the lethal Afghan cocktail of heat, dust and vibration. Lack of time and spare parts meant we had no choice but to leave them – and, perhaps more critically, the ten men they were carrying.

We also had a problem with soft sand. Every so often one of our number would end up axle-deep in silicon, the only way out coming through the use of shovels and plenty of elbow grease. Already the temperature was over forty degrees Celsius, hot enough to be uncomfortable even while merely driving along, more than unpleasant when it came to manhandling tons of steel out of a dune. The sweat stains started to grow under my arms.

To protect my eyes I wore goggles. Across my mouth was tied my *shemagh*, a square piece of cloth. Constantly tugged at by the breeze and jolted by the shaking, it kept slipping down, exposing my skin and lips to the blistering dry heat of the desert.

To try to reduce our vulnerability to attack, and sand, we started to take a higher line through the terrain. It was nearly to be our undoing. My driver, Joe Cummings, was trying his best not to let the WMIK get away from him – the high centre of gravity created by the heavy gun platform on top meant he was slipping and sliding all over the place. He became more engrossed in halting our lateral progression than he was on concentrating on our forward momentum. It was this that almost saw us drive into a wadi and crash thirty metres to the parched earth below.

Thank God someone was looking ahead.

'We're going over. We're going over!' Yasir yelled as we

approached the precipice. Our interpreter was right. We were about to arc lazily through the air towards a certain, messy death.

He got ready to jump. I got ready to jump. What saved us was that all the shouting had made Joe panic. A small thin man, Joe's nerves had got the better of him and just inches from the edge he managed to stall the engine. We sat there in a sweat, and not just from the baking sun.

For eight hours we continued on our bone-jarring passage across the wasteland before reaching our destination. The lie-up was some five kilometres from our military objective the next day and we got there with barely an hour of daylight to spare.

Guarding our makeshift camp was a similarly ramshackle affair. There was little love lost between the two groups of Afghans. The ANA accused the ANP of being sympathetic to the Taliban. The ANP believed the ANA little better than Western puppets. The ANP had no standard operating procedures. The ANA came across as a bunch of trigger-happy cowboys. With our local colleagues patrolling the perimeter we were scared stiff of one group shooting up the other, a so-called green on green (rather than a blue on blue, which describes a friendly fire incident involving only ISAF troops). In the end we split the two sides up, one dispatched north of our location, the other south, the buffer in between: us Brits and the Estonians.

That evening I ate with General Durani and talked about the task ahead.

He had sent for me. In his mind, because I was supposed to be mentoring the ANP, he owned me. When he wanted something, he asked for Beattie. And I was answerable to him. I was there to support and guide the ANP. And the General was at its head.

We discussed the attack.

Yes, we had to clear Garmsir of the Taliban, but we also had to leave the Afghan forces in control and ready for counter-attacks. The more benign the environment in the town, the more chance there was of the local population returning to their homes and jobs. Hundreds, perhaps thousands, had fled to the countryside after the Taliban first put the government forces under pressure in early May. As the inhabitants hopefully came back, the intention was to recruit them into a local defence force. This militia would allow the Afghan 'professionals' to be deployed elsewhere.

All well and good in theory. But even if our mission succeeded militarily, it still depended on the Helmand chief of police and the Governor putting resources into the area, and living up to their fine words about rooting out corruption and destroying the many ad hoc alliances made between town officials and the Taliban.

'Tomorrow we fight together,' said the General. 'And when we win we will be famous and the Taliban will go.'

As I walked away I couldn't help but think the fighting might actually be the easy part, with the hard part brokering the peace. Once again I was wrong. Nothing would be easy.

Paddy was waiting for me. The son of a career soldier who rose through the ranks, he was serving with the Blues and Royals (part of the Household Cavalry). He was stocky, but not particularly tall, with short black hair. His Irish heritage was hidden by a Home Counties accent gained during his dad's time in England. With a cigarette routinely clamped in his mouth he gave off an air of calm, a smile rarely far from the surface.

His good humour would be sorely tested in the days to come.*

Paddy gave us the final orders for the next day's offensive. We would launch our assault at 06:00 hrs on 11 September 2006, exactly five years to the day since the al-Qaeda attacks on the twin towers in New York, the subsequent war on terror being the pretext for us being in Afghanistan at all.

He said the Pathfinder Platoon was due to rendezvous with us

---

* I was later to find out that our paths had crossed before. Paddy was part of the Household Cavalry reconnaissance screen that I had rushed past with Colonel Tim Collins on our dash to the town of Al Medina in Iraq in April 2003. Paddy would also be the one who told me the Household Cavalry's nickname for the Colonel was 'the American Tourist'.

in the morning and secure our form-up position (FUP) before the assault. It was good to have these guys about.

Part of 16 Air Assault Brigade, most of the platoon's members come from the Parachute Regiment. In terms of experience, reputation and training, they are second only to the Special Air Service, indeed many of them make the transition to the SAS. Their main role is as a reconnaissance unit, acting on the front line, and often beyond it. Unfortunately they would only be with us to cover the beginning of our operation, not the middle and end.

'Once we start, Doug, I'll need you to make sure the ANP are directed to the northern canal crossing. Once that's secure I'll send in the ANA to clear the buildings west of the crossing and then we can start to work southwards.'

Southwards towards the district centre (DC).

'Understood, Paddy,' I said.

'Just remember, I don't want you involved in the fighting. Just get Sam in a position where he can call in air support if needed.'

I knew Paddy was worried. He was the man at the top of our particular tree and he was going to take the fall if we didn't succeed. He had plenty to think about. Discipline within the ANP was shaky at best and the men of the OMLT led by Tim were short on infantry skills and influence.

But which commander is ever happy with the resources at hand on the eve of battle? Our task, like generations of soldiers before us, was to make the best of a bad job.

I wished I had a good reply for Paddy to lighten the mood, but none came. All I said as I headed off to get some rest was 'Inshallah'.

I had been expecting to get no sleep at all, tossing and turning, vivid thoughts racing through my mind, umpteen battle scenarios playing themselves out in my head. But in reality I was out like a light.

SEVEN

WHERE DID IT ALL GO WRONG?

(GARMSIR, DAY 1)

My blissful slumber didn't last long. All too soon I was shaken awake by a hand on my shoulder. I rubbed my eyes. Sam was standing over me. It was 02:00 hrs and my turn for stag, listening to the radio. There would be no more rest that night. The temperature had fallen rapidly as darkness descended and it was now perhaps just ten degrees. The others were asleep around me; some hunched in the vehicles, more curled up in sleeping bags on the ground, or in the case of the Afghans, in blankets. There was the odd grunt and groan, one or two faint sounds of snoring, but overall the impression was one of peace. Looking up I could see a stellar display from the cosmos. It was spellbinding, mesmerising.

Two and a half hours later and morning arrived for everyone.

The stars were still high and bright in the sky. We were due to be at the FUP by 06:00 hrs, but sixty minutes after that we had only just got there; once again we had been caught out by the environment, or rather I had. It was my wagon that got bogged down in the sand. I cursed my luck.

The FUP afforded us our first look at Garmsir. Not the DC – that was still some three kilometres south of us – but at least the north-eastern fringes. The odd hut and building became groups of buildings, the flat sandy landscape starting to give way to vegetation supported in its precarious battle for life by the Helmand River and parallel canal which ran north–south, straddling the town.

As promised, the Pathfinders were already waiting for us. Suddenly, without warning, they opened up with their .50-cal machine guns, rounds of tracer streaking through the now quickly brightening sky in a curve towards the canal bridge. Then came the whoosh, whoosh, whoosh of Javelin missiles being fired. They had plainly seen something we had not.

'Well, that's our element of surprise bloody well gone,' said Paddy over the Personal Role Radio (PRR) that all British troops carried. Not that there had been much secrecy in the first place; even despite our convoluted route, it was hard to hide 30 vehicles and nearly 200 men on a flat, open desert plain.

Paddy was drowned out as the enemy fired back. The telltale whistle and then crump of a 107mm rocket filled the air.

It landed a good 400 metres short of us but was followed up moments later by a second round and then a third, each closer than the one before. Looking about me I couldn't see anywhere to seek cover. That's the bloody annoying thing about deserts.

The incoming 107mm ordnance sounded a bit like fireworks being set off. The shells produced a strange warbling noise that made it very difficult to work out where they were coming from and, perhaps more importantly, where they were going to land. The rockets hit the ground at a low angle and explode, sending red-hot shards of body casing spinning through the air in all directions. When you're caught up in a nearby strike in a closed vehicle it feels like you're being pelted with stones. When you are outside, you die.

The enemy was getting our range and we were in danger of taking casualties.

'Enemy left. Enemy left,' the PRR crackled again.

'Not seen,' came a cautious, disembodied reply.

'Six hundred metres due south, in the buildings, enemy moving left to right, permission to engage.'

'Wait!' The wariness was there again.

All the vehicle commanders had their binoculars locked to their eyes, scanning the same patch of ground, looking for insurgents.

'This is Tim. Do not fire. Those people are civilians moving away from the area. Acknowledge.'

We did. The hunt for the source of the 107s continued.

Paddy told me to speak to the General and get the ANP formed up ready for the assault on the canal crossing.

'Happy to move in any bloody direction as long as it's away from here,' I answered.

I drove over to where the General stood with his second-in-command, Colonel Gulzar.

'Taliban,' said the General, pointing towards a position west of us, close to where some of the locals were fleeing.

'They're civilians,' I insisted. 'The Taliban are by the canal crossing further south.'

'No, no, Taliban over there,' he repeated more forcefully.

It took me a few moments to work out exactly what he was trying to say. Durani wasn't pointing at the people, but at some huts. He was convinced our first target, the crossing, was not where I thought it was, some 1,000 metres away pretty much south, but was in fact much nearer, a mere 400 metres to our right. One of us had got it completely wrong and the General was certain that person was me. As was the Colonel.

'We will attack there,' said the General triumphantly.

They had put doubt in my mind and I wasn't going to change their opinion any time soon. I told them to hang fire while I gave Paddy the bad news.

I could see him thinking it through, concern etched on his brow; here we were, stuck out in the open, the element of surprise gone, 107mm rockets landing amongst us, sixty minutes late for H-hour (the time the operation was due to start) and now we weren't even sure of our intended first target.

'I need a second opinion from Tim,' he decided.

But Tim and the OMLT were rather preoccupied. He'd worked out where the 107s had originated from and was directing fire towards the source. He clearly had other things to worry about. Paddy made up his mind.

'Doug, take the ANP to the start point and we will speak again when you are there.'

I explained to him I was doubtful that once the ANP started moving they would stop again till they reached the objective, be it the right one or not.

It was like a cavalry charge. Eight ANP vehicles stretched line-abreast across the desert, eight men in each. Within seconds they were going hell for leather, towards a small mound, which was the start point – and there did indeed seem little chance of them stopping, or being stopped, before first blood had been drawn. I kept my vehicle to the left flank so I could retain some sort of visual contact with the rest of our forces. Chipper Davidson's Land Rover was just to my rear.

It was just like *Top Gun*, me playing the Tom Cruise character Maverick, Chipper taking on Anthony Edwards's role as Goose, my wingman, the faithful number two. A quiet, diligent Glaswegian, who wore glasses and had greying hair, Chipper was a territorial sergeant-major in the Royal Regiment of Scotland. His job was to cover my arse, to get Beattie out of the mess he was bound to end up in. The idea was simple. Chipper and his crew (driver Michael 'Geordie' Elgie from the Army Air Corps and Steve Chambers, the gunner, a Royal Marine) would remain a 'tactical bound' behind, scanning the terrain, looking for trouble. If our vehicle came under attack they would either stop to lay down suppressing fire so we could withdraw, or they'd race to our assistance.

The start point came and went. No one slowed down.

'Fuck it,' I said to Joe. 'Just keep going.' Over the radio: 'This is it, Paddy. They're not stopping. Our battle begins here.'

And so it did. Small-arms fire started to crack over our heads, then strange cigar-shaped objects streaked our way; rocket-propelled grenades (RPGs) detonating all around us.

I couldn't fully register what was going on. It didn't seem like danger, just noise. But a direct hit from an RPG and we would all have been dead. In my Land Rover Sam New stood in the back using the general purpose machine gun (GPMG) to give as good as he got. Joe was driving, careering headlong into the mayhem, worried most of all that we would get left behind.

Out of my view the Pathfinders had already taken their leave.

One hundred metres from a drainage ditch, just short of the crossing, the ANP vehicles slewed to a halt. Out of each tumbled seven men; within seconds the vehicles were racing back the way they had just come, leaving the poor bloody infantry to take the objective. The ANP dismounts were just north of the crossing and clearing a small building. Moments later and they disappeared into the ditch. My WMIK together with Chipper's had stopped out in the open. The 107mm rounds started to target us again. Then I heard a slightly different sort of explosion: incoming Soviet-made 82mm mortars.

Strange, I thought. After spending so many of my younger years during the Cold War, preparing for an onslaught from the Soviet Union that never materialised, here I was, two decades later, in mortal danger from its hardware. Maybe the bastards would get me after all.

Chipper moved his vehicle to take some sort of cover behind what looked like a sheep pen made out of mud. It wouldn't provide much protection from fire, but perhaps a little from view.

I got back on the radio to Paddy. He said he had contacted Kandahar to report a 'Troops in Contact' or TiC. This was our 'get out of jail free' card. Under British rules of engagement, soldiers could only consider calling in air support once they had been fired upon. We didn't need telling twice. Sam was on to it.

'We have two AHs en route to us. They'll be ours for ninety minutes. Any targets?'

As well as being a mean gunner, Sam was also our Joint Tactical Air Controller or JTAC. His call sign was Widow 77. All JTACs in Afghanistan were known as widows. Using his tactical satellite (TacSat) comms equipment he could speak directly to the pilots being sent to our assistance.

The AHs were the latest attack helicopters, American-built Apaches, flown by the Army Air Corps.

No, I didn't have any targets yet. I could hear the crackle of Kalashnikov fire at the crossing just 150 metres away, but could see very little because of the high-sided ditch running in front of it.

There was only one thing for it – to go forward to join up with the ANP and find out exactly what was happening. That way I would be able to relay the detail back to Sam and we could make full use of the aircraft.

'Stay here, Sam. When I call, bring the vehicles over with Chipper. Just keep your bloody head down.'

I grabbed my rifle and a couple of the phosphorus smoke grenades that hung from the Land Rover's side before sliding feet first into the dry drainage channel at the same point the policemen had gone from view.

Running along it, bent over, head hunched deep into my shoulders, I came to a group of ANP, huddled together, waiting for their turn to advance and attack. Several more were laid spread-eagled over the side of the ditch. Intermittently they would stand up, fire a burst from their AK47s, then duck back down. Every so often, with a thunderous bang, one of them launched an RPG towards the high ground the Taliban held and that dominated the crossing.

Further down the channel I found Colonel Gulzar. Through Yasir I asked him what the hell was going on.

He told me his men had driven some Taliban away down the ditch. They were now cornered at the point where the trench met the crossing. I sneaked a cautious look over the top of the sandy parapet and saw perhaps eight of the enemy up on the hill. They were using the same tactics as the ANP – raising themselves up to fire a long stream of 7.62mm bullets, then getting back down out of sight. They too had RPGs, not to mention the rockets and mortars that had harassed us on the plain. If only the Apaches were here now.

Then further along the ditch, to my left, the firing intensified. I pulled at Yasir and we followed a handful of ANP as they headed towards the commotion. Within seconds we ran headlong into more ANP firing wildly at the four Taliban who had been cut off by the fighting. One was clearly wounded, badly. Blood had soaked his clothes and the ground around him. The other three were trying to drag him clear but they were trapped with little place to go.

It had become a Mexican stand-off; the ANP and Taliban blasting away at each other, both sides waiting for the other to break and run. Given that in general Afghans can't shoot – they might have the weapons, but they don't have the training – I sensed this could be a long job. Not so. Just then there was an explosion and a cloud of dirt erupted in my face as an RPG fired from no more than eighty metres away detonated close by. Too close. Two of the policemen were thrown off their feet. In the confusion the Talib at last had their chance. Turning their backs on the policemen, they scrambled over the side of the ditch, hauling their colleague after them, and staggered towards their comrades on the high ground.

I dragged myself up the bank and took aim, trying to calm my breathing, blinking furiously to get the dust and grit out of my eyes. My targets were some 200 metres away by now. I fired, pulling back three times on the trigger of my SA80. It was zeroed for 300. The trajectory of the bullets should have been pretty much flat. No need to aim high or low. All three shots missed by a mile.

Bang, bang, bang.

I fired again.

I missed again.

Fuck, fuck, fuck, I cursed myself. By now the enemy had changed direction; heading south towards some buildings. They shouldn't have been able to. They should have been lying dead in the dust.

Back in the ditch Colonel Gulzar approached. 'Crossing clear. Now time for the ANA to move in.'

'No way,' I shouted in reply. 'You must take the high ground too.'

'You bomb it. Then the ANA goes in,' the Colonel retorted.

After a heated debate I shouldn't have had to go through, I persuaded him to complete the task.

Under RPG covering fire, ten of the ANP charged from the ditch, the front three firing at the hill as they moved. But there was no return fire. Were all the enemy dead or injured? Unlikely. Had they retreated? More probable.

I got on the PRR to Sam and asked him to relay a message to Paddy, who was now way out of radio range: unleash the ANA. Then I hauled Yasir out of the ditch and we sprinted after the ANP, who had by now reached the top of the hill. Once more they were shooting, this time at Taliban positions in some dwellings further west. Bullets streaked past us as we huddled amongst the policemen. They pointed out exactly where the danger lay: a small group of houses surrounded by a walled garden. Peering over the parapet towards the dwellings I could see at least four fighters in and around the buildings. And in worryingly untypical Afghan style they seemed to have got our range. I fired at one of the windows. As I did so a Talib came into full view. I continued to shoot and he fell back out of sight.

Crawling back from my firing position I cast an eye around the Taliban positions we had just overrun. There were plenty of blood trails. Pieces of flesh. Body parts, big and small. But no corpses.

For our part, one of the policemen had been wounded in the

arm, another hit in the back with some shrapnel, but so far that seemed to be it.

I looked further afield and became more confused about the layout of the land. It just didn't seem right.

At that moment Sam's voice came over the radio. 'Doug, the AHs are on station at the crossing but can't see us. Can you give me a target and confirm the grid?'

I stared up into the clear sky, searching for the Apaches. There was no sight or sound of them.

I yanked out my map and peered down at it. Then, for the second time in twenty minutes, I cursed myself.

'We're in the wrong bloody place,' I mumbled to no one in particular.

'Sam, we've fucked it up. The crossing we want is 600 metres south of us. Get Paddy and come to this crossing we've just secured. I'll meet you in a minute.'

The ANP had attacked the wrong position and I had let them do it. What a bloody disaster. Thank God we hadn't taken more casualties.

I ran down the hill in time to see my vehicle, plus those of Paddy and Chipper, and the other two British WMIKs, pulling up at the crossing. The wrong crossing. With them were the Pinzgauer, an all-terrain utility vehicle, then produced by BAE Systems but originally of Austrian origin, and the white 4x4 of General Durani.

'What are the AHs doing now?' I asked Sam.

'They're engaging targets at the correct objective, boss,' he said curtly, a scowl on his face. I wasn't in any position to wipe it off.

I reached Paddy. As I told him of the cock-up, there was a scream. A wounded Afghan policeman was being dragged down the hill, shouting out in pain at every jolt.

Corporal Anthony (Tony) Cowley jumped from the Pinz to meet him at the bottom of the slope.

I watched Corporal Cowley go to work. Tony was a slightly nervous man, who flinched instinctively at the sound of gunfire, but he was utterly professional. As rounds from small arms, rockets and mortars landed about him he kept his attention steadfastly focused on his patient.

The Afghan had been hit in the shin by a high-velocity round. He continued to cry out in pain until Tony jabbed a needle into his thigh, a syringeful of morphine shooting into his body. The effect was nearly instantaneous and the man went quiet. I turned my attention away from Tony's job and back to mine.

'Paddy, the problem is that these lunatics can't read a map, they don't understand grid references, they have no command-and-control structure, and no idea what we are trying to achieve.'

If it sounded like a whinge, then that is exactly what it was.

'So what do you suggest?'

'Well, we need to be at the front, at the point of contact. If we stay at the back then we have no influence on what is happening until it is too late and a mistake has been made.'

'All right, understood. But from now on you take Sam with you. Don't let him out of your bloody sight again.'

It was agreed. Chipper and I would have to re-cross the ditches and then head southwards towards our original objective. Paddy would be coming too, while Tim and the ANA tried to make progress down the western side of the ditch.

We were almost back where we started.

As we moved off, our three vehicles kept in close to the banking of the drainage ditch which ran north–south, offering limited cover. My map and compass stayed out. I wasn't going to screw it up again.

Ahead of us appeared another track, cutting from left to right; one I was confident, for what that was worth, would lead us to the correct crossing. But the open ground was also about to give way to more trees, a network of smaller irrigation trenches and fields of corn (also known as maize) with crops taller than a man. Perfect ambush territory.

We decided to take the next part of our journey at speed.

Pedals to the metal, we burst out from behind the banking and on to the track, veering right, westwards, driving as fast as we could towards the crossing half a kilometre away.

The flat dusty surface soon morphed into deep ruts, furrowed in winter by tractors and carts, and now set as hard as concrete in the baking sun. But the quality of the road surface was about to become the least of our problems.

At that moment the ground around us erupted in small fountains of dirt, 7.62mm rounds boring into the caked earth, throwing up large clumps of soil. Twisting in my seat I could make out the enemy eighty metres or so away, off to the left. The threat of ambush had become reality. An RPG whistled past the back of my Land Rover and over the bonnet of Paddy's. Was it my imagination or could I make out the yellow writing on the side? More grenades exploded just feet away in a line of small trees.

The suddenness of the attack took my breath away. I scrabbled for a response, my brain whirling as I tried to make an assessment of what was happening and concoct a plan for dealing with it. It seemed to take a lifetime but the processing must have been completed in an instant. However, deciding what to do was only the first part of the battle. I still had to convince my body to go through with it. Reality seemed suspended. It was as if I had become an observer, looking at myself from a distance, as if I were both a film star on the cinema screen, and the guy in the audience watching the movie. Unconsciously I was searching for someone to give me guidance, permission to engage, to shout out orders. But there was no one.

Finally, finally, mind conquered matter.

I spun my GPMG anticlockwise towards the enemy and fired a ten-round burst. But instead of the bullets ripping into the Taliban position, I watched in horror as they churned up the soil no more than twenty metres in front of me. I could have blamed it on the unstable, forward momentum of the Land Rover, but the truth was nerves had got me by the balls. It was all I could do to get the shots away. Forget about them being on target.

The sweat came in profusion. Beads of moisture ran down my brow, stinging my eyes. My hands were slipping on the stock of the GPMG. I felt physically sick. I was sure the enemy was about to get our range, and the resulting carnage would be my fault. My fault because I had led us into a trap and my fault because I had not dealt with it quickly enough. It was not something I did very often, but there and then I prayed to God, pleading for some divine intervention.

It came in the reassuringly familiar forms of Paddy and Chipper.

They had managed what I hadn't, and brought their weapons to bear with some accuracy. Meantime Sam was crouched in the back of our wagon, trying to call in air support. As he did so, more enemy fire came towards us from a second position by the canal. There was no way we were going to be able to move any further forward.

Our small convoy ground to a halt and I half-jumped, half-tumbled out of the Land Rover and into cover amongst the trees.

I couldn't see the enemy, but their positions were given away by muzzle flashes from their weapons. I blasted away at the flickering lights.

Sam shouted out that if we could hang on for five minutes the Apaches would be with us.

Paddy's plan was that when the helicopters arrived we would use their covering fire to make a dash for the crossing.

As we ducked the incoming rounds we were joined from the north by a section of the ANA, shooting back at their countrymen, if not comrades, with RPGs and AK47s. With the Taliban's attention diverted I got back into the WMIK, ready for our breakout.

Then the Apaches turned up. I can't remember what I heard first – the sound of their rotor blades or the roar of their 30mm cannon. As they entered the fray empty cartridge cases rained down on us. The helicopters stayed high enough to avoid the small-arms fire, making the occasional short dive to take on specific targets, their rotor blades making a sharper noise each time the aircraft dipped. As the onslaught continued the ANA soldiers leapt to their feet. Not to pursue the attack but to cheer and hug and pat each other in celebration of our air superiority. Paddy unwittingly found himself in the middle of the mêlée. I'd never seen him move so fast. He wanted out of the scrum. Forget friendly fire. He was in imminent danger of receiving a life-extinguishing bear hug from a wild-eyed, smelly, bearded Afghan.

The fire from the enemy positions faltered, either because the AHs had forced them back or because the Taliban were too astonished by our male bonding to shoot at us. We took the lull as our cue. We were off.

The intention was to drive right up to, and then over, the crossing without stopping, praying it hadn't been mined or booby-trapped.

Fifty metres from the canal we were greeted by yet more small-arms fire from our flanks, but the helicopters were doing a good job of covering our backs and they soon suppressed it. At the same time more ANA soldiers engaged a small building that dominated the crossing point. Everywhere I looked there seemed to be contacts.

At last the prize became clear. Not a bridge, but a dam, with water-release valves on the northern side. On the far side of it lay a road running north–south along the canal. Beyond that, more buildings, and more cornfields.

My heart almost jumped out of my chest as we sped past an empty Taliban bunker and on to the dam. It was 11:30 hrs. We had been fighting and moving for four and a half hours, yet only now had we reached our initial objective with the DC still some three kilometres distant. Chipper followed our example. So did Paddy. The ANA and ANP also started to emerge from various directions, converging on the crossing. Tim was there too.

The Apaches – the real battle-winners – were disappearing into the distance, black specks against the clear, pale-blue sky.

Their pilots had offered to stay on, but it seemed certain we would need them again later, so they were cleared to return to Kandahar Airfield to rearm and refuel.

Within minutes it seemed as if later had already arrived. Whistle, crump. Whistle, crump. 107mm rockets landed around us yet again. So did the mortar rounds.

As I scanned the ground to the south an enemy soldier jumped out in front of me, emerging from a cornfield, the crops as high as a man. He was no more than fifty metres away. On his right shoulder there was a tube with something jammed into one end; it was shaped like an elongated bulb, grey in colour. He'd got an RPG launcher and the warhead was pointing straight at me. A fraction of a second later he fired.

First I saw a flash, then came the bang. It was really quite hypnotic. The RPG flew right over the top of our vehicle. Way, way too late I ducked, the missile already far beyond, striking the ground next to the Land Rover of Sergeant-Major Tommy Johnstone.

I swung my GPMG round to bring it to bear on the man trying to kill me. He was dressed in traditional loose-fitting clothes, the colours a mix of white and brown. Wrapped around his head was a turban, a long swathe of cloth hanging from it over his left shoulder. In my mind he seemed to be in his mid-thirties, but telling how old an Afghan is, is far from easy. The grind of daily life, the dirt, the sun; they conspire to age a person way beyond their years. Not that he was likely to have been very old, the average life expectancy in Afghanistan being just forty-four. He looked like a peasant farmer, but in a country of such dismal poverty most of the men did, and indeed were.

The man stared back at me with intense brown eyes. There was no fear.

This time I didn't hesitate, didn't analyse. His sharp outline became blurred as I refocused on the small foresight at the end of my weapon and squeezed the trigger. It was almost an innocent act, a drill, a bit like being on the firing range, shooting at a target made of metal. The weapon bucked into life as I released a five-round burst, the links and empty cartridges spewing out of the gun to my right, landing on the floor of the vehicle, joining a growing pile of spent cases. The bullets exited the barrel at a phenomenal speed, travelling towards the Talib at more than 800 metres per second. That didn't give him much time to get out of the way.

If that first volley had been wide or high then perhaps, maybe, he would have had a chance of escape before I fired again, but it wasn't. It was spot on. I lifted my eyes up and away from the sight and gazed down the road. As he came back into focus I saw the result of him being hit by at least three rounds. Two had caught him square in the upper body, the impact causing dust to fly up from his cloak, as if someone were beating a rug. The third round hit him in the head. I couldn't quite tell where. It didn't really matter. His skull shattered, parts of bone, blood, brain, hair and flesh spinning out in all directions.

The force of the impact threw him back into the cornfield and out of view. For the first time in all my years of soldiering I had killed someone. There was no doubt about it. I had taken a life. Perhaps during what had gone before that day I'd already taken others. Maybe the fighter at the window who fell from view was a victim of mine. But this was definite – no question.

And personal. I was face to face with the enemy. Close enough to identify features, distinguish some blemishes, certainly recognise bravery and determination.

It set off a whole train of thoughts.

Was he married, like me?

Did he have children, like me?

Were members of his family counting down the days till he came home, like mine were?

Perhaps he had an absolute belief that everything he was doing was just and right, and that God was on his side as he defended his homeland against an evil aggressor. Now he would meet that God, having died for his cause. My encounter with my maker was back on hold, but for how long? What was waiting round the next corner for me? Another enemy who this time would be quicker than me? Luckier than me?

If any scrap of the romanticism of Lawrence or Mayne had been left inside me, it instantly evaporated. The tearing-apart of another man's body banished it completely.

War is about dirty disgusting realities that are rightly an affront to most people. It is about blood and guts and pain and distress. Nothing more. Welcome to Afghanistan, summer 2006. The country where Defence Secretary John Reid said he hoped the British would not have to fire a shot.

But there was no time to dwell further on the personal and political aspects of war. There would, I prayed again, be plenty of opportunity for that in the future. For now I still had work to do. Funny that I was paid to kill people. Strange to describe it as work – so anodyne a description for such a brutal reality.

A moment later and I loosed off another five-round burst, then another, then more still. If there were any other Taliban in that cornfield I was going to shred them before they had chance to repeat what their erstwhile colleague had just attempted.

Chipper, Tim, Steve and Paddy were now all firing in the same direction. Even Joe was engaging with his SA80.

I glanced across to see the vehicles rocking back and forth from the kick of the top-mounted .50-calibres. They reminded me of the nodding donkeys you see in oilfields. The chorus of fire was quite deafening.

All of a sudden there was the most excruciating pain in my ears. Sam had joined the attack, his weapon directly over my head, the noise from it ricocheting around my skull. Because of the cacophony of noise he couldn't hear my shouts of anger.

I jumped out and went to the back of the truck. 'For fuck's sake, Sam, are you trying to deafen me? Bloody well tell me when you are going to shoot over my head.'

'What?' yelled Sam. 'I can't hear a thing. It's all this shooting.'

Exactly, I said to myself.

Return fire from the cornfield had dried up and our fusillade petered out too. Only then did the ANP and ANA start to emerge from the cover they had taken during the firefight, more than happy for UK plc to sort things out.

Not so Sean Langan. He'd been darting about filming the mayhem, ignoring the bullets and bits of bombs. I was already becoming used to Sean's presence and didn't mind it. He wasn't asking for our help and we weren't giving it.

Our position was just west of the canal, the centre of Garmsir still almost three kilometres to the south. To get there we would have more outlying settlements to move through, more of these bloody cornfields to cautiously circumvent. Hemming us in to the left, the east, was the canal. To the right, the west, about one and a half kilometres away, the Helmand River.

The river sustains the province. In a region of arid, sandy emptiness it is a vivid-blue ragged slash flowing first north to south before cutting across Helmand towards the south-west. On each side it is bordered by greenery; fertile land the Afghans have created for themselves by the use of irrigation ditches and canals. This green zone extends away from the water for anything from a couple of hundred metres to a kilometre or more. At the edge of this narrow strip of lushness the vast barren desert sits there patiently, waiting for the rains to fail, the meltwaters from the uplands not to arrive, and therefore its opportunity to smother colour and hence life. Not that the desert was all bad, at least as far as we were concerned. There might not have been much cover out in the open but at least you could see your enemy coming.

Not so next to the river. Amongst the trenches, trees and crops crowding the meandering waterway there was every opportunity for the enemy to lie in wait. The Taliban could be as close as ten metres away in places and we would not have a clue. It frightened the life out of me.

*

Paddy called Tim and me together to remind us of his intentions. He wanted us to clear our way south between the two watercourses, right down to the DC . . . by nightfall. But it was clear that our orders from Kandahar to lead from the back were not going to work if we were to have any control at all over the Afghans. Paddy recognised that rapid, offensive movement would give us the most likely chance of overwhelming the enemy. What we had to avoid at all costs was becoming bogged down in close-quarter confrontation.

'Tim, I want you and the ANA to work westwards towards the high ground here,' said Paddy. He indicated a point on the map some two kilometres north of the DC and perhaps 500 metres in from the river.

'Doug, you are to continue going down the road next to the canal with the ANP, clearing these villages.' His finger hovered over a series of habitation symbols.

Paddy would travel with us, along with the JTAC, acting as link between Tim and myself. The rest of the vehicles would follow too, while Tim went off cross-country on foot with the ANA soldiers.

Our orders understood, all we had to do was explain them to the Afghans.

I approached the white 4x4 of the General. As he opened the door an avalanche of cold air tumbled out, spilling down my legs and on to my feet. I could have stood there all afternoon. Via Yasir I told him what was going to happen. As I was beginning to find out, his solution to any problem was to bring in air support – in this case to bomb the DC. I said that wasn't possible as there was no way of telling how many civilians might be left. He had little sympathy for my argument.

'It doesn't matter,' he said. 'Women Talib, old men Talib, children Talib. Just bomb them all like the others did.'

He was trying to persuade me some of our allied colleagues had previously gone into the town, apparently using, shall we say, more robust tactics. I couldn't quite believe what he was suggesting and wondered whether something had got lost in translation.

A quarter of an hour later and the ANA soldiers still hadn't moved off. Paddy and Tim were in animated discussion with their leader, who was being urged on by his men. It was the typical Afghan way. Decision by committee – no real sense of a command structure and no trust in or loyalty to the guy giving the orders. If an Afghan soldier doesn't like what he's being asked to do, then he doesn't do it.

'They claim it's too dangerous,' Paddy said exasperatedly.

'Well, Tim had better get it sorted pretty damn quick before they start mortaring us again,' I snapped.

After much negotiation, a deal of sorts was done, Tim having gathered together a breakaway group of five ANA troops. The tension between the ANP and those ANA left behind rose to boiling point, with General Durani and Colonel Gulzar shouting at the ANA soldiers. They told them just how bloody useless they were and that they should hand over all their ammunition to the ANP so the policemen could get on with what needed to be done.

Enemy firing started again and once more it seemed to be coming from the east of the canal, somewhere near the spot where the Apaches had rained down their cannon shells. The Taliban had obviously regrouped.

I was standing behind a high wall when an RPG round struck it, sending masonry flying into the air and bits of dust and grit into my eyes. The ANA responded by firing long bursts from their assault rifles, which had more chance of bringing down birds than killing the enemy. General Durani started screaming and cursing an ANA soldier who was enthusiastically blasting away nearby, using up bullets the General felt his men could have expended rather more effectively.

This berating and a repeat of the RPG strike finally gave the rest of the ANA some impetus. At last they too agreed to go with Tim, probably because it was safer than staying where they were and possibly because they also wanted to get out of range of the General.

Twenty more soldiers had already been tasked with staying at the crossing. If the insurgents wanted to outflank us, this was the obvious point for them to cross. I could do without that surprise, thank you very much.

We all moved off together, including Tim and his men, advancing past the buildings, setting fire to each one as we cleared them, and skirting the cornfield where I had shot the man with the RPG. As I walked, I looked around for the body, but there was no sign of it. No blood, no flesh, nothing. Perhaps I'd missed him after all. No, that wasn't possible. I didn't miss. Definitely I didn't. He must have been spirited away by his colleagues.

Tim peeled off, taking the ANA soldiers westwards, leaving me with the General, the Colonel and around forty of their men. The rest of the ANP forces were either at the crossing with the ANA, guarding the vehicles, or had become casualties of war. We seemed to comprise a worryingly small force given the immediate challenges we faced and it didn't take long until the ANA ran into trouble, confronted with RPG, 107mm and 81mm shells, and small-arms fire.

Over the next hour they would get within grenade-throwing range of the enemy and suffer a steady stream of casualties, the dead and wounded dragged and carried back to the crossing; the corpses dumped by the roadside, the injured tended to by Corporal Cowley, who quickly became familiar with a hideous range of penetrative injuries caused by a murderous mix of bullets and shrapnel.

As Tim's battle ground on, I continued down a track parallel with the canal road. It was a slow ramble in the Afghan countryside, interspersed every so often with an unscheduled stop while the policemen concentrated fire into a building until the enemy either died or fled. It wasn't a pretty tactic and perhaps not the way I would have cleared buildings, but it seemed to be working.

We came to a narrowing of the track. On one side, the ubiquitous cornfield. To the other, a row of buildings. More ambush territory. If we were attacked from the crops there would be nowhere to run or hide, our backs would literally be up against the wall. I had an idea though. Why not try and set fire to the crops and flush the enemy out that way?

I removed my rucksack, and took a red phosphorus grenade from it, pulling the pin ready to throw.

Red phos is the main munition British troops have for generating smoke. Its predecessor was the white phosphorus grenade. Not only did that produce smoke, but it was also an offensive weapon; pieces of the burning element would be flung through the air upon detonation. Any that stuck to human flesh would continue to burn, right through skin and muscle, straight down to the bone. It was almost impossible to pick off or extinguish.

'Phos!' I yelled into the radio.

The grenade disappeared into the field and exploded. Sparks flew into the air and the area slowly became shrouded in smoke. I grinned at General Durani, a look of achievement painted across my face. It was a little premature. The smoke cleared and then nothing. No trace of flames flickering and catching. What a complete waste of time. The grenade had done just what it said on the tin and no more.

The General grinned back. Or was he smirking? I walked away sheepishly, my embarrassment and anger greater than any fear of the enemy.

The advance seemed to be going well. Tim and his group had finally taken the high ground, despite the ferocity of the fighting and the casualties. The ANP with me and the General were making progress south, keeping parallel to the canal road.

It was difficult to assess what the enemy was up to. The best we could manage to do was rely on what the General reported back. I don't know how he did it, or what sources he had, but he always appeared to be well informed on what was happening to the enemy. He told us we had killed a Taliban local commander and five of his men. The enemy was retreating, the General said, leaving just pockets of resistance to slow our progress.

And slow it they did. At that moment another RPG struck the ground no more than twenty metres away. The ANP returned fire en masse. I dived for cover and crawled towards a small ditch where the General and Colonel were already taking shelter. We watched as a dozen ANP converged on an old fort just across the track from us. Sam had already earmarked it as a possible enemy position and earlier he'd called in an air-strike, Harriers swooping in and dropping a couple of 500lb bombs on it.

Clearly the enemy had survived the onslaught and decided it was time to re-engage. Hauling myself back to my feet, I joined the assault.

We were no more than thirty metres from the fort walls when there was the dull explosion of a grenade – theirs, not ours. We were halted in our tracks. Face down in the dirt, I studied my immediate environment. There wasn't much to look at. Absently I flicked aside a couple of pieces of earth. I was lying in a ploughed furrow. The field should have been full of crops ready to harvest, but none seemed to have been planted. It left me feeling more than a bit vulnerable. The two Afghan policemen with me decided to make a dash for it. I tried to put down some covering fire with my SA80 as they stumbled away.

Then it was my turn. I pulled the pin of another red phos grenade and flung it towards the fort. It exploded and smoke billowed skywards. I forced myself up and headed in the same direction as the Afghans. It was only twenty metres to the building they were now sheltering behind, but it seemed like a hundred.

I was happy to reach cover but it seemed I was one step behind the Afghans as they took the smoke as their cue to regain the initiative. Shooting from the hip they were expending ammunition as if there were no tomorrow. If I were the enemy I would have been inclined to go for a tactical retreat. But then I was not the enemy.

I looked on as the ANP took casualties. A policeman towards the rear fell over backwards. He was grabbed and yanked at by a colleague but it was clear he was dead. Forcing myself up off my knees, I ran to the left to join the attacking party and started firing my rifle from the shoulder. Enemy fire raked the ground in front of me. Bang. A grenade exploded. Bang. There was another one. This was now close-quarters fighting, with both sides using RPGs at little more than spitting distance.

It is hard to believe I wasn't hit. There was so much metal flying around that it seemed a certainty I would become a casualty. I would have put money on it. I can only liken it to being caught out in a rain shower and not getting wet. Impossible, but there it was.

We were now up against the fort's outer wall, trying to melt into the mud, ready to storm the building. In the British Army this is something that is practised time and time again. Not so with the Afghans. I was loath to go in first and clear a room, lest a grenade was thrown in behind me by an over-exuberant member of my own side, but there didn't seem much alternative.

I looked back the way we had come. I could see Durani and Gulzar on their feet, surveying the scene like a pair of Wellingtons at Waterloo.

I pulled an L109 high-explosive grenade from my belt, checked my magazine was full and my bayonet attached.

Glancing around I saw no one else had moved. It would be down to me. I removed the safety clip and pulled the pin, then threw the grenade through an opening. There was a boom and I was about to follow it in when firing came from my right. Some of the Taliban had found another way out and were staggering from the fort, trying to get away. The ANP cut them down, unhesitatingly shooting them in the back.

Calm followed. I crawled through a hole in the wall to find

another of the enemy dead inside. Already his equipment was being shared out amongst the policemen.

I looked down at the body. He too seemed like a farmer, very dark skin, and a very long beard. He looked much like the man I had killed an hour earlier. In fact he also looked similar to most of the policemen who were on my side. He was dressed in the same way and had the same basic equipment.

'Punjabi,' said Gulzar from behind me.

'How do you know?'

'Because despite what you Westerners think we do not all look the same.'

I sat down in the shadow of the fort, completely knackered. The nervousness of combat, the 45-degree heat and the body armour had left me drained, exhausted. My legs ached, my head throbbed from the noise, I was covered in cuts and bruises, my pasty white skin had darkened through a mixture of sun, dirt and dust.

I got hold of Paddy on the radio and told him our location. The fort was a stone's throw from the canal road and less than a kilometre from the DC. The building must have been there for centuries, the wattle-and-daub battlements baked solid over hundreds of years by the relentless heat, impervious to almost everything thrown against them. Until today that was. The 500lb bombs called in by Sam had taken their toll.

I congratulated the General on the success of his men.

But he was already thinking ahead. 'We will now move on the DC and get to the police station. That is where the Talib have withdrawn to.'

I wasn't so sure. There were still plenty of buildings along the canal road and I didn't want to bypass them only to find the enemy on my tail sometime later. But nor did I have the strength to argue.

I asked the General what would happen to the bodies of the dead.

'We will give them back to the village elders and they will return them to the Talib for burial.'

This was a sense of honour between the two sides I did not expect. Perhaps it came about because there wasn't actually much that differentiated them. Afghans take a pragmatic approach to fighting. Their loyalty can be bought, people often choosing sides on the basis of who they believe will win and deliver them the best future.

I trudged back to the wagon and asked Sam if there was any cold water.

To my astonishment there was. I drank it greedily. Looking at my watch it was still only 14:00 hrs.

The ANP were now making a beeline straight for the police station in the DC and we were still alongside the canal. Paddy wanted to clear further along the waterway before turning right and also heading for the DC. I was to lead in my WMIK. Chipper would be second, Paddy behind him. The Sergeant-Major would stay back with Tim's vehicle, the Pinz and the Estonian EOD (Explosive Ordnance Disposal) team as well as the Afghans' vehicles.

We headed tentatively south, the road now running along the top of a dyke, raised above the surrounding countryside. Nine men and three unarmoured Land Rovers – sitting ducks.

After twenty minutes we came to a spot where in the near distance we could easily see the point where the road running through the DC hit the canal, a cluster of buildings next to it. Crossing the water was a rickety footbridge, enabling inhabitants of outlying parts of the town to reach the centre. Just short of the crossing we dismounted and started to clear the houses on foot. We weren't taking chances. Grenades posted through the doors, then in with a burst of fire. At first there was no resistance. That didn't last long. Suddenly there was a cacophony of fire from the east, perhaps some sixty metres away. Bullets whizzed overhead.

As we tried to lock on to our targets Paddy shouted out my

next orders. 'Get into the DC. See what the ANP are up to and try and get a contingent to come out here and secure this position so we can come and join you. Go.'

I wasn't going to hang about to see if he changed his mind.

Leaving the mayhem behind us we drove slowly into town. Garmsir wasn't like anything you'd see in the UK. Even at its best it would have seemed a shabby, ramshackle sort of place, certainly Third World. And it certainly wasn't at its best now.

God, look at this, I thought.

The buildings we'd been sent to liberate were barely that at all. These were no steel, glass and brick constructions, architect-designed or with a sense of modernity and function. This was a town built of mud. Single-storey shops and homes with flat roofs, little more than boxes. Most had security shutters to protect the windows and doors. Almost without exception these had been forced open, twisted and wrenched from their frames, the contents behind them either looted or strewn about on the street. There wasn't a soul to be seen. One or two desperate-looking, half-starved dogs were the only signs of life.

A tat, tat, tat brought me back to the task in hand. We were being shot at from enemy positions to the south. It was only as the buildings became more numerous that we felt some sort of safety, the closeness of the structures putting us out of view of the enemy. But I still felt nervous. In such a hemmed-in environment there is so little time to react to threats – I drew my pistol from the door holster, ready to respond.

We reached the other end of the main drag, close to the bridge that marked the western end of the town and crossed the Helmand River. I was reluctant to go much further in case the enemy had stayed around to defend the crossing. As we turned back I caught sight of two Afghans with Kalashnikovs waving at us and pointing down a side street. I recognised them. We followed their directions, coming quickly to the police station where, as promised, we found the ANP, the Afghan national flag already flying from the roof. Through

Yasir we ordered a contingent of policemen to go and lend weight to Paddy's action.

Moments later he came through on the radio.

'I want to blow the canal footbridge. Am waiting for the OK from KAF. Stand by.'

There are some decisions that commanders on the ground can make and some they can't. This was one of the latter. It needed to be referred up. Demolishing the crossing could be a double-edged sword. Yes it would protect our flank, denying the Taliban an easy opportunity to attack from the east. But it would also form an obstacle to any reinforcements coming to our aid.

We sat and waited, the crack, crack of small-arms fire still breaking the peace every few minutes.

Then the medicine arrived. Out of nowhere I was presented with a brew, a soldier's nectar, a cuppa. Tea, green, not black, but no less welcome for that.

I drank slowly, savouring every drop. With me was the General. I wanted him to arrange a checkpoint in the main street. The job of doing this fell on the shoulders of one Major Shahrukh, an ANP officer I had not come across so far that day.

Shortly afterwards a loud explosion interrupted our tea party. The footbridge was no more.

Three-quarters of an hour later and Sam, Joe and I were on the road again, moving towards the bridge over the Helmand River. Two members of the ANP had beaten us to it. They were standing around casually, seemingly without a care in the world.

Overlooking this benign scene was a hill fort in which the ANA had installed a command post. It was ancient, reputed to have been built during the time of Alexander the Great, a huge man-made knoll with a small bastion on top. It reminded me of a funny story Namir told me. Apparently Helmand still had a tourist department. One of the 'attractions' was a similar Alexandrian fort in the town of Gereshk. A guide turned up every day, ready to show people round. But for the past twenty-five years there had been a shortage of visitors. I wondered why.

I climbed up the hill. It was now 17:00 hrs and darkness, plus a degree of coolness, was not far away.

The view was commanding. It would be a key position to hold to beat off any counter-attack. We returned to the police HQ. Paddy and the remainder of the force, including the Estonians and the OMLT, had arrived. So too had Tim.

A counter-attack was a real possibility. It was decided we too should set up a command post in the fort. Sam removed the TacSat equipment from the WMIK and hauled it to the top. From then on, we would refer to the fort as JTAC Hill. He would spend the night there. So would I. Joe would remain at the foot of the fort along with Chipper and his crew and vehicle, ready to make a quick withdrawal if needed. Everyone else would bed down at our hastily formed base in the town's school next to the police HQ.

Then we talked about Garmsir day two. Despite our best intentions this was not going to be a quick operation. The next day's goal was to drive the Taliban to the 42 northing, a line of latitude on our maps, some three kilometres further south. Once we had cleared that far, a stream between the river and the canal would become our defensive line. The ANP would provide forty men for the next day's op. The ANA, fifty.

Of course an army marches on its stomach and Paddy was doing his best to ensure a re-supply of food and ammo. And the helicopter wouldn't return empty. The Afghan casualties would be loaded on board for the start of their long journey to recovery.

For my crew there was finally the chance of some scoff. In normal circumstances army rations are about as far from fine dining as you can get. But these weren't normal circumstances and after eleven hours of almost continuous contact the grub was like nouvelle cuisine. Joe had some hot food. Sam and I couldn't face the wait for boiling water and went for the cold-buffet option. Lamb stew in a bag. Rip open and serve. The Chateau Lafite was brewed up on the portable stove, NATO standard – strong, with two sugars. The perfect end to an anything but perfect day.

EIGHT

UP CLOSE AND PERSONAL

(GARMSIR, DAY 2)

'What targets have you got for me?' yelled Sam over the din of the firing, huddled in the back of our Land Rover.

Where do I start? I thought to myself.

Day two for us had begun pretty much where day one had left off – pinned down by Taliban fire.

I looked south down the canal road.

The six of us, in two vehicles, had only travelled a few hundred metres along it when the shooting began from the east of the waterway, bullets and grenades flying towards us from at least two locations to my left. More fire was being directed at us from almost straight ahead. There was another enemy position to the right of that, south-west of where my WMIK and that of Chipper now stood stationary. Fire rained down on us from at least four different locations. It was hard keeping count.

'What targets have you got for me, boss?' Sam asked again, this time with a degree of annoyance in his voice.

I knew I had to let go of the machine gun and start fixing some co-ordinates.

The American F-18s were less than ten minutes away and

they needed to know where to put their bombs. We had only just put in our request for air support, but they were almost with us, the aircraft having already been airborne when our call for help came in.

I crouched down and orientated myself with the plan, matching the map to the ground laid out around me. One, two, three, four: I identified the positions the Taliban were engaging us from. I started shouting the grid references to Sam above the racket. Paddy heard too, back in the DC. He was listening in to the chaos. I could see Sam scribbling down the numbers, marking the points on his aerial photo of the area.

Sam was shouting at me again. 'I need an order of attack, boss. And you have to tell me where the friendly forces are.'

I heaved myself up so I was standing in the commander's seat, trying to get a better view of what was going on. The ANP, some 150 metres ahead of us and 50 metres in from the canal road, were pinned down by fire from the two locations to the west of the canal, our side of the canal. As I looked on, I could see the solitary figure of Major Shahrukh on his feet, shouting encouragement to his men. It was a thankless task.

Crack.

A high-velocity round whizzed just above my head. I slipped back into my seat.

'Which one do we drop first?' urged Sam.

'Target one, buildings south of the ANP. Grid 93124476. Target two, south-east of our location. Grid 94494482. Targets three and four to follow.'

Sam leant over the top of the vehicle, thrusting the photo towards me, his blue eyes holding my gaze. He was still in his mid-twenties, a mere youth to my mature, wizened, hard-won forty. But this wasn't about age as much as experience and here in Afghanistan Sam was already a veteran.

'Boss, this is important, double-check with me the forward location of the friendlies.'

I pointed out where I thought everyone was. I asked him if he was happy with my references.

'Well, it's your call. You're in charge.'

It wasn't the reassuring answer I wanted to hear, but he was right. It was my decision and I had made it.

I tried to keep talking over the radio to Paddy about the mire we were in, not easy as I also needed to keep firing the GPMG towards the enemy east of us.

Where were those planes? From being just minutes away to being overhead seemed to be taking an age.

Then I heard Sam talking to the pilots again. 'Redball 29, this is Widow 77. The town of Garmsir is marked as Darveshan on the map, but known as Garmsir. For this engagement we will refer to it as Garmsir. Roger so far, over.'

'Roger, Widow 77,' came back the reply.

Then more complications from Sam: 'Our location is south of Garmsir, on the western side of a canal that runs north-south to the east of the town.'

It sounded like a complete jumble of information. I hoped the pilots were getting their heads around it.

It seemed so. The answer from the sky was as before. 'Roger, Widow 77.'

'We are two British Land Rovers pinned down on the canal road, taking fire from four enemy positions.' Sam continued to explain the lay of the land to the Americans as they converged on the targets.

Flying high, they had a good view of the battlefield despite their immense speed. 'Widow 77. Yes, sir.'

It was slightly surreal. Every second or third response from the pilots was suffixed with a dash of politeness in a deep Texan drawl.

'Widow 77, we have two unidentified vehicles on a canal road running north–south and six enemy positions. Request smoke to confirm your location and that of friendly forces. Over.'

Sam threw a blue smoke grenade out of the back of the truck, at the same time warning the Americans that the Afghan police didn't have anything similar to mark themselves out, but that they were just some 150 metres or so south and west of our vehicles.

Again the reply came in the affirmative. 'We have smoke and have positively identified friendly call signs. Starting attack run on target one.'

'Roger, give thirty seconds and stores,' said Sam.

He wanted the pilots to let us know when the first 1,000lb bomb was released and on its way. This warning wasn't so we could keep our heads down, but so we could put our heads up, checking the location of the strike and whether the weapon had the desired effect.

The situation was getting serious. Mortar rounds had started to land around us and 107mm rockets were detonating nearby. We needed something to disturb the enemy action and the F-18s were it.

'Boss, that's thirty seconds and stores,' said Sam relaying the information direct from the attacking pilot.

Sam raised his binoculars to his eyes. I let go of the GPMG and did the same, curiosity and fascination taking over from the natural instinct to hit the deck. As Sam and I stared towards the intended target, Chipper's vehicle took up the slack, continuing to fire at the enemy to our east. The lead plane filled my circular view. It was coming in fast and steep, from height, slung beneath it a stubby, fat cigar.

After what seemed an endless dive, the two parted; the plane pulling up from its screaming descent, the cigar continuing down on its relentless path towards destruction both for itself and anything in its way. It exploded no more than 250 metres away from the ANP, the bomb disappearing from view as the ground came up to meet it. An instant later there was an eruption of dirt, the fountain of debris expanding as it flew skywards. A second or so later the sound reached us, a low crump, rumbling out across the landscape.

It was impossible to imagine what it was like immediately

around the epicentre of this earthquake. It looked as if anyone close by would have been vaporised by the heat, cut to bits by the shrapnel, reduced to jelly by the shockwaves, or buried by the mass of material churned up in the blast.

Sam sent the message back. 'Good strike, target one. Target two now.'

I was worried. Looking around I saw Major Shahrukh had surfaced again. He was leading the ANP towards the small group of farm buildings that was our first co-ordination point and close to where the enemy and air strike had met each other.

I wanted the policemen to use the aircraft to cover their movement but it was a dangerous game. Get too far ahead and they would risk being bombed as the second attack took place. I said nothing and started firing again.

The next F-18 swooped in and another bomb was released on a journey of death. This time, just 150 metres away. And this time I felt the blast. It only hardened the impression that survival for those under the onslaught was impossible. We had created some breathing space.

Sam called the fighters back in to strafe targets three and four. The ANP had taken advantage of the disarray to continue their advance and had achieved the first objective of the day, taking a cluster of buildings along a small stream half a kilometre south of the Garmsir DC. Confronted by the F-18s, small-arms fire and RPGs the Taliban had retreated 350 metres to a second row of buildings. We too seized the moment, using the lull to start off down the track, trying to get parallel with the ANP. A couple of minutes later and we passed a large building just the other side of the canal. I wasn't unduly worried. I gambled the enemy would not come so close to confront us. I was wrong. As we slowed down, we were opened up on from little more than fifty metres away.

An RPG crashed into a wall just behind us. A few metres ahead lay a right turn that led to the farm buildings the ANP had just cleared to. We were covered in mud and dust.

My response was far from inspirational. 'Fuck. Fuck, fuck, fuck.' I was scared witless.

I started firing wildly with the GPMG.

A second RPG slammed into the ground to our left. I saw something out of the corner of my eye. A red-hot, razor-sharp piece of metal jammed into the dashboard.

That did it.

'Joe, take the right. Now. Move!'

Chipper was immediately behind us, Steve letting loose with the .50-cal as their wagon heeled hard over in the turn.

We careered on till we got to the buildings. They were in a horseshoe shape, built around a courtyard, the main dwelling on our right surrounded by yet another large high wall. Forget white picket fences and privet hedges, it seemed as if everything in this damned country was surrounded with a large high wall. We charged in and pulled a U-turn to face back the way we had come.

The noise subsided as for the first time in two hours we were sheltered from the shooting.

The ANP were still there, occupying the main house. It had a high roof, offering a good vantage point of the enemy territory that lay ahead.

I wanted to stop and let my heart calm down and take stock of what was happening across the whole front. But there was little chance of a rest with the ANP already re-engaged with the Taliban. I dragged myself out of the Land Rover and entered the compound with the tallest building. It was clear this had been enemy-held just minutes earlier. There were a number of pots and pans strewn about. Also a pile of small-arms ammunition dumped in the dust. In one corner was an area planted with flowers – but this wasn't a bed of roses, it was a crop of poppies.

Three flights of steps later and I was on the roof. But my arrival hadn't gone unnoticed. Some bastard had seen me and started to give the low parapet behind which I was hiding his full attention, probably with a Soviet-made Dragunov sniper rifle. The ANP answered my tormentor with a volley of fire from the roof of a smaller building just to my right. Trying to ignore the man attempting to kill me I scanned the ground south of where we were. I picked out several Taliban positions, all of them good targets for the follow-on air support Sam had requested, the F-18s having already left. I knew a B-1 bomber was on its way. The problem was that whilst I had eyes on the target, Sam, sitting with the TacSat, didn't have the same line-of-sight vision, and because he would be talking to the pilots he couldn't speak to me on the PRR. However Joe was standing in the compound. I used him as a go-between.

He relayed the target information back to Sam as I called it out. I had to get this spot-on. For the B-1 crew there was no visual element to this as there had been with the F-18s. Their plane flew high, way beyond the range of the enemy, at least a mile up, and its bombs were guided by one thing – my grid references. The pilot would receive the co-ordinates I chose via Sam, via Joe. These would be programmed into the GPS-guided munitions and that was that. Bombs away. Get it wrong and 1,000lbs of high explosive could land on you as easily as anywhere else.

Sam said the first weapon had been released.

Ten seconds.

It was a strange experience.

Twenty seconds.

Counting down the time, waiting for all hell to break loose.

Thirty seconds.

There was a huge explosion some 200 metres south of where I was lying. First came the picture – a moment later, the sound.

I felt a sense of exhilaration and power.

What was to stop me remaining here all day and relying on air support to do the dirty work? Give me a ring, guys, when it's all over and the enemy is in submission.

No wonder General Durani had been so keen the previous day on using air power.

A second 1,000lb device dropped close to where the first had just done so much damage. The incoming fire started to slow. As it did, the policemen rose to their feet and restarted their advance, leaving the relative safety of the complex, Shahrukh leading from the front, Durani and Gulzar looking on from the sidelines.

As I watched, I talked, telling Paddy over the radio that my two vehicles would rejoin the push south, keeping in line with the ANP attack. We drove away from the shelter of the farm buildings and back on to the canal road. This might have been a good idea as far as mentoring and supporting the Afghans was concerned but it did little to keep us out of trouble. In our elevated position we were sure to attract the attention of some keen young Taliban fighters out to impress their commander. And so it proved, our status as a bullet magnet reconfirmed, rounds fizzing past us.

Minutes later the cavalry was back on the scene, another pair of F-18s replacing the B-1, hitting targets further down the road around another canal crossing. Under the cover of the American planes we managed to push on a further 800 metres before the ANP advance ground to a halt. They had reached another set of buildings and were fighting at close quarters with its defenders. We pulled up level, the battle raging 100 metres to the west, sitting ducks to any further enemy attack. Taliban fighters started to emerge from the woodwork and now they had us back in their sights.

We were being shot at from two sides. Sam had put down his TacSat radio and picked up his rifle. The small-arms fire from the enemy was supplemented by RPGs, one striking the bank protecting our western flank no more than five metres away, the shrapnel spinning over the top of it, just missing our vehicles. We must have looked like fish in a barrel. That's certainly how it felt, exposed, vulnerable, the only option being retreat, but we couldn't do that without leaving the twenty ANP to fight it out unaided, unmentored.

Quite how none of us were hit I will never know. I could put it down to the Taliban's poor marksmanship, but how did they all miss all of the time? Didn't the enemy deserve a bit of luck every now and then?

There were plenty of close calls. The wagons were getting peppered. Mine was hit repeatedly, one bullet even severing the coax cable connecting the radio to the handset as Sam was using it trying to request more air cover. He sat there with a quizzical look on his face, trying to figure out why he had lost all contact. Then, in that web of fire both incoming and outgoing, the realisation of what had happened dawned on him. With a smile on his face, or was it a nervous grin, he held up the mic, the cut cord hanging limply from it.

The moment of hilarity was only brief and he quickly dropped back into the bottom of the vehicle to find the spare lead and get his comms reconnected. There wasn't a panel on the vehicle that had not been holed and the engine compartment had also been pierced. This was fast becoming a lightweight Land Rover.

I heard Chipper shout out above the mayhem.

'Sir, I need your spare tyre,' he yelled.

'What for?' I answered. As soon as the words came out of my mouth I knew how stupid they sounded.

'Because I can sell it as knock-off in a Glasgow market. Why do you think?'

I looked over to see the rear offside tyre of Chipper's Land Rover deflated, the whole vehicle listing badly. His own spare was no better, flat after being shredded by shrapnel and bullets.

There wasn't much time to think, but I did find a second to marvel at what these soldiers from the Logistics Corps and the TA were about to do: carry out a wheel change in the most hostile of environments.

We had now been pretty much stuck in the same location for two hours. We had stopped because the ANP had stopped, so I decided I had to go and find out what was happening.

'Joe, I'm going over to the ANP positions to see if I can get them moving again.'

I grabbed my rifle and a couple of extra grenades that were hanging on one of the many straps strung across the front bulkhead of the vehicle. With Yasir close behind, I stumbled off across a piece of recently harvested ground, towards Shahrukh. He was some 100 metres away, once again standing tall in the face of the enemy aggression.

Crouched at his feet I looked up and asked why progress had stalled?

'Because we need to clear the walled garden at the end of that compound.'

Raising my head ever so slightly, I chanced a glance in the direction he was pointing.

'Tell him we need to go one step at a time,' I ordered Yasir. 'First we must secure that hut on the right.'

'Then off you go,' was Shahrukh's matter-of-fact response.

I got the impression that the Major wasn't too happy with this British upstart telling him how to fight his war.

I didn't seem to have much choice. Despite Shahrukh's enthusiasm, the ANP's tactics were woeful. There was no one else but me to show them how it was done.

We moved forward past a clutch of policemen. They stood silently, looking down at a bundle of rags at their feet. Protruding from one end of the black cloth was a mass of dark hair, framing a weathered face. From the forehead, past the eyes, down the nose to the upper lip, everything was normal. But then the observer was suddenly confronted with a twisted, contorted jumble of flesh, bone and blood. This victim of war had had his jaw shot off; judging from the damage, probably by a large-calibre bullet. If I needed a reminder of the random, unforgiving nature of battle, here it was: another young man who was not going to be going home to his family, to enjoy time with his relatives, to regale his children, nieces and nephews with stories of his time at the front.

We moved on; along a drainage ditch, taking accurate fire, until we were just 100 metres from where the enemy was holed up. Halfway between them and us was the single-storey building I had told Shahrukh needed to be taken first.

Not that he seemed to care. Perhaps he had got bored of waiting, but he was on his feet again, leading a charge towards the garden, two of his men just behind him. There was a crescendo of fire, RPGs exploded, and then silence. The job was done. The garden and the main compound were clear. Which only left my objective, off to the right.

Hunched down in the ditch I released the magazine from my SA80, checked it was full and snapped it back into place. Holding the pistol grip I slotted the bayonet over the muzzle of the weapon, covering the flash eliminator. Taking one deep breath, and then another, I forced myself up and out towards the building. All around me the ANP were firing. I was scared. If the Taliban didn't get me, I faced the prospect of being shot in the back by my supposed allies. I was carrying out the task on my own and I had no idea what the enemy had in store for me.

I was halfway there when an RPG slammed into the wattle and daub ahead of me. Quickly I looked back over my shoulder. Shahrukh was grinning at me like a Cheshire cat, firing his AK47, as if urging me on, as if saying I was going to be safer going forward than if I came back. I got to within a few metres of my destination, firing too. As were the enemy, who didn't want to be left out. I could see muzzle flashes and hear the sound of automatic weapons just ahead of me. I had hoped the Taliban would retreat. But they hadn't. I was going to have to go in. I pulled a high-explosive grenade from my patrol vest.

Trying to control my breathing I removed the safety clip and looked at where I would throw it. Normal practice would have been to run up to the wall beside the entrance of the building and then post the grenade through the door. But fuck that. This wasn't normal. There wasn't anyone to support me. I wasn't going to go any closer, thank you very much. A good lob would do. Yanking out the pin I chucked it towards the opening. I had four seconds to wait before detonation. I was spot-on direction-wise, but it didn't go the distance. Shit. I buried my head in the hard ground as it exploded well short of the target. I cursed myself before launching another bomb. This time I was luckier. Good direction again and this time it bounced out of sight through the open door. I heard the detonation and sprinted forward following the path of the grenade. Engulfed by dust and smoke I opened fire, spraying it all round the room, my heart thumping in my ears. In one corner, through the gloom, I could just make out the prone body of a Taliban fighter. Perhaps he had died a moment ago, maybe the earlier air-strikes had done for him or it could be he'd been shot by the ANP. He seemed far beyond help, but I was going to make sure.

Just as we had been taught.

I leant forward and thrust my bayonet towards the man's body as hard as I could. I aimed for the centre of him, forcing my rifle on to him, the bayonet into him, but the gloom made it hard to know exactly where I made contact. There was barely any resistance, the sharpened blade, sliding deeper, quickly disappearing. I heard the metal slice through the flesh, felt it break bone and cut gristle as it glided further in, right up to the hilt. Did I hear a small gasp from the man? I don't know, perhaps it was the devil inside me playing with my imagination. When it could go no further, I twisted the bayonet to increase the damage.

Just as we had been taught.

I kicked at the body, pushing away clothing, placing my foot on his shoulder. Only then, as my eyes became accustomed to the light, did I see exactly where I had struck him. The blade had entered the man's neck at the top of the spine, the tip now protruding just below his larynx, drops of blood running down the grooves. I pulled hard and the weapon slipped out, a small piece of windpipe coming with it. I didn't give it a second thought.

Just as we had been taught.

There was a commotion to the rear of the building. Some of the other Talibs who were finally fleeing were being shot at by the ANP who had moved up behind me.

The ANP were now in a strong position. They had taken the large walled complex; I had helped them clear the smaller building to the west, and they were also stretched out along the drainage ditch they'd used to cover their advance. We were still taking heavy fire from another building out to the south-west but I was confident the policemen were up to the task and would use their momentum to clear this too, the last hurdle before they got to the southern canal crossing. I headed back to the Land Rovers to see if we could get some more air support to cover the last stage of the advance. What had the crews been up to? The huge pile of spent cartridge cases at Chipper's feet seemed to tell the story.

I was starting to feel more confident. We seemed to have the measure of the enemy. I allowed myself to relax for a minute.

Then Paddy came on the radio. 'What is going on? The ANP seem to be withdrawing? Can you confirm? They are now some 100 metres north of your position and moving back all the time. I suggest you use the next set of air-strikes to cover your own withdrawal.' It was more of an order than a request.

I was confused. Withdrawing? Having just made such good progress?

As the A-10 Warthogs arrived Joe and Geordie spun our vehicles round on the narrow track, tyres slipping on the gravel, trying to find purchase. We raced back north towards the farm compound from where I had called in the earlier B-1 strikes, still being engaged by the enemy to our east and from the southern canal crossing. I barely noticed. I was furious about the ANP's retreat. Hard left and we were back where we had started. I jumped out of the vehicle and marched over to Shahrukh, Durani and Gulzar.

'What the fuck is going on?' I demanded, the frustration bubbling up.

'We are low on ammunition, we haven't eaten, and while we do our bit the ANA are not moving,' replied Gulzar.

'We can't take that position until we have a chance to rest and get more ammo,' added Shahrukh.

They were correct on all counts, but I couldn't hide my anger. Here we were handing back ground we had just spent three hours fighting for. Three hours during which we had taken casualties, lost men.

'How long, General? How long before we can get on the move again?'

'An hour.'

I passed our problem on to Paddy, asking him to confirm whether the ANA had begun their advance. They should have been pushing forward simultaneously to the west of us, but they hadn't. The ANA soldiers were still in the DC, refusing to fight.

As I digested this new information a large man struggled into the room, carrying a huge, filthy-looking plastic bucket; behind him another arrived laden with a stack of bread.

This was the meal. Chicken and rice served straight from the swill trough to the hungry policemen. They each dug into the communal pot with one hand, scooping out the food and placing it on the bread held in the other. It wasn't that long ago that the same strong hands had been manhandling the dead and the dying.

Shahrukh gestured towards the food. 'Please.'

'No thank you, Major. I'm not hungry,' I lied and stepped back out into the harsh sunshine. Sam said we had two attack helicopters on the way. By my calculations they would be on station just as the ANP were wiping their mouths clean. News too from Paddy. The ANA had finally been persuaded to start their advance south. Now we seemed to have some sort of cohesive force, there was a real chance we could get down to the 43 northing and hold a line from the canal in the east to the river in the west.

As the ANP tucked into their meal I dragged myself up on to the high building once more to look for targets for the AH. I knew our main stumbling block was the large building out to the south-west that the ANP were about to clear when they had been distracted by their stomachs. I also knew that the enemy still held the southern canal crossing. These were the points we'd hit next.

When the attack helicopters arrived they were not alone. Flying between them was a lumbering CH-47 Chinook. As the Apaches hovered overhead, standing sentry, the CH-47 lowered itself down towards an open patch of desert to the north of the DC, out of sight of our party and more importantly the enemy's prying eyes. It took just a couple of minutes to offload supplies and transfer the injured Afghans onboard. Then it was up and gone.

Freed from their guard duties the Apaches turned their attention towards the Taliban, systematically going through the latest target list. They began to pound the enemy with cannon and rockets. What made the Apaches different to the Harriers and F-18s was that they could self-designate, choose their own additional targets based on what they saw happening on the ground around them. And they weren't shy about doing so.

After forty minutes Sam warned me the helicopters would not be able to stay much longer. We had to get moving. But the ANP seemed disinclined to go anywhere.

I went to find Gulzar. 'Colonel, we have to go now or else we will lose the initiative and the air support will have been wasted.'

'Five minutes,' he said. 'Give us five minutes.'

We didn't have five minutes.

I needed to kick-start the operation. I got through to Paddy. 'I am going to make a dash for the southern canal crossing with the two Land Rovers. I'll try and secure the area, while you get the ANP and ANA to advance down to us. Just don't let the bastards shoot me on the way.'

My plan was to race the kilometre and a half down the road to the crossing, drive out the enemy from the buildings there and then hang on till the Afghans got their act together and reinforced us. I was just praying the Apaches had taken their toll on the enemy positions.

Joe gunned the engine and we broke cover from behind the enclosure, hurtling down the short track to the road junction. As we careered on to it, I flung a smoke grenade to try and give my vehicle, and more importantly Chipper's, cover from view as we made the turn. It didn't do much good. Within seconds we were being shot at from all sides. Myself, Sam, Steve and Chipper blasted back as best we could, Joe and Geordie struggling to keep us on the straight and narrow, desperately weaving around the potholes that threatened to derail our mission. Bullets smacked into the Land Rovers, churned up the road, whizzed over our heads, but somehow failed to hit any of us. As we headed south we also came under RPG attack, but thankfully they were landing behind us, their operators failing to account properly for our speed when launching. I was firing forward, trying to engage the buildings by the crossing while Sam was blasting away at the walled garden. Chipper and Steve had responsibility for the east of the canal. I could tell by their rate of fire that they had their hands full. The Americans would call this a 'target-rich environment'. Me, I just thought we were in the shit. We flew past the point where we had been pinned down that morning. Over the radio the six of us screamed information at each other.

'Watch the pothole!'

'Enemy position south-west!'

'Keep firing!'

'Mind the bloody debris in the road!'

'Reloading. Loaded. Stoppage. Fuck!'

It was chaos, like something from an old war movie that everyone says is so unrealistic. But it was happening. To us. Still we charged on.

In just that short distance to the crossing, I twice reloaded my GPMG, each time replacing the empty box with a full one containing 200 rounds of 7.62mm belted ammunition. Firing five-round bursts it didn't take long to get through the bullets.

I knew I was taking a chance with both my plan and my weapon. The barrel was in serious danger of overheating, but there was nothing for it; the only way we were going to make it to the crossing was if the enemy kept their heads down because of the weight of our fire. We had to keep shooting and moving, shooting and moving.

Just twenty metres short of the buildings at the southern crossing we dropped the vehicles into a dip at the side of the road, where a track led into a field. As we skidded to a halt I flung my door open and jumped out, grabbing my pistol and a grenade from the lashing cords on the dashboard.

I sprinted towards the nearest of the two houses. It was a single-storey building in an L-shape. In the middle of the L I could see two doors. There were also a number of very small windows, above head height, covered by cloth and wood. The roof was flat and the building was protected on the eastern side by high banking. It was only as I got there that I wondered if I had made a mistake. Here I was, a 9mm pistol in my right hand, a grenade in my left hand, about to try and clear the house ahead of me. But no rifle. It had been a snap decision, grabbing the sidearm from the door holster in almost the same movement as I tumbled out of the vehicle. It was the quickest and easiest thing to do rather than turn and take the SA80 out of the rack behind the two front seats. But now I was feeling under-gunned. I slumped against the wall beside one of the entrances. Resting against the dried mud I looked back at where I had come from. The other five were still in the WMIKs, shooting in all directions. Why hadn't anyone come in support? Hadn't I been clear in my orders for them to follow and support me? Actually, had I given any orders or was I making this up as I went along? No matter, really. They were there and I was here.

I spun round and kicked at the wood. It flew open with little resistance and I rushed in, firing my pistol twice. The dark room was empty with no other exits. I ducked back out into the intense light, squinting as I went. On to the next door. Again I kicked out. Like the first it gave way easily and I darted inside. This time I wasn't alone. Three Taliban were scrambling to get out through an entrance at the back. The one closest to me was the first to react, twisting towards me and firing a burst from his AK47. The bullets tore into the door jamb, wood splintering all around me.

I staggered backwards, desperate to get away, firing eight, nine, perhaps ten shots from my pistol as I tried to escape. Had I hit him? Had I hit any of them? I thought perhaps I had, but I wasn't going to stop and find out. Screened by the wall I pulled the safety clip from the grenade and then yanked out the pin. Keeping low, I leant forward and threw it into the room. The explosion was deafening. Smoke and dust blossomed out of the opening. In the moment it took for things to settle I ejected the now-empty magazine from the bottom of my pistol, before forcing in a full one containing a further twelve rounds. My heart thumping, the sound of blood rushing through my ears, I jumped back into the building, only to see, through a door opposite, the enemy running across a field, keeping the structure between themselves and the rest of my guys. I watched as they fled. If I had hit one of them it must only have been a flesh wound, as they showed no signs of being impeded. I didn't bother shooting at them again. Already they were out of range of my Browning pistol. If only I had had my rifle.

But my job wasn't done yet. There was the second, smaller, building to clear, too. As I ran the few metres up the banking and over to it I saw it had already taken a hell of a battering. There were holes of all shapes and sizes in the walls, loose stones around the edges of the door. I pulled a second grenade from my patrol vest. Out came the safety clip, out came the pin. I posted it through a window.

One.

I had a thought.

Two.

What if this sorry-looking structure wasn't strong enough to contain the blast?

Three.

I started to leg it.

Four.

The grenade exploded just as I reached the shelter of the first building. Immediately I retraced my steps and fired into the single room. There was no one there.

I moved to the back of the hut to look out southwards. The canal crossing was to my left. Straight on continued the road we had just driven down. Three hundred metres along it there were yet more buildings, part of yet another complex surrounded by yet another high wall. A kilometre away would be the notional 42 northing. Not our objective for that day but the private goal Paddy and I had set ourselves for securing the town. Further still I could make out a tree-line and wooded area that met the road on the diagonal, running south-east to north-west.

The shooting outside had eased off. I headed back to the Land Rovers.

I informed Paddy of our situation. He came back with the less-than-welcome news that the ANP had yet to leave their dining hall and the ANA, rather than fight due south from JTAC Hill by the river, were instead converging on us. What was it with these people?

Then the brief lull came to an end. The enemy fire picked up and this time the small arms were being supplemented by mortar shells as well as the ever-predictable RPGs.

Shit, I thought. Here we were, just the six of us, 1.5 kilometres forward of the rest of our forces, incoming from three sides. My plan seemed to be unravelling.

Could things get any worse?

Suddenly they did. We started to receive fire directly from the north, a round thudding into the ballistic matting covering the door of my vehicle. Fuck. Had we bypassed a pocket of the enemy? Had they managed to get behind us?

No. We were now being shot at by our own side. Despite telling Paddy to warn the ANA and ANP that we would end up between them and the enemy, the message plainly hadn't got through to everyone, the consequences of the Afghans not having a decent command-and-control system suddenly all too clear. Unbriefed or uncaring some of them were now pumping fire at the crossing, engaging the moving targets around the two buildings. Us.

'For fuck's sake, Sam, the bloody Afghans are shooting at us!'

There wasn't much we could do about it. We still had the real enemy hitting us from the east, south and west. We were in a hole. A bloody big one.

'Sandstone 28, this is Widow 77. We're at the crossing and taking fire from friendly forces. Can you talk to Gulzar and Durani and get them to control their men? I'm going to throw blue smoke to mark our position.'

Paddy responded in the affirmative. 'Be advised that two Harriers are on their way to you. Can you get Sam to speak to them?'

I looked at Sam.

'Already on to it, boss,' he said.

I threw the smoke grenades as yet more bullets zipped around us from the north. I was getting pretty pissed off.

We were completely isolated and the ammunition situation was getting critical.

We had been stuck for the best part of forty minutes now. All fifteen of our blue smoke grenades had been thrown to try and show the friendly forces exactly where we were. I contemplated withdrawing just as we had done that morning. Our lives were now at grave risk. But in theory we should have done all the hard work; making our bold move, taking the crossing and repelling the counter-attack. If only the ANA and ANP could stop shooting and start advancing, then perhaps we could still strengthen our position.

I hunkered down again to speak to Paddy. Through it all he remained calm and his coolness gave me a degree of reassurance. At least there was someone in the middle of things doing his best to keep the whole thing together. When we'd finished talking I decided we would stay.

'Five minutes, guys,' I shouted, using the Afghan unit of time. 'Five minutes and the ANP should be here.'

In fact it was ten minutes before we saw figures approaching across a field just to our north. And it wasn't the ANP, it was the ANA.

They advanced past the Land Rovers and up into the shelter of the buildings I had cleared. Then they let loose at the enemy to the east of the canal, little more than fifty metres away.

Their arrival brought another lull in the proceedings, the enemy drifting away to cover and safety.

Behind us, ANP vehicles began to appear, trundling down to the crossing, carrying supplies and men, amongst them Paddy, Gulzar and Durani.

Sam said the two Harriers were still inbound to us, but because we were no longer receiving fire, he was at a loss to know what to do with them.

'Get them to hit those buildings over to the east of the crossing and then the tree-line to the west.'

'I can't do that, boss. If we can't positively identify the enemy positions we can't just speculatively drop bombs.'

'Yeah, but we know they are there somewhere,' I said in frustration.

'I know, but rules are rules,' was the reply.

Of course Sam was right and I knew it.

I guess I just wanted someone else to take the responsibility for making the decisions for a while. 'OK, OK, fair enough. So what do you suggest we do with them?'

'A show of strength, and a quick shufty to our south to see the lie of the land.'

'That'll do. Call it in.'

I looked around at the rest of the guys. They all appeared more relaxed, having dismounted from the vehicles and let the Afghans take over the securing of the site. I assessed our ammunition stock. We had fired an extraordinary amount of bullets. Cartridge cases littered the ground around the vehicles, glinting in the sun. They were piled high inside the vehicles. Empty ammo boxes were strewn all about. I tried to work out how many rounds we must have fired. Eight thousand? Ten thousand?

Walking over to Paddy, I nodded at Chipper, acknowledging the effort he and his crew had put into the battle.

I gave Paddy the rundown on what had happened, leaving out the bit about my heroics with the pistol, and suggested ways of fortifying the area. He told how the ANA had taken prisoner a wounded Taliban fighter. Intent on dispatching him with a 7.62mm round to the head, they were only stopped by the intervention of Sergeant-Major Johnstone. Paddy also confirmed that the whole of the ANA force had worked its way south-east across to us instead of clearing the ground south of their starting position. We now had a staggered line to defend, running from JTAC Hill just south of the western end of Garmsir across to us at the canal crossing. It was not ideal.

Suddenly there was a yell. 'IED!'

Geordie had found an Improvised Explosive Device. He pointed to the road. A slightly raised, barely noticeable, area of ground ran across it, hiding a command wire. At one end the wire disappeared into the trees. At the other it was linked to a couple of hastily hidden anti-tank mines, one stacked on top of the other. And we had driven right by the bloody thing. But for the grace of God our war should have been over. The Taliban must have been too busy dodging our bullets to set off the bomb.

Our attention suddenly turned skywards as the two Harriers screamed overhead heading south parallel with the road. After two low passes – the show of strength – they climbed and circled the area, having a good look around and relaying back to Sam what they saw. It seemed that for now the Taliban were keeping their heads down. Not that this stopped the ANA and the ANP from fighting – each other.

Durani and Gulzar were in a screaming match with the ANA commander over who was supposed to be doing what, where and when. The pair were berating their army counterpart for not showing them enough support earlier in the day. After they had bollocked him they said he and his men should stay at the crossing and protect it through the night.

He on the other hand was having none of it, yelling that his troops were going to withdraw to the DC. Paddy was going to have to get this sorted. Somebody was going to have to stay at the crossing or else all the hard work would again be for nothing.

After much forthright discussion a deal was done. The ANP would leave ten men at the crossing, whilst a couple of dozen ANA soldiers were to be posted at a building just to the west of it. Surrounded by plenty of lush vegetation it provided as much cover as the Taliban could ask for, if they thought of mounting a counter-attack. As for us Brits, we were all going to retreat to the town, though Paddy promised we'd make regular vehicle patrols to the crossing during the night.

As Paddy dished out the orders to the commanders, Durani and Shahrukh wandered over to look at the IED, which remained untouched as we awaited the arrival of an Estonian bomb-disposal guy. The pair squatted next to the device to get a better look. After a moment or two of gesturing and debate Shahrukh suddenly leant forward. It became clear he had his own views on how this threat should be made safe. He lifted up one of the two mines, turned it over and yanked at the wires attached to its base. They came away. There was no explosion. Pleased with this result, he picked up the mine, rose to his feet, walked to the canal and threw it in. Even before the ripples had disappeared another Afghan policeman picked up the second mine and dumped that into the water too.

'Problem solved,' I said to Paddy, daring to relax for a moment.

We had been fighting for eight hours. I was exhausted. Drenched in sweat, I stank to high heaven. I was caked in dust and blood, and was hungry and thirsty. My mind was also in overdrive, thinking about what I had done, the man I had bayoneted, how we had managed to escape unscathed, how stupid I had been trying to clear those buildings on my own. Most depressingly of all I knew I would be coming back down this road the next day as we tried to reach the 42 northing.

Not that we were in a bad position at that moment.

We had advanced two kilometres along the canal and seized the southern crossing, which we hoped to hold overnight. The ANP were also still manning a checkpoint close to the town centre, at the eastern end of the main street, where we had blown the footbridge the day before. And further north the ANA were in post at the first canal crossing, also captured on day one. Just thirty hours or so earlier in fact, but oh didn't it seem so much longer than that.

Given the all-clear by Paddy, our little convoy pottered back towards the town. On the way the Estonians rushed past us in the other direction. I didn't have the heart, energy or inclination to stop and tell them the IED had already been disposed of. With a smile and a wave I bade them on their way.

Back at base Chipper and his crew headed off to find the rest of the OMLT. I told Sam and Joe to get on with some admin.

Admin in the army is not quite what it is in civilian life. It means sort yourself out. Clean your weapons and your vehicles, check your equipment, stock up on ammo, dust yourself down. It also means have a shit, shave and shower (as if), get fed and watered, catch forty winks, if you can. Do everything you need to do so you will be ready to get back to work when you're ordered. That's what admin means in the army.

I wanted to sit down with the guys and do my own admin, but I knew if I did that I would struggle to get up again and I still needed to see the Afghans.

With heavy legs, I trudged over to the police HQ. I found the General, Colonel Gulzar and Major Shahrukh sitting at the front of the building having tea. Hovering close by were several policemen there to act on the whim of the General, to fetch him more tea, pass on his orders, protect him.

And then, just beyond this circle of lackeys, was a young man standing on his own. More a boy really. In fact, I suspected he was a rent boy, or a 'chai boy' as the Afghans referred to them; there to be ordered about by the men and, when required, to provide sexual pleasure, although I couldn't imagine Gulzar, Durani or Shahrukh behaving in such a manner. The boy was fresh-faced and shaven. He looked timid. At some stage, as he aged, his sexual attractiveness would wane and he would be replaced by someone else, someone younger. For him the abuse would be over. Instead it was likely he would himself become a fully fledged member of the police and probably turn into an abuser too.

It was something I had heard about before in Afghanistan – the regular exploitation of children by people in power. The country was rife with it, particularly in poor rural areas like Helmand. Families with little or no money, food or prospects, sold their sons. Sometimes it was done for hard cash, sometimes for favours. Often parents would be made an offer they couldn't refuse.

When I first arrived in Helmand I was told a story about a high-ranking provincial official who it was claimed gouged out the eyes of a villager because the man had refused to let him sleep with his five-year-old son. It was a shocking story, made even more so because it was believable.

For me as a dad, it was a hard thing to understand, harder still to actually witness. But what could I do? We were not here to impose our ways on these people. A change in attitude might or might not come about many years down the line as the country dragged itself out of the dark ages through education and economic growth. But at that moment in time our job was to help defeat the Taliban. We could only look on aghast at their ways of doing things, then grit our teeth and get on with the task at hand. Though sometimes I couldn't help but wonder whether we were fighting on the wrong side. Would the peasants not be better served by the Taliban and their version of Sharia law? Perhaps a harsh regime would actually protect the exploited rather better than we would ever manage?

As I reached the General and the others, they stood up, smiling, big grins across their faces. They were obviously pleased with the way things had turned out. Durani gave me a big hug, patting me on the back. The Colonel wrung my hand vigorously. The Major stood back waiting for Durani to release me from his clutches before he too came to congratulate me.

'Today we killed the Talib commander,' the General said triumphantly. 'His men are scattered everywhere and there is no one to lead them. We will be safe here for a while.'

'I thought we killed the local commander yesterday?' I queried.

'Ah, different commander. Yesterday we also killed thirty-five fighters. Today we killed twenty-two Talib.'

How did he know these things? Where did the information come from?

'Are you sure?'

'I have a friend who lives in the Talib-controlled area. He counts the funerals. One burial. One dead enemy.'

I stayed on for some time with the three of them. Drinking tea, talking about the day. The actual act of conversation was difficult, every word having to be passed through the mouth of the interpreter. But in order to get the job done it was important to show these men commitment and loyalty, whatever the obstacles. Without them we were not going to hold on to Garmsir, and for some reason they seemed to respect me. Perhaps my endeavours had gained me some street credibility in their eyes. Not that I was the only one who was worthy of recognition.

'Shahrukh, why do you not take cover? Why do you stand in the face of the enemy? Fire when everyone else is diving for the ground?'

'I am their leader. It's important they see me stand my ground, lead by example, show them I'm not afraid of the Talib. There is no other way.'

'You're a brave man, Major, but you really should protect yourself when the shooting starts.'

'This is my fight, not yours,' he replied. 'I don't want you to fight for me, just help me. And anyway today you too were standing in the face of the enemy attack. Why did you not take cover?'

He had a point. He must have seen us parked on the canal road, attracting fire like bees to a honey pot. Perhaps he thought that was the way things were done. I wasn't in much of a position to argue otherwise.

By now it was 17:30 hrs. The sun was sinking over the horizon and the heat was decreasing from furnace-like to just bloody hot.

In the distance there came the sporadic sound of gunfire, the odd explosion of RPGs and mortars. But for the first time in the day and a half I had been in and around Garmsir I wasn't under fire or the threat of fire. We had driven the Taliban to a point where they could not reach us with indirect ordnance (fire directed without line-of-sight contact, usually from long range). But there was a lot more to do to secure our position. We still needed to push our defensive line further south and that was going to be the next day's task.

After the chaos of battle comes the quiet time when you have chance to think. And thinking can be far from healthy. Thoughts criss-cross your mind at breakneck speed. I survived today, but will I tomorrow? I have cheated death once, twice, who knows, several times; must I do it all again? I felt physically sick.

I also struggled to understand our position as far as HQ at

KAF was concerned. Throughout my years in the army I always imagined that when it came to battle it would be me and the might of the British military taking it to the enemy. That I would be part of a large British force, friendly faces everywhere I looked, strength in numbers. Behind me a logistical and organisational set-up ensuring I had the right equipment, enough ammunition.

This was not the case in Garmsir. We had barely any of this. We were a handful of soldiers, far from base, further still from home, fighting for survival. It was air-strikes that were keeping us alive. Without them, at best we would have been pushed out of the town. At worst we would have been injured or dead. All these thoughts bounced around my head as I headed back to the British camp.

On arrival I found Corporal Cowley and the Estonian doctor fighting to keep alive the Taliban prisoner Paddy had mentioned. Helping was Sean Langan.

The patient, a young Pakistani, was lying out in the open on a makeshift stretcher. His hands were cuffed together with a plastic pull-tie, the sort you use at home to secure lagging to your water pipes.

The Talib might have been critically wounded but the fight had yet to leave him completely. A little earlier he had made a grab for the weapons of those battling to save him. Now his future looked grim: the colour was gone from his cheeks; he was becoming increasingly unresponsive; it was clear he needed to be evacuated as a matter of priority, but of course he wasn't a priority. Paddy had already found that out. He had asked for a helicopter, but there wasn't one to spare, at least not one for the enemy, not that day. The best chance of getting him casevaced* was on a flight lined up for the next morning at first light. It was hoped to get a Chinook to us, loaded with ammunition. If he was still breathing the Taliban casualty could go back on that.

* Evacuation of military casualty.

Not that there was any sign the rest of us would be leaving any time soon either.

The members of the OMLT were anxious to get away. They had been up against it over the past forty-eight hours, as had I. But the difference was they were almost at the end of their six-month tour of Afghanistan, whilst I was only halfway through mine.

I could see why they were keen to get back to the relative safety of Bastion.

From my experience military tours can be divided into three parts.

The first is characterised by an eagerness to get on with the job you have been trained to do. This phase might last a month or so. Phase two goes on for the majority of the rest of the time. You have got to know your environment and its challenges and you feel more confident, you start to take greater risks.

Then there's the final phase. The one the OMLT members were in. With just a matter of weeks, perhaps days, to go before the end of a tour, you start to look forward to going home, to seeing your loved ones. You have put in all the hard graft, taken your chances and got away with it. You are still alive and you're going to do your damnedest to keep it that way. Bugger those orders from your superiors sending you back into the firing line.

With nightfall I finally got the chance to do my own admin, eating, cleaning, restocking.

But there were also other duties to perform. As promised, Paddy sent us out in turn on patrols to the various ANA and ANP outposts. I also took my turn on radio stag, monitoring the chit-chat from across Helmand, listening to the seemingly endless contacts and cries for support as men battled each other in this most inhospitable land. Over the top of it all came the repeated moaning of the prisoner. He was close to death and more than once we summoned Corporal Cowley to come and resuscitate him after he stopped breathing. Had the Afghans been guarding him he would surely have been dead already – if not at their hands, then through neglect. Though quite why we kept him alive was a moot point. I wanted to give him morphine but wasn't allowed to, as the medic said this would probably hasten his demise – not necessarily a bad thing, I thought. If he had been an animal he would have been shot, put out of his misery. Instead all I could do was sit there and listen to his pain. He was a dreadful sight, and in the end I took some pity on him. As he was unable to move because of his injuries, and watched over by an armed sentry, I decided to remove the cuffs. Taking my bayonet, I sliced through the plastic. If he was going to die in a strange place, surrounded by the faces of his enemy, then at least he was going to have a degree of dignity.

The night dragged on. It didn't seem to matter whether I was on duty or not. Time passed at a snail's pace. Rest was elusive, sleep almost nonexistent. When I closed my eyes I saw images from the day. Death. Injury. Blood. Bullets. Battle. And now I was also thinking, no chance of dreaming, about home. I wondered how Margaret and the children were doing. What were they up to, unaware of the situation I found myself in, believing I was manning a desk? I tried to block it all out, but the pictures and thoughts kept coming back, vultures circling my mind. What if I never returned? What if I had already said my last words to my wife? Sent my last email? Seen my children for the final time? What if. What if. What if.

I found my eyes welling up. I wiped my arm across my face, smudging the dust and dirt covering my skin with tears. Too much time to think. Damn it. Too much time.

NINE

TAKING CASUALTIES

(GARMSIR, DAY 3)

Another day arrived and another run down the canal road awaited. It seemed as if a pattern was being set.

But before the off, there was time – I made a point of it – to check and recheck we were ready for whatever the enemy might throw at us.

I looked down to my left. The door holster was full, my pistol sitting snugly inside it. Casting my eyes in an arc I came to the GPMG, a box of 200 rounds of ammo already attached to it, and two more boxes ready for rapid change: one at my feet, the other under cargo netting on the bonnet. Then there were the phosphorus grenades and the high-explosive grenades, L109s. Two of the latter were tucked into my vest, two more hung from plastic cuffs looped to the dashboard. More still were in the door next to my pistol, plus blue smoke grenades. As I sorted myself out so did the others. Each of us had a way of stowing our equipment so that when the time came we knew where it was. Routine was the key. The day you put something in a strange or different place would be the day you needed it in a hurry and reached for it only to find it wasn't there. I was determined not to let that happen.

For Sam and Chipper, their final bit of admin was to have a smoke. A moment of calm before the madness started again.

I gave the order for the two Land Rovers to move out, leaving the school – our base. As we rolled out of the compound I started thinking. Not about the day ahead, but about whether now was the moment to start smoking. I never failed to be envious of how at ease those taking a quick puff could be. It might be murder and mayhem all around but there are plenty of soldiers who find some peace in a fag. I had seen it many times before. In Brecon for example, after a long, wet, bruising forced march, chilled to the bone, blisters burst and skin rubbed raw by ill-fitting boots, there would always be those who managed to draw solace from their cigarettes. They were the ones amongst us who could put the pain and discomfort to one side simply through a quick fix of nicotine. What was doubly galling was that they managed to give off an aura of warmth, despite being as sodden as the rest of us. It amazed me that I had never really been tempted before. Now I was desperate to be part of the club. I tried to look on the bright side. In a way I had just had the benefits of smoking without the addiction. Just thinking about cigarettes had diverted my attention from the dangers that the next few hours were bound to bring.

The journey was quiet. There was no RPG attack at the checkpoint at the eastern end of the DC. No shooting as we drove steadily down the road towards the southerly crossing. Nothing as we passed the hotspots of the previous day: the track down to the farm complex; the point at which we had been pinned down in the morning; not even at the crossing itself.

When we pulled up, the Afghan policemen looked in a hell of a state. The strain showed on their faces. They looked exhausted. The result of a night spent living on their nerves, contacting the enemy just often enough to be allowed no rest or relaxation. There with them were the ANA soldiers. Instead of remaining at their posts in the small house west of the crossing, ready for a Taliban counter-attack, they had all walked out and come to join the ANP. Luckily the Taliban had not noticed this less-than-tactical withdrawal, the subsequent gaping holes in our defensive line, the lack of depth. If they had, the first we would have known about it was as they strode into town.

I jumped down from the wagon and yelled out for the senior ANA officer in charge to come forward. No one moved. I shouted again. Still nothing.

It soon became clear why no one of any authority was coming to talk to me. It was because there was no one of any authority there. The previous night after we left, so had they, the ANA officers buggering off back to the town, the job of keeping order instead falling to some weary-looking conscript who seemed barely old enough to be fighting, let alone left in charge.

With him in command, no wonder the ANA had decided to abandon their positions.

The whole thing was totally unacceptable. I wasn't annoyed just with the Afghans. I was also pretty pissed off with the OMLT members. It was their bloody job to mentor these people; their job to ensure the tactics and plans we suggested were put into practice.

Through Yasir I told the ANA soldiers to get back out to the house west of the crossing. I needed them out there so when we advanced south they would at least be able to cover our right flank.

But at that moment it didn't seem as if there would be an advance. With just fifteen minutes till H-hour, Shahrukh and his men had still not turned up.

It was frustrating and depressing. It looked like everything would turn to shit once again.

H-hour came and went, and still no policemen. I got back on the radio to Paddy and asked what the hell was happening.

'Doug, they will be leaving any minute. Their ammo re-supply has only just arrived and they're still dishing it out.'

At 10:15 hrs they finally appeared. It wasn't much of a force, just twelve of them led by Shahrukh, a mere fraction of the sixty men the ANP had in and around Garmsir. By the time you took out people to guard the positions we had already taken, those available to capture new ground were worryingly small in number. We needed reinforcements but there was no sign of them coming. We had to go on with what we had.

Four of the policemen started to push down through the small village on the eastern side of the canal. The other eight with the Major dropped into a shallow, dry drainage ditch beside the road and also headed off south. We stayed put, waiting for the first engagement of the day. We didn't have many minutes to wait. The ANP had gone no more than 100 metres when the firing started up, the shooting coming from several sources: the walled complex some 350 metres due south, the tree-line to the south-west and from buildings to the east.

It was time we helped out.

I ordered Chipper's vehicle to come up level with ours. 'Steve, I want you to engage the enemy south-east of the canal with the .50-cal.'

'OK, boss, but I can't see the bastards.'

'Follow the canal south until the end of the buildings on the east of it. Seen?' I asked.

'Seen.'

'Continue further south until a large tree-line meets the canal. Seen?' I asked again.

'Seen.'

'Two knuckles left of that junction is a large tree, higher than the rest. From the base and left of that tree there's some rubble. There are muzzle flashes coming from it. Watch and shoot. Watch and shoot.'

Steve didn't say anything, but his answer came a couple of moments later when the .50-cal kicked into life, rounds of heavy-calibre tracer winging their way towards the target I had identified, slamming into the ruins.

'Steve, keep your fire directed there. Chipper, you join in if needed.'

I looked over my shoulder at Sam. I wanted to know if he had yet declared a TiC so we had an excuse to request air support. 'Done,' came the reply. Which was just as well because we weren't going to be going anywhere till the cavalry arrived. I tried to work out a target list. First I wanted a couple of bombs dropped on the tree-line to our south-west. Then another on the pile of rubble Steve was shooting at. The idea was to make the Taliban in the walled complex feel isolated as we hit their colleagues to the rear. The hope was they would withdraw rather than risk getting cut off.

But suddenly we had more immediate problems. A mortar round landed close by, sending chunks of the road spinning away from the point of impact. This was followed by small-arms fire just to our left, east of the crossing; I guessed it was these fighters who must be spotting for the mortar teams much further away. We needed to deal with them. I ordered all guns to open up on the buildings to the east, no more than fifty metres away. We could not call in an air-strike this close to our location. We would have to sort the problem ourselves. I gave each gunner a target area; an arc within which to contain their shooting.

'Rapid fire!'

The .50-cal and the three GPMGs opened up in unison. The noise was phenomenal. So was the damage. The buildings started to disintegrate in front of our eyes; small, then much larger, holes began to appear in the walls, dust flew into the air, chunks of brick, stone and mud fell to the ground as the structures were eaten away.

The return fire stopped but we kept shooting for another couple of minutes before I called a halt.

'Watch and shoot.'

The Harriers had just arrived on station, circling high above us, waiting for Sam to give them the lie of the land. This always had to be done before an attack; to make sure the pilots were looking at the same battlefield we were fighting on. It wasn't necessarily a straightforward task. We were viewing things from a stationary position at ground level. The pilots were way above, flying at several hundred miles per hour. There was bound to be confusion, and with thousands of pounds of high explosive about to be dropped it was critical that confusion was cleared up. I wanted the first 1,000lb weapon dropped on the tree-line 800 metres to our south-west. But all the Harrier crews could make out was a wooded area more than a kilometre away.

Same thing, different perspective. We needed to get it sorted. Yes, it might take more time than we on the ground would have liked for the planes to finally engage their targets, but better that than causing death, possibly ours, by friendly fire.

At last the pilots were happy with what they were seeing.

The first attack run started.

A plane flashed along the horizon, converging on the tree-line, as always flying perpendicular to our line of attack, never down it. As so many times before I looked on as the bomb separated from the aircraft and lazily tumbled towards the ground. It disappeared from view, then came the explosion. I saw a flash that a split second later was engulfed by an expanding cloud of smoke. A second or two after that and the sound reached us.

Sam reported back to the pilots; the strike had been a good one.

Four more times the planes streaked in, hitting the targets I had designated for them. Four more times I was presented with the same visual spectacle. I had no compassion for the Taliban, but I couldn't help wondering about the hellish nature of being subjected to such a bombardment.

It was time for Shahrukh to start advancing again.

I gave the thumbs-up to Colonel Gulzar, who was standing by our vehicles, and he passed on the message. His men restarted their progress along the ditch.

We moved too, staying abreast of the ANP. It helped that the Harriers were still on station, ready to give cover if our progress stalled again, though it seemed the mere presence of the

Harriers was enough to persuade the Taliban to keep their heads down.

Sam shouted from the back of the wagon that we also had the chance of support from a B-1 if we needed it. The bomber was on its way south for another mission and could be diverted to us for just a few minutes. This gave me some confidence and we continued our crawl along the road. There was a worry though. I had not had any details of the rest of the ANA contingent, which Tim was supposed to be leading south from the DC towards the wood to the west, our right.

As we edged forward I radioed Paddy for an update.

His response should not have come as a shock, but it was no more welcome for being half expected.

Not only had Tim and the ANA failed to begin advancing south of the 43 northing, they hadn't even got to the start line. In fact they were still in the DC. I cursed silently. Here we were again, six British soldiers, twelve members of the ANP plus two of their commanders, out on a limb with no support on our right flank. It went against everything we had been trained to do. But yet we had made progress. We were now 300 metres south of the crossing and just 700 metres from the 42 northing, the final objective. I should have thought about halting but then we would be giving up the initiative. The Harriers were gone but Sam said the B-1 would be overhead in ten minutes. If only we could stay out of trouble till then.

It wasn't to be. With the RAF's departure, the Taliban had regrouped and firing started up again from several locations, the heaviest engagement still coming from the woods. I needed the ANA to get in there and clear them.

I radioed back to Paddy. 'How long till the ANA are ready to head south?'

The answer wasn't particularly encouraging. Yes the ANA were finally on the move. No they had still not reached the start line, where they should have been two hours previously.

Sam shouted down. 'Boss, the B-1 is here. What do you want it to do?'

'Drop a bomb exactly where you are firing.' I pointed towards the edge of the wood where Sam was directing his GPMG. I turned and thrust the aerial photo towards him, indicating the spot I wanted targeting.

I double-checked the map co-ordinates before giving them to Sam.

'We are going to get a couple of 2,000lb bombs followed by a pair of 500s,' said Sam.

I confirmed the co-ordinates again.

If the Harriers had been a shock for the enemy, this was going to be a visitation from hell. At least with the smaller jets, they probably had a second or two to take cover as they saw the aircraft coming in on their attack runs. With the B-1 there would be no warning. A mile or more high, it was barely visible, a black speck in a vast expanse of blue. The bombs would come out of nowhere. There would be no chance to react.

The B-1 unleashed its firepower.

I remember the strikes as if they were only yesterday.

The first bomb I didn't see land, my head still buried in my charts. But I heard the reaction to it around me, gasps and shouts coming from the mouths of the Afghan policemen as it detonated. I glanced up just in time to see dust, debris, trees, earth and I suppose people – or at least bits of them – start to fall back to earth. The second device exploded. The effect was the same. It was as if a whole section of the wood had been lifted up and deposited somewhere else. The sight was awesome. It reminded me of the old news footage I had seen from Vietnam, where the US pilots tried to carpet-bomb the Vietcong into submission. This was far short of what happened back in the 1960s, but it gave some insight into the sheer scale of the destructive firepower available to us in Afghanistan.

The firing from the enemy didn't just slow, it stopped completely. I knew people must have died; more must have been injured. But I wasn't about to start thinking about them. The military objective had been achieved, this was war and they had been shooting at us. Better them dismembered, disembowelled, decapitated, flayed, than us.

I called to Sam to get the B-1 to repeat the task.

Seconds later and there were more gigantic explosions in the same area as the first two, sound rumbling out across the landscape.

We started to move forward. The ANP seemed to have taken on a casual air. They were standing tall, their rifles slung over their shoulders. To the east, our left, the other four ANP men had stopped at the edge of the village that spread down the side of the canal from the crossing. I was far from certain they had managed to clear it all of Taliban, but at least they offered some protection to our flank.

I sat in my seat, the butt of the GPMG set firmly in my shoulder, my finger resting gently on the trigger guard, swivelling in a small arc to scan the ground ahead of us.

Sam was doing the same behind me.

We were now perhaps 500 metres from our ultimate objective. The ANP were closer still. It seemed to be within our grasp.

Bang. Whoosh. Bang.

An RPG round detonated just to our rear.

'Contact right. No, left. Fuck. I'm not sure. Did anyone see where that came from?' I screamed into the PRR.

A second, then third, round slammed into the ground too close for comfort. They actually seemed to be coming from straight ahead of us down the road. The RPGs were soon joined by more small-arms fire from a whole host of positions. We were exposed and in trouble. I tried to duck down behind the dashboard for some shelter. I didn't need to direct our return fire. The guys had no shortage of targets. From the ditch the ANP also started to shoot back, Shahrukh running up and down screaming at his men to fight.

It was getting out of control. The enemy had the measure of us and RPGs were falling all around. Sam and I watched in grim fascination as one grenade hit the ground no more than twenty metres to our right before skidding and bouncing towards our wagon. It stopped just a couple of metres away. I wanted to dive out of the way, but I was transfixed, I couldn't do anything. As still as a statue, I was completely focused on the device; Sam was the same. We waited for it to explode. We waited to die. We waited some more. Nothing happened. I shook myself out of my torpor.

It is hard to describe just how bad the situation was.

The small-arms fire and RPGs being directed towards us had now been joined by mortar rounds. We had no cover and the enemy was attacking us from at least three sides. We couldn't move forward because that would have taken us deeper into trouble and going back wasn't much of an option either; this wasn't the place to do a three-point turn, not least because both drivers would have to put down their weapons to do so, thus encouraging the Taliban to take even more potshots at us. And suppose we did manage to turn and run, what about the Major and his eight men? They would be left for slaughter. The only way we were going to get out of this was for the ANA to get a fucking move on and take the pressure off us.

That's if we survived that long.

I spoke to Paddy again. 'If Tim doesn't get the ANA going, then we're fucked.'

Paddy told me the ANA were almost at their start point and should be with us in twenty minutes. He said I should be able to talk to Tim direct.

I didn't have twenty minutes. I didn't have ten. The enemy was winning the firefight and rounds were thudding into the vehicles all about me. I glanced around and saw a slight dip in the road ahead of us. It wasn't much, but might just offer a degree of protection at least for the lower half of the WMIKs. We edged forward.

Crack, crack.

Two bullets came through the dashboard.

Crack.

There was a scream.

'I'm hit,' was all Joe managed to say.

I looked across at him. A third round had followed the first two through the dashboard, then between the spokes of the steering wheel, and eventually had found its target, British flesh, striking Joe in the arm.

'Are you OK?' I yelled. I knew it was a stupid question.

'I'll be all right,' Joe said as with his one good hand he fumbled for a field dressing jammed into his webbing.

There was nothing I could do to help. More of the enemy were now approaching us from the east over some open ground. There were perhaps a dozen of them moving rapidly across the field towards the eastern side of the canal and a position where even they could not miss with their RPGs.

'Sam, shoot those fuckers over to your left,' I screamed as I too blasted away at them. If they made it to the water then the game was up. We were completely ignoring the bullets flying towards us from the south and south-west. This was now the priority. If we didn't get them, they would get us. There was certainly no time to get on the radio to Paddy again.

Such was the intensity of the contact that the 200-round box I had fitted to my GPMG first thing in the morning was empty. So was the one that had been on the bonnet. So was the one that had been at my feet. I needed Sam to pass me more ammo from the back of the Land Rover but he was too busy shooting to help.

I fell out of the vehicle and ran to the back. Curled up in a ball at Sam's feet was Yasir, a look of complete horror painted on his face. I swore at him to pass me some ammunition. He handed over three boxes of 7.62mm link and I scrambled back to my seat. As I did I could see that Joe was still trying to stem the flow of blood from his arm. He wasn't having much luck. He had also gone terribly pale. He was going into shock.

'Sandstone 78, this is Widow 77. We have a British casualty, are under intense fire and need immediate casevac. Over.'

'Roger, Widow 77. Wait. Out.'

I reloaded my gun. 'Joe, you had better get out of the wagon and find some shelter.'

With that he hauled himself out from the driver's seat and crawled round the Land Rover before huddling up against the rear wheel. I just hoped he would be OK till help arrived.

For what seemed like an age Sam and I continued shooting. Finally, finally, after we had expended hundreds, perhaps thousands, of rounds, the enemy started to pull back, leaving four bodies lying motionless in the field.

But we weren't out of trouble yet. We were still being shot at from at least four locations, we still couldn't move anywhere and we had a casualty.

'Sam, any chance of any air cover?'

'Not yet, boss,' was the unwanted reply.

Paddy was back on the radio. 'Widow 77, this is Sandstone 78. Estonians will be with you in five minutes.'

'Roger, Sandstone. Tell them to engage targets to the east as they come down the road.' I looked back and could already see two vehicles up at the crossing, starting to move towards us. 'Come on, you bastards, come on.'

And so they did. In no time at all they had pulled up level with us, to our left, offering some cover from the shooting coming from the east. Out of the back of the second armoured truck jumped Corporal Cowley with a couple of the Estonians. They heaved Joe to his feet and unceremoniously dragged him away. Almost as soon as they arrived the vehicles had turned round and roared off back the way they'd come.

In the mayhem the ANP had begun to pull back towards us. They were little more than thirty metres to our front now, still in the ditch. I told Yasir to tell Shahrukh that his men had to stay where they were, otherwise this would become a rout.

There was another scream and then frantic shouting in Pashtu.

En masse the ANP policemen rose to their feet and started shooting at the wood. All except two. One was hunched over the other, who was lying at the bottom of the ditch. Failing to get any response from the casualty, the first tried to hook his hands under the victim's armpits and haul him away from the fighting. But the body was completely limp, making it almost impossible to move. It was clear the victim was beyond help; shot in the head, he had probably been dead before he hit the ground.

Despite the fire coming our way, I watched intently as the rest of the policemen now crouched down around him too, keeping under cover, assessing the loss of another of their comrades, counting the growing cost of the battle for Garmsir.

'Doug, this is Tim.'

I was brought back to my senses. 'Tim, where are you?'

'I'm at the start line, about 200 metres west of the canal crossing. I've got about forty ANA soldiers with me. I could come straight to your position as we are not under any fire.'

'No, don't do that,' I warned. 'Or else we will all end up getting shot to pieces here. I want you to work your way south towards the tree-line and then start clearing along it. That will take the pressure off us and the ANP.'

Our situation had barely changed in two hours. Ammunition was low and we had been using the guns continuously for sixty minutes. Sam said there was still no chance of air support and he had returned to his weapon. I kept firing too, but tried to make a mental note of targets should the air situation change. Tim was now the key to how things turned out. Once he reached the trees should we start our advance again? It was difficult to see how we could. The ANP were exhausted and demoralised, and we were all still in danger of being outflanked. Added to that I was short of a driver and I couldn't see one emerging from the ranks of the OMLT in the next few minutes.

I looked around to see how Tim and the ANA were doing. It wasn't what we had discussed. Rather than move south and slightly west till they hit the tree-line, the ANA were coming south-east towards the building complex some 400 metres down the road. What had happened with the wood? I got Tim's response over the radio.

'Doug, we are going to suppress the enemy from the complex and then attack over the open ground to take the pressure off you.'

I didn't give a shit. It was his shout. He was in charge of the ANA. Just as long as he achieved the desired result.

Sam interrupted. Two F-18s were now on their way to us, but it was good news, bad news. They wouldn't arrive for another forty minutes.

'Why so bloody long?'

'Because they're coming from another job. They have to land at Kandahar, refuel and rearm before heading here.'

At least that would give Sam a bit of time to fix the TacSat, which had just stopped responding. He ducked down to sort it out, hopefully just a change of batteries needed and not the whole thing wrecked by a bullet. Steve was also having problems. His .50-cal had jammed and he was frantically trying to clear it. This was a constant worry when the weapon got hot through overuse. Chipper was trying to distribute ammunition between the two WMIKs, which left only Geordie trying to kill the enemy, using just his rifle.

Bang, bang, bang, bang.

The ANA fired a salvo of RPGs towards the wood and used it as cover to start their assault from the buildings. Tim led from the front with the ANA commander close behind. Viewed from where I was, it looked good. The men were well spread out, crossing the ground, using a technique known as fire and manoeuvre. Two hundred metres on and I lost sight of them as they disappeared into thicker foliage. But I could still hear the shooting. By now the enemy had turned almost all their attention to what was happening in and around the trees. The Taliban to our south had given up firing at us and had redirected their weapons towards the ANA with ferocious intensity. I tried to distract them by firing at their position but with little success.

For some twenty minutes the battle raged. Then failure.

The first I knew of it was when Tim came on the radio. I could hear the strain in his voice. It was sobering and hinted at what they had been through out of our sight.

He just informed. He didn't explain. 'Doug, we're going to have to withdraw to the buildings.'

'Roger, Tim. Will you then stay at the buildings and cover us as we pull out? We'll put down fire till you get there.'

'OK, will do.'

I was about to tell Shahrukh what was planned, but he was already on the move. His men were coming back along the drainage ditch, carrying their dead comrade between them.

Now all the unwanted attention had reverted back to us. I willed Tim and the ANA to hurry up before we lost our breathing space to get out of there. Chipper started to turn his vehicle round, ready to make a break for it up the road. When he was in position I got in the driving seat of my vehicle and did the same.

The ANA reached the building complex.

'Tim, this is Doug, we are on our way. I suggest you get out, too. I don't think we are going to be able to organise any sort of ordered withdrawal.'

'Roger that, Doug. The ANA are in full flight now anyway. I'm going with them.'

We threw smoke grenades to cover our departure and hoofed it out of there. As I had feared it had become a rout and the enemy chased us on our way. As we sped down the road towards the crossing, I saw the ANP continuing to drag the dead man with them. The ANA were running in a similar direction, making for the buildings to the west of the crossing.

Durani and Gulzar were there to meet us as we arrived. I saw the worry in their eyes but I wasn't in the mood to speak to them. After the euphoria of yesterday they now seemed to realise just how precarious things were. They could see we had been beaten and at some cost too.

Feeling completely deflated I approached Shahrukh. He was standing over the lifeless body that lay on a brightly coloured blanket. I could see the policeman had more than just the wound to the head. There were several bullet holes across his chest. Yasir whispered that the man was one of Shahrukh's relatives.

I asked him to tell Shahrukh how sorry I was.

'I warned you the enemy was too strong here. I said we did not have enough ammunition and equipment. And now one of my men is dead. My cousin is dead.'

There was nothing I could say. Any residue of optimism I had about the situation evaporated to be replaced by a cloud of guilt. These are the moments when the doubts set in, times when it is impossible to take anything positive from your actions. You are in charge and the buck stops with you. The cost of failure is death. Of course success can also cost lives but at least there you have a trade-off: the giving of life for the achievement of an objective; the reassurance that the sacrifices were not in vain. You cannot say that about defeat. You have lost. People have died and the survivors are looking at you for an explanation. Why did you do this? Why did you do that? Why the other? Then you start to question yourself. Am I a bad leader? Did I make decisions no one else would have? Am I culpable? It is a lonely experience. When you are closer to the top of the ladder than the bottom you cannot use the excuse 'I was only following orders'. In fact it is the opposite. You gave the orders. And the consequences of those orders weigh on your shoulders.

I went back to my vehicle. Sam was standing beside it.

'The F-18s are almost with us,' he said. 'What do you want them to hit?'

I didn't really care. They were too late to save our situation. Too late to prevent the need for Tim's near-suicidal attack on the tree-line.

I told Sam to get them to drop some bombs 'around this area'; 'in the vicinity of that building'; 'somewhere over there'.

He was having none of it. He wanted specifics, but he understood the mood I was in and came to my rescue. 'Boss, the planes have multiple rockets as well as 500lb bombs. I think we should hit the woods with a set of six rockets and then drop a bomb on our original target, the house at the 42 northing.' He made it easy for me to agree.

As Sam waited for the planes I wandered towards Durani and Gulzar.

The General was pretty philosophical about what had happened and the loss of one of his men. He understood what we had been trying to achieve and he realised why it had not been managed. But he wasn't in a position to offer me any good news. 'The Taliban are sending in fresh fighters from Jugroom.' He was talking about the village to the south-west of where we were, perhaps two kilometres away – the Taliban 'capital' for the area. 'Every time you bomb them and kill them, they send for reinforcements. They are also spreading the word that today they destroyed two ISAF vehicles on the canal road.'

It wasn't true, of course, but to them it was good propaganda. War is not just about what has happened, but about what people think has happened. And today everyone seemed to perceive the Taliban had won – including us.

It had been an hour since our hasty retreat. The F-18s had been and gone. The air-strikes were accurate, but more about us venting our anger and frustration than gaining military advantage. We helped the ANP shore up their defences before we decided to leave. We mounted up and continued back down the canal road to the town. We had been in Garmsir just three days and already this was an all too familiar journey.

We didn't go back to the school. Our camp had changed. Paddy had moved our base to the town's agricultural college. In terms of salubrious accommodation it was no more welcoming, but in military terms it was much more satisfactory, offering increased withdrawal routes in case we were overrun. I had no confidence we wouldn't soon be needing them.

Paddy was waiting to meet us. He gave me the low-down on Joe's condition. My driver had been extremely lucky. The bullet had entered his arm and been contained inside the muscle without hitting anything important. Bone damage and exit wounds are the things to worry about and in this case Joe had avoided both. It was the perfect wound for getting a pint. All he would have to do was roll up his sleeve at the bar and tell anyone interested how he single-handedly defeated the Taliban.

As we spoke I could see Tim over Paddy's shoulder, looking forlorn. He was amongst a group of the ANA and the OMLT.

'How's he doing?' I asked Paddy.

'Feeling it. You know the ANA commander with him was killed and I think his men are giving Tim a hard time about not bringing back the body.'

'What do they bloody well expect?' I said with fury.

By Tim's actions and example he had saved the lives of the ANP and the Land Rover crews. How on earth could he be held responsible for leaving the dead man out there?

'Perhaps if the ANA hadn't been so quick to turn and run, they might have been able to bring back the body themselves,' I spat.

Paddy offered no response. He was already trying to think ahead. 'I'm worried about the morale of the OMLT and the ANA, not to mention the ANP's constant shortage of ammunition. You, Tim and I are going to have to have a chat about what we do next. I'm not sure we have the forces to push home any advantage we might still hold. For that matter I don't even know if we can hang on to the town.'

I approached Tim as the group around him disbanded. He looked a different soldier to the one who had left the DC just hours earlier. A beaten man. The tall athletic frame was gone. Now all I could see was the stooped body of an old man. His shoulders were hunched, his eyes listless and his head down. It was only later that I found out a bit more about what had happened. As the foliage had become thicker and the advance harder, the Afghan soldiers turned and ran. That left just Tim and the Afghan commander to take the fight to the enemy. They battled on but the wall of bullets became impenetrable. The result was inevitable: the Afghan commander cut down in front of Tim. There was nothing he could do to help. He tried to drag the man's body back through the undergrowth under intense fire. He was bound to fail. The saving grace? There had only been one fatality and not two.*

'How are you doing?' I asked.

'Hi, Doug.' He spoke in a hushed, deliberate tone. 'That was a close call today. I'm not sure quite how I am feeling. You know they want me to go back out there and get the body of their commander.'

---

* For his actions Tim was awarded the Conspicuous Gallantry Cross. This is his citation: 'On 10 September 2006, Lieutenant Tim Illingworth deployed with a small team in support of a joint Afghan Police and Army operation to recapture Garmsir District Centre. During two days of heavy fighting, Lieutenant Illingworth and his team were constantly under fire whilst motivating, directing and advising their Afghan colleagues who successfully re-took Garmsir. Later that week an Afghan Police patrol supported by Illingworth's team, was ambushed. One British casualty resulted. In an effort to relieve the pressure on the Afghan Police, he led his Afghan company commander and a foot patrol to neutralise the enemy position. This inspired his Afghan Army colleagues who were reticent to advance on the heavily defended enemy position.

The Afghani resolve to continue failed after three days of heavy fighting. Seeing this, Lieutenant Illingworth went to the front of the Afghan troops and moved alone to within 30 metres of the first enemy position under heavy fire. Soon after the company commander was killed. Lieutenant Illingworth took up the commander's rocket launcher, firing three rounds into the main enemy position in full view of them. He himself narrowly missed being killed. All but one of the Afghan force abandoned Illingworth, leaving him exposed and under withering fire. In spite of his isolation, he attempted to assault the enemy position expending seven magazines of ammunition. The enemy fire was unrelenting. He regrouped and rallied the remaining force to continue. Lieutenant Illingworth's bravery and example over seven days was well beyond the call of duty. His role was to mentor rather than fight. However, understanding the importance of Garmsir, he placed himself in a position of utmost danger to influence events. His outstanding courage, leadership and selflessness in pressing home his attack upset the enemy ambush and saved many lives. Such inspiring and raw courage from a relatively young and inexperienced officer was exemplary and justly merit the award of the Conspicuous Gallantry Cross.'

From the way he said it I knew he was actually thinking of going.

'No way, Tim. You would just end up taking more casualties. Perhaps we will be out that way again and we can pick him up then.'

This was what Tim wanted to hear. A sense of honour and duty was making him contemplate the mission; he just needed someone to help talk him out of going through with it. His eyes turned watery. There wasn't much I could do.

'Mate, you saved our lives out there today. We wouldn't have got back otherwise. Thank you. Why don't you take yourself away for a while, somewhere quiet, think things over.'

I could see he was already slipping back into the events of the day. He nodded and turned away silently.

It must be the measure of an officer that he can share the pain of his men and understand their anguish. That after the heat of battle he can re-run the confrontation in his mind, rather than blot it out. Not so as to dwell on events and let it pull him down, but to empathise with the others; to see what went right and what went wrong and to come back from that in a stronger frame of mind. It is not easy. It takes some strength of character. And to my mind Tim possessed that in spades.

I watched as he walked towards the college building.

Left alone, I had a chance to assess our new billet. It was a single-storey building, eighty metres or so long and five metres deep. There were equally spaced, door-less openings all along it, leading into bare rooms. Each of these rooms had a window, again without shutters or coverings. There was a flat roof made of concrete with an overhang to the front. It was under this that most of the men were busying themselves.

Chipper and Geordie had rejoined their mates from the OMLT and were in animated conversation.

Corporal Cowley and the doctor were completing an inventory of the medical equipment, so they knew what to order for the next re-supply.

A signaller was doing the same for the ammunition and other equipment. I wanted to remind him to request the spare wheels we needed for the Land Rovers.

Another OMLT member was tending a fire he had started to burn the discarded bloody rags of the wounded. Despite the heat of the day it was still strangely comforting to watch the flames.

The Sergeant-Major was taking charge of putting in place trip flares at various entry points to the compound so we would get early warning of anyone sneaking in.

Most of the Estonians were at the far end of the building sorting out whatever Estonians needed to sort out, though one was engrossed with Sam, looking over our vehicle. His name was Claus and he was a captain in charge of bomb disposal. But he had another talent that was of particular interest to us. In a previous life he'd worked as a mechanic and that made him our saviour.

We had noticed a leak from the engine bay when we got back and the pair of them were trying to find the root of the problem. The liquid turned out to be coming from the water cooler. The starter motor was also on its last legs, having been hit by bits of shrapnel. Claus was happy to sort things out, but he needed the parts. More for the signaller's re-supply list.

It was time to talk tactics. Paddy called Tim and me over to him. We ran through the current situation.

The ANP were down to just fifty fighting men. The ANA had eighty but morale was poor and they were now without a commander. We still held two canal crossings and the ANA had men on JTAC Hill. Our base at the college was to the west of the DC and we had access to the bridge over the river if we needed to make a hasty getaway. At least our position was far from being fixed. (In military terms being fixed means not having the ability to move freely, either because of the constraints of enemy forces, the environment or equipment. This was the situation the guys at platoon houses in places like Kajaki, Now Zad and Musa Qala found themselves in, essentially confined to their defensive positions by the Taliban who surrounded them.)

The big imponderable was the state of our foes. They had taken a severe beating not just from our firepower on the ground but also from the air. Yet they didn't seem to be losing strength or effectiveness. Either they had already been here in even greater numbers than we thought when we arrived or else they were calling in reinforcements as the General had suggested. Perhaps both.

'I am now expecting the OMLT to be relieved some time tomorrow night,' said Paddy, before continuing: 'Therefore I think it might be a good idea to consolidate our positions tomorrow, rather than carry out any more offensive operations.'

Tim agreed. 'If we ask for defensive stores to be added to the re-supply list then we can spend the day securing our perimeter and create strongholds at the checkpoints.'

'I agree that we need a rest,' I said. 'And I also think that we will not be able to clear any further south and hold on to it. I think we have gone as far as we can but we need to maintain aggressive fighting patrols to make sure the Taliban don't sneak back too close to our positions.'

'OK, but those will have to be done with the OMLT's replacements whenever they arrive.'

I remembered something rather important. 'I'm also going to need another driver.'

Paddy went off to tell KAF what was on our shopping list.

It looked as if the rest of the evening was going to pass off peacefully when there was a screech of tyres and a plume of dust as Gulzar's car flew into our compound. Behind it was another ANP vehicle, a flatbed with several men clinging on to the sides. At their feet, yet another casualty of war: a policeman with a bullet wound to the head.

'What happened?' I asked Gulzar.

He explained that the Taliban had indeed sneaked back to some buildings a mere sixty metres from the southern crossing. Now they were sniping at the defenders.

Corporal Cowley took control of the injured man. Paddy

went straight back on to his TacSat radio to call KAF and request the Incident Response Team (IRT), the same medical team that had arrived earlier that day within thirty minutes of Joe's injury being reported.*

We were told to send a nine-liner. This is a list of questions and answers used to calculate a casualty's condition and the urgency of treatment. It didn't take long to work it out. The wounded policeman was classed as T1, top priority because of his head wound. Without prompt help, he was going to die.

Army medics, like their colleagues in civvy street, work on the principle of the golden hour. Emergency teams do everything they can to reach a casualty and get him to a medical facility within sixty minutes. It is of some comfort to British soldiers to know that, should they get hurt, there are doctors, nurses and helicopters ready to come to their aid as quickly as possible.

And the Ministry of Defence rules were that in Afghanistan those same procedures, that same help, should have been equally applied to our coalition colleagues, local forces included.

Yet for some reason it took four hours for the IRT helicopter to arrive. Four hours during which Tony Cowley and the Estonian doctor did what they could to keep the man alive. To their credit the man was still breathing when he was carried aboard the Chinook. By the time the aircraft landed at Bastion he was not.

The truth is that in war terrible things happen. The helicopter and the IRT were probably already tasked on another job. But that didn't make things easier to explain to the dead man's colleagues. In their eyes I feared they would think he had been left to his fate because of his nationality.

I headed for my bed. It was away from the main college building, past my Land Rover, just the other side of the compound

---

* The Taliban prisoner was also evacuated that day and treated at Camp Bastion. Later he was handed over to the Afghan National Directorate of Security in Lashkar Gah. His eventual fate is not known.

perimeter in a cemetery. In a macabre sort of way, my pit for the night was fitting for the circumstances. I lay down in a half-dug grave, perhaps twenty centimetres deep. There was a pile of soil running along one side. I placed my rifle along it.

Lying on my sleeping bag in the shallow trench, trying to ignore the stink from my shirt, I shut my eyes. I soon wondered why I had bothered. It was to be another long fitful night. What sleep I did find still didn't offer an escape from Afghanistan.

Our two WMIKs were at the southern crossing. All around us there was incoming fire. Bullets, RPGs, mortars, rockets. I knew we had had it. There was a huge explosion. Both vehicles erupted into churning balls of flame. It was an inferno, like hell itself. I woke in a panic, sweating profusely, and looked up at the stars.

TEN

A CALL TO PRAYER

(GARMSIR, DAY 4)

I hauled myself out of the grave, scratching at the vivid red bites that seemed to be all over me. I'd seen some black ants scurrying about on the ground the previous day when I had been searching for a bed, but not given them much thought. But obviously they had taken offence at me having the nerve to share what was clearly their nest and had consequently made their feelings known by an assault on my person under cover of darkness. As with the other nights I'd been in Garmsir I still had my uniform on, my boots laced up, ready to go. I had slept – if that was what you could call it – with my Kestrel body armour draped across my chest. During my tossing and turning it had slipped off and ended up as my mattress for the night. I reached for it and shook off some of the dust before putting it on. It resembled a sleeveless jacket, a Velcro fastener off-centred at the front keeping it tight to the chest and large zipped pockets at the front and the back. Into each fit Kevlar plates, almost thirty centimetres square, designed to stop a direct hit from a high-velocity round fired from an AK47 or the like.

I hated this bit of kit.

It was fine if your job was standing on street corners talking to civilians, waiting for that rare contact with the enemy; perfect for almost all of the thirty years we had spent in Northern Ireland. But I found it hopeless for the kind of situation we faced now – a real pain in the arse.

When wearing it, it was difficult to properly shoulder your rifle, and then almost impossible to use that weapon accurately if you had your webbing over the top of it. Lying down in the prone position was little better, probably worse. Add the weight of the thing to the whole equation and you ended up with a piece of equipment that, though designed with safety in mind, actually ended up hampering soldiers. What is the point of having kit that makes you more, not less, vulnerable because it hinders the ability to protect yourself, to move out of harm's way, to defend yourself through the use of your weapon?

Such was its degree of unpopularity that I had heard some units in the field decided, depending on role and circumstances, not to wear the body armour at all. Others wore the old-style protective jackets that were lighter and allowed for freer movement.

I didn't have that choice though. Colonel Charlie Knaggs had ordered that everyone leaving the PRT base in Lashkar Gah should use it. So that was that, more to wear, more to carry in the scorching heat. Forget about wrapping yourself in cellophane; this was the way to sweat off a few pounds.

It was now just after first light, about 05:00 hrs. Paddy had decided I should lead a clearance patrol to make sure there were no Taliban infiltrating the town immediately to the north. Through the night there had been a couple of stand-tos where the alarm had been raised over possible incursions. At least one of the trip flares had been set off. No one was seen, perhaps it had only been hapless animals that strayed through our security cordon, but we were going to go and check the area anyway.

I gathered together my team of four, all from the OMLT. Steve, of course, I knew. I couldn't put a name to the others.

The plan was to move the 200 metres or so to the edge of the built-up area, scan the ground ahead and then move across the top of the town before heading back to the centre. Personally I didn't think we would find anything – the enemy didn't know our strengths and I didn't believe they were brave enough to come so close – but we were going to operate as if there was someone out there. We moved off warily.

The area we headed through was made up of tightly packed shops and houses, many with courtyards surrounded by high walls. There were plenty of small alleyways leading in all directions, zigzagging between the buildings. Open sewers and drains ran along the edges of the dirt walkways. There was rubbish and filth everywhere, debris too. Barely a property had not been damaged by mortars or rockets. The town had been targeted by indirect fire for the past six months and it was showing its scars; there were pockmarks and holes of varying shapes and sizes everywhere you looked. For several buildings the regular bombardment had been too much and they had crumbled to rubble and dust.

Our progress was deliberate, slow. At each turn two soldiers would scan the way ahead, scribing an arc through the air with their rifles as they tried to spot anything suspicious. At the all-clear, the second pair would sprint forward and find some cover ahead before encouraging the first two to make a similar dash and leapfrog past them. I drifted between the two teams. So it went on as we made our way through Garmsir's northern fringe.

It took us almost thirty minutes to reach a vantage point from where we could take in the open ground beyond the dwellings.

I peered through my rifle sight, but could see nothing. I looked again and still all was quiet. But I had missed something.

'Movement to the north,' shouted one of the men.

I had a third look. He was right. Perhaps 200 metres away a small group of people was moving across a field. Were they the enemy?

Then out of the corner of my eye I saw something moving much closer, no more than seventy-five metres away. I swung my rifle round. It was a bizarre image: magnified four times, there was an old man in a wheelchair, propelling himself along a track. Around him, a handful of children, running this way and that.

I refocused on the original group I had seen. I could now make out they were elderly men. They were all heading in the same direction.

At that moment another two men appeared in an alley to my right. People were coming out of the woodwork. For a moment I couldn't fathom why. Then I worked it out. They were on their way to prayer, heading towards the town's mosque. It was not the mosque you might expect. No gleaming dome, no huge structure dominating its surroundings, just a low single-storey building that looked very much like every other one in the town. The religious significance of a mosque is not in its appearance but its designation. Label something as a mosque and it acquires the full aura and protection of the Muslim faith.

I tried to talk to the pair as they shuffled past. But without Yasir it was not going to be easy.

I offered them a greeting.

'*Salam alaikum*.' Peace unto you.

'*Alaikum salam*' came the reply. Peace unto you too.

It was as far as we got before they wandered by and on to their service.

I stood where I was for a while, watching as more and more people made their pilgrimage. I reckoned we had seen at least fifty adults plus a number of children. This was good news. Because ISAF was in town and because the town was now out of range of the Taliban, some of the local population had returned. This was the whole point of our little exercise. Push the enemy back so they could not inflict any damage on Garmsir, and encourage the inhabitants to re-enter an environment where they would be relatively safe. The only problem was: would we have enough men to secure the town in the long term? I wasn't sure.

Even so I was enthusiastic about what I had seen and keen to get back to Paddy so he could report it to KAF. I hoped it would strengthen our case for a greater investment of men and resources. If we could show some sort of success even with our limited manpower, who knew what was possible with a bit more commitment from the bosses.

We returned some ninety minutes later. Paddy was as excited as I was. He was also pleased we had not come across any trouble. So were the other members of the OMLT. They had been standing to since we went out on the patrol and now they could rest easy and devote some time to themselves. Food was a priority for several.

They set up their small stoves. Some of the devices were gas cookers; others used hexamine solid fuel blocks. The menu didn't really change. In fact it wasn't really a menu. It was sausages and beans, lamb hotpot or chocolate pudding. Not unusually more than one of the soldiers began the day with pudding.

They started heating up water for their 'boil in the bag' meals. When the food was ready the water would not go to waste. It would either be used to make a brew, or to wash and shave in. One or two got their razors out, but tea seemed to be the favoured option. Several of the men seemed more than happy with their four days' growth of facial hair. Some had already sprouted fully fledged beards.

Finishing my own breakfast I picked up my helmet, body armour and rifle and trudged towards the camp's perimeter. I also had my shovel. Well away from the others, but still in sight of the sentry, I dug a small hole, dropped my trousers, squatted and went about my business. Job done, I cleaned my hands with the alcohol gel we had been issued and went back to see what had changed.

At 07:00 hrs Paddy made his sitrep to KAF: outlining what we had found on patrol; asking about the OMLT relief; whether the re-supply was still due at 10:00 hrs?

He went through the points methodically and clearly, one by one, till he got to the end.

He was told to wait for the responses.

'Roger out,' he said and the radio went silent.

I could just imagine some young signaller, new in theatre, only just starting his eight-hour shift, sitting there thinking, who the hell is Sandstone 78? I was right.

The radio burst back into life. 'Hello, Sandstone 78, this is Zero. Please send location status and operation name.'

You couldn't make this shit up. Here we were fighting for our lives in the arse end of nowhere and as far as some people at HQ were concerned we didn't even exist. We must have been so far down the list of priorities that we didn't even get a mention at headquarters' handover. Forget about the public back in the UK not having a clue about what was happening in Afghanistan, it seemed half of those who were supposedly in command didn't know either. If you told people how bad things were they wouldn't believe you.

Paddy went through it all again. If it had been me I am sure I would have given the disembodied voice a piece of my mind. But Paddy played it straight, refusing to get riled.

The morning moved on slowly, with at last a chance to have a proper look at the wagon and the weapons.

I sorted out Joe's kit which was still stashed in the vehicle. After rifling through it for socks – you can never have too many clean pairs of socks – it was put under the watchful eye of the company quartermaster-sergeant (CQMS).

I already missed Joe. He had been uncomplaining throughout, even though he was thrust into a job he had never been trained for and probably never expected to do. A TA soldier with the Intelligence Corps, he had had no previous experience of driving a WMIK, but stepped up to the mark in the best traditions of the British Army. I just hoped I would get chance to speak to him before he was shipped back to the UK.

The morning continued to unfold slowly.

Things remained quiet. Relatively. Just before 08:00 hrs there was the sound of small-arms fire down towards the southern crossing, but it was just an exchange of noise that petered out after a few minutes. What we had been listening out for was the detonation of RPGs. This would have signalled a more serious contact and probably resulted in us mobilising to help.

Fifteen minutes later Gulzar's vehicle appeared round the corner. Just like the previous night it was followed by the flatbed truck. The exchange of noise had claimed a casualty. And a serious one at that. Corporal Cowley moved quickly. He directed the Afghans as they hauled their comrade out of the van and moved him to the building. He too had been shot in the head. Involuntarily he had adopted a foetal position and his body was shaking, wracked by spasms. He was groaning. I left the medic to deal with it.

Paddy was already drawing up a nine-liner to send back to KAF. The Colonel said the latest incident had been almost a repeat of the one last night. Taliban fighters had crept back into the buildings just east of the crossing and opened fire. The damage done, they vanished into the maze of alleys. Gulzar asked me for reassurance that help would come for his man. Fingers crossed, I said yes. I still hadn't told him yesterday's victim was dead. Given the four-hour delay in emergency evacuation, I didn't really know how to.

And once again there was going to be no immediate arrival of the IRT. Paddy was told they were busy elsewhere. The only option was to put the casualty on the re-supply helicopter due at 10:00 hrs, still more than an hour and a half away. I doubted he would live that long.

I tried to settle down and have something to eat. It's difficult to have your breakfast when a man is moaning in agony nearby. Welcome to the army, son. Sean Langan had joined Corporal Cowley to help. There was nothing I could add. I decided to take my food over to my Land Rover – still grounded whilst it awaited new parts. I was parked next to a wall that separated the agricultural college from the cemetery. I had just got settled when there was shouting from the other end of the compound. Looking up I saw camp security had been breached.

There were four of them, dark-skinned, their clothes simple yet in seemingly good condition, their feet bare. Children. Aged between perhaps eight and twelve. Healthy-looking. Their curiosity had got the better of them. They had dared a frontal assault on the might of the British Army.

The oldest of the group was pushing two of the younger ones on what seemed like a small market-stall trolley. It was strange to see such innocence in such a hostile environment. The kids were an obvious draw for several of the soldiers, a distraction from war perhaps, a reminder of their own children. One or two of the OMLT members smiled and tried to approach the youngsters to say hello. The four little warriors pulled back, curiosity tempered by apprehension. What did they make of us? Lumbering giants all dressed in camouflage, carrying weapons, foreigners in their land.

I kept my distance. I was wary of having them amongst us, for several reasons. Firstly it is a fact that insurgents in Afghanistan, just as in Iraq and other conflicts around the world, use local children to gather low-level intelligence. Already these children would have known how many we numbered, what vehicles were parked up in the compound, how easy it had been to walk through the front gate.

Then there's the ever-present danger they would become casualties of the fighting. If they latched on to us too tightly they could end up as collateral damage. Perhaps not so much here at our base, but when we were on patrol, as we moved through the town. If we were shot at, they would be in the firing line too.

Finally there was the risk to their health from general soldiering duties; driving about, checking weapons, handling explosives, grenades and flares. Accidents happen. My mind went back to Op Telic in Iraq.

Some British troops in that campaign had got into the habit of throwing rations and sweets to children as they drove past in their vehicles, even though since the Bosnian conflict army operational standing orders has banned such behaviour. The kids had come to expect the treats and would gather along the roadside whenever a convoy came into sight. They would jostle each other to get hold of the goodies being chucked out. As far as the men were concerned, it probably made them feel better about being in the country, the idea they were brightening up the lives of those who had only bleak futures ahead of them. It all seemed harmless fun.

All harmless fun that was till two eight-year-olds, pretty girls with raven hair and big brown eyes, jumped out behind a Land Rover to grab food dropped in the road. They never saw the eight-tonne truck following close behind – the eight-tonne truck that killed them. It was a bloody tragedy.

From then on Colonel Collins made it known the practice must stop. He didn't want to see the deaths of any more children. Three years on, here in Afghanistan, nor did I.

Just before 10:00 hrs Corporal Cowley supervised the loading of the patient into the back of an Estonian vehicle for the short trip out to the helicopter landing zone. The truck was chosen for the room it had in the back and its soft suspension. Not that the ride quality was likely to make much difference to the final outcome.

'How is he?' I asked.

'As good as dead, sir,' Tony replied. 'No chance at all, not now. I'm surprised he's lasted this long.'

Pinned to the man's chest was a handwritten note from the Estonian doctor for the medical team back in Bastion, outlining what had been done and what drugs had been given. I later found out it had been written in Latin, the doctor believing this was the international language of medicine.

The small convoy drove slowly out of the college grounds.

I watched from my Land Rover as the Chinook loomed into view, coming in to land on the open ground just west of the Helmand River. As it descended, a vast cloud of sand and dust rose up to envelop it. The technical term for such a storm is a brown-out. Just like the white-out you get in a blizzard.

As the dust settled a little, I could see the medical party carry the patient up the ramp. They didn't return empty-handed, coming out with a couple of portable stretchers. It seemed someone expected us to be taking more casualties. Then the rest of the supplies we had requested were offloaded, including the Land Rover spares. There was also some human cargo: a new driver for me and two majors. One from the OMLT who had come to see how bad things really were; the other from the Psychological Operations team. He and his colleagues were responsible for chipping away at the Afghans' psyche, eroding support for the Taliban and promoting the Afghan government line. They'd do leaflet drops, meet tribal elders, give away wind-up radios.

Whilst the CQMS oversaw the distribution of the supplies, Paddy and I decided it was time to go back to the ANP base at police HQ and tell Durani and Gulzar what we needed them to do over the coming hours.

But our first job was to inform them of the condition of their casualties; that the one from the day before was dead and the other, just loaded on to the aircraft, was, save a miracle, heading for the same fate.

Colonel Gulzar shrugged his shoulders. I was always amazed at how the Afghans could deal with death. To them it was God's will. No real analysis, no pondering on how to avoid the same thing happening again. Just a fatalistic approach.

The Colonel asked how he could get the bodies back. He said the men had both lived in the same village and the elders would want them returned for burial. Paddy made a note.

Tea was brought and the conversation continued. Paddy told them how we had bumped into locals earlier that day. Neither seemed surprised. He also explained that we had now received defensive stores and the priority was to get them set up at the crossings we held.

'What is happening with the Talib, General?' I asked Durani, knowing of his contacts with people on the other side of the lines.

'They are regrouping with forces from the Laki area. They also have a new commander. Soon they will be strong enough to attack us again.'

'Have we had any effect on them at all then?'

'Yes. You have killed a lot of them. Eighty, perhaps ninety, in the past three days, but there are more coming over from Pakistan all the time.'

I looked across at Paddy. We both knew there were other British troops far south of Garmsir tasked with intercepting men and machinery being sent from across the border. I hoped they were doing their job.

We stayed with Durani and Gulzar for some time, both of them trying to convince us the town could not be held by Afghan forces alone and that they needed ISAF support. This led Paddy on to what was going to happen next.

'In the next twenty-four hours replacement British forces and more ANA soldiers will arrive to help with the defence,' he said. 'They'll work slightly differently to the way we have been doing things. While the British will patrol to the east and west and keep a base in the centre of town, more responsibility for front-line fighting will be down to you Afghans.'

I chipped in. 'General, I think it's time you went back to the police HQ in Lashkar Gah,' I said, trying to explain he needed to co-ordinate things centrally from there. His presence had helped galvanise his men into action over the past few days but now he would do more good back at the provincial capital. There was the bigger picture to think about. Colonel Gulzar could handle things in Garmsir.

After a moment's thought he conceded this was the best plan.

'Will you send down more men and ammunition?' I asked.

'Hmmm,' came the response.

'What about the southern crossing?' said Gulzar. 'I've already lost two men there because of the Taliban sniping. What shall we do?'

It was Paddy's turn to reply: 'Tomorrow, depending on what

time the relief arrives, we will mount a fighting patrol to go into the buildings east of your position and attempt to clear them. I will try and confirm this with you later tonight when we have more details on the replacements.'

I sighed to myself. In my head I knew I would be leading the operation. Paddy and I were going to have to stay on to offer some continuity and the op was likely to be given to the ANP, with me at the front. I wondered which Brits would be arriving to go with me? Specially trained infanteers or another assortment of characters from all sections of the army?

We were asked to stay to lunch but respectfully declined. It was probably the right decision. The day before we had seen a dead donkey lying by the side of the road. The following morning it was not there. We both had the same thought. It had become the meal. What did surprise me was that again the policemen were tucking in to fresh bread. Where was it coming from? Was it being shipped in? The answer came as we left the police station. We passed a bakery doing a brisk trade, not just with the ANP but also the ANA and what seemed to be some locals. If the baker was a local himself and not someone brought in specifically by the police to provide the men with food then this was a good sign. Garmsir was starting to reopen for business.

Back at our small camp it turned out everyone was busy. Most of them were out and about variously delivering HESCOs (collapsible cubes made of plastic and wire that when filled with earth and rock made immovable objects, useful in building up defences), barbed wire and sandbags to the various checkpoints we now had operating in and around Garmsir.

Claus, just his legs sticking out from under the bonnet, was still working on my Land Rover; at least I assumed that was what he was doing.

Paddy started chatting to the OMLT major as he ran through his list of questions about the story so far.

The psy ops major was engrossed in conversation with an elderly man. He turned out to be the caretaker of the new agricultural college being built in another part of the town. But no work had taken place for months; indeed there were no workers to do the job. They had run off taking their tools when the fighting started back in April. But still the man stuck doggedly to his task, convinced that one day things would get back on track.

I saw the major hand him one of the wind-up radios as a gift. The recipient gave a toothless grin. The Afghans were desperate for news of any sort. As for the radios, we could afford to be generous, we had stacks more of the damn things to give away.

For the next couple of hours I did next to nothing, just chatted idly and watched as Claus finished the work on my vehicle.

Then Paddy stalked over. He had a face like thunder.

'What's the matter?' I asked as he approached.

'You won't bloody believe it, but the Pathfinders who have been providing protection to our eastern flank out in the desert are pulling out tomorrow. And it gets worse. The troops in the south near the border are also being withdrawn.'

I couldn't believe it. 'That's ridiculous. How on earth are we going to hold the town now? The enemy will be all over us.'

'I know,' said Paddy. 'And there's more. Nick [our contact back at KAF, effectively the man running the show] has been moved to another task. We are now being controlled by an OMLT liaison officer, a young captain with little or no idea about what the hell is going on here.'

Paddy stormed off to speak to Al Stocker back in Lashkar Gah.

That morning I had felt confident our mission was succeeding, and being taken seriously by KAF. Now I felt the opposite. The confidence drained out of me and disappeared into the Afghan dust.

I needed to do something to ease the frustration. I shouted at Sam and the new driver. We were going on a road trip. Down to the southern crossing to see how the ANP were doing digging in. It was an unremarkable journey. As we arrived, it was plain to see progress, of sorts, had been made. HESCOs were arranged round the two buildings cleared by me on the second day. Uncoiled razor wire was also strewn about, and just to the eastern side of the crossing a couple of young sentries were manning a freshly dug ditch.

I surveyed the scene but couldn't muster any enthusiasm for the work that had been done. My heart wasn't in it. What was the point of making all the effort, the sacrifices, if at the end of the day the top brass were going to turn their backs on us? Adrenalin keeps you going during battle; so too does commitment and loyalty to your colleagues. But there is more to it than that. An idea that you are doing what is right, that you are helping people; the belief that someone higher up the pecking order is backing you to the hilt; it gives you a sense of purpose, reassurance. It spurs you on. But when these things disappear, so does the drive. You are left feeling deflated, demoralised. Tiredness kicks in, mental and physical. It was happening now. I was finding it almost impossible to give anything more to this campaign. Just as we had made some real inroads, we were being cast adrift.

We headed back to base, nothing said, watching out cautiously for the enemy. But there was nobody around.

The mood was little better back at the college. Indeed, from people's demeanour it seemed worse. Soldiers were sitting around staring glumly into the middle distance, grinding their feet absent-mindedly into the dirt, picking at their nails, massaging their weapons.

'What's up, Paddy?'

He ushered me to one side, out of earshot of the others. 'There's no relief coming tonight. The OMLT will be here at least another two days. They didn't give us a reason, just said they won't be coming.'

No wonder Chipper, Geordie and the others were looking so dejected.

The news only reinforced the collective sense of abandonment. Ours was a forgotten struggle in an under-reported war. Soldiers are always at their happiest knowing what they have to do, what they have to do it with, and when it will be done. Without this basic information morale and effectiveness suffer. It's called the mushroom effect: 'Kept in the dark and fed on shite'. Of course I should have been able to reason with myself that there was some great strategic reason why we had become a side-show; perhaps other guys were having it much tougher than we were elsewhere in the province. But I found it hard.

The only way I knew out of this malaise was through work. I told Paddy I would formulate a plan for the next day to clear the buildings east of the crossing, and warned Chipper he was going to be part of it. I sat with Sam, working out our best method of attack. I would have liked to have the weight of numbers to do it conventionally, clearing buildings one by one. But they weren't available. The best we could hope to do was outflank the enemy, cut them off from their comrades and supplies. Our strongest cards were the two WMIKs and air support. They had to be at the heart of whatever we did. In the end I decided my vehicle would cross the canal and follow a track south-eastwards so we would come in behind the village from the eastern side. Chipper would be right behind me. The ANP would do the legwork of actually clearing the village. After Paddy had radioed in the plan to KAF and they had given it the green light we were set to go. H-hour would be 11:00 hrs.

I crouched down by the bonfire. What had begun as a way of incinerating the used medical equipment was now a repository for all our waste. Flames flickered and died, only to be replaced by new ones as more material was piled on. It was mesmerising. Dare I say it, relaxing.

'How are you doing, Dougie?'

It was Sean Langan.

'Yes, good. And yourself? Got a bit more than you bargained for, eh?'

'You're right. I've run out of tape and am having to re-record over the material of us leaving Lash and driving across the desert. Any chance of doing a quick interview with you?' he asked.

I agreed. For ten minutes I spoke about the war according to General Doug Beattie, 1 R IRISH. I covered it all. How I would do things differently. How the Taliban were getting stronger. What I thought of KAF. I even got on to politics, grumbling that MPs and government had no idea how their policies affected the men on the ground.

After my rant we sat and had a coffee.

We spoke about our lives, how he had found himself back in Afghanistan for a second time, what he was trying to achieve. He was an interesting man. I was glad he was there to record the moment. I just wondered how his documentary would turn out. And whether I would live to see it.

It had become dark and there was actually a slight chill in the air. Intermittently a few gunshots punctured the silence. This was about as calm as it was going to get. I laid out my sleeping bag. This time not in the grave – the ants had defeated me – but between the rear wheel of the Land Rover and a wall. As the night closed in so did the thoughts. Wriggling around, attempting to get comfortable, I tried to imagine myself back home – going shopping at Tesco, walking down the High Street with Margaret, having a pint at the local, watching Ireland play rugby. I wasn't sure I would be able to manage any of it. I seemed to be collecting unwanted baggage at a terrific rate. Would I ever escape what I had seen and done? Tomorrow I would be killing again, perhaps not with my own hands but with the bombs and rockets I would have to call in. This wasn't the First World War, it wasn't slaughter on an industrial scale, it wasn't the trenches, but everything is relative. This was my reality. My conflict. My Battle of the Somme. I drifted off into some sort of sleep.

ELEVEN

A QUESTION OF ETHICS

(GARMSIR, DAY 5)

There were three of them – no, four. Out in the open, just to the right of the building I had seen several Taliban fighters using as cover; repeatedly darting out of it to fire short bursts towards the Afghan policemen who were fifty metres in front of us.

The enemy were also using RPGs. As I put my binoculars to my eyes again, a blast shook the ground in front of our position.

'Geordie,' I yelled. 'Bring up the 51mm mortar.'

He ran forward, hunched over, carrying the short tube in one hand, a bag of bombs in the other; they were a mixture of smoke and high-explosive rounds.

From where he was, crouched down beside my vehicle, he wasn't able to see the human targets who were becoming ever more brazen, standing out in full view, squirting bullets in our direction, and now only occasionally disappearing back into and behind the house probably to reload. I estimated they were some 400 metres away. It would be up to me to relay back the firing information to Geordie. I could see where his weapon was pointing and it didn't look good. I shouted out instructions.

I glanced down again to see him adjusting the weapon's range to 400 metres and then turn it forty-five degrees clockwise. He bedded it into the soft sand so the recoil would not throw the bomb off its intended trajectory. He was ready.

'I want you to fire a smoke round so I can see what you are like for line. I will bring you in from there.'

Geordie knelt up and dropped a shell down the barrel, grabbed hold of the firing lanyard and pulled it sharply. There was a *whoomph* as the mortar kicked into life and the smoke bomb shot out. I kept peering through my binos, waiting for the impact; waiting, waiting. There it was; a plume of white smoke billowing up from a point some seventy metres in front of the enemy position, drifting lazily towards them.

All four men were in view once more, three standing, firing with their rifles, the other down on one knee about to unleash another RPG.

'Good line, Geordie. Try adding another 100 in range and this time go with the HE [high explosive].'

Chipper stood ready with another round as Geordie made the necessary changes. He took the bomb, safety pin now out, and dropped it down the tube. Bang. The second mortar was spat out.

What I expected to see was the round dropping somewhere close enough to the enemy for them to be brought to their senses, forcing them to dash for cover. What I actually saw was an impact as precise as any I had ever witnessed. The bomb landed no more than five metres from its intended target, just to the right of the group as I looked at them.

All four were flung to the ground as if rag dolls; either thrown off their feet by the force of the blast or cut down by shards of flying shrapnel and lumps of rock. Probably both.

'Great shot, Geordie. Keep it there,' I shouted, professional pride overcoming any sense of revulsion, shock or horror at what I was seeing. For good measure Steve continued pumping away with the .50-cal.

My attention remained glued on the site of the explosion. Two of the men were motionless. The others were moving; one only just, the second writhing about. Then there was another bang, and another. And another. Geordie had fired three more HE rounds. The first of these landed almost exactly where the first had exploded, almost within spitting distance of the man who had been frantically twisting and turning on the ground, desperate to get away but disabled by his shattered body. Now he lay completely still. The next two rounds landed well short, but it didn't matter; the damage had been done.

Our advance had started just after midday, our team made up of the usual suspects: we Brits manning the two WMIKs, plus Major Shahrukh and sixteen of his men. Eight of the Afghans led by Shahrukh were to enter the village, located just east of the southern crossing, clearing the houses as they went. The other group of eight would head out along a track that ran diagonally south-east from the crossing and around the back of the same settlement, almost encouraging the enemy to open up on the policemen so we could then engage with our heavier weapons as we followed behind. The track was rough and narrow, barely wide enough for a single vehicle. On one side, to the right, were the village buildings; to the other was a low bank that gave way to fields of corn and other vegetables. Dismounted, the earthen parapet would give us some protection as we advanced on foot, not so when we were in the Land Rovers, our heads and bodies jutting out, making inviting targets. This wasn't as bad as it sounded though. Having shelter is all very well, but not if it leaves you unable to see the enemy coming until they are all but on top of you.

I gave the thumbs-up for the ANP to move off, the first group quickly disappearing into the maze of alleys, buildings, walls and compounds. The rest began a casual amble down the track ahead of us, rifles slung over their shoulders, RPGs sticking out of backpacks like loaves of French bread; to all intents and purposes it appeared as if they were off on a unit outing, not about to fight the Taliban. When they had moved some fifty metres we started to follow. Gulzar walked next to us, giving orders to his men through his handheld radio.

It didn't take long till our stroll in the country was rudely interrupted; a burst of gunfire coming from our right. Instinctively I dropped down behind the dashboard.

'Talib!' I shouted.

'Not Talib,' Gulzar replied. 'It is the policemen clearing buildings.'

Slowly I raised my head.

We continued our crawl along the track. One hundred and fifty metres on and the buildings to our right thinned, then disappeared as the village petered out. We were left with a clear view of the open ground in front.

There was more firing, and this time it was from the enemy. Taliban fighters in built-up positions almost a kilometre to our east must have seen us as we drove clear of the village and some of the taller crops. I called Paddy on the radio, asking him to report a TiC.

Steve was answering back with the .50-cal, tracer rounds streaking through the air towards the enemy.

Sam was doing likewise with his GPMG. He shouted out to me. 'Boss, we will have a B-1 with us in twenty minutes. It's coming straight from KAF.'

We were now drawing fire from a building to the south, much closer. This became my immediate priority and I ordered Geordie to engage with the mortar.

I peered again through my binoculars at the four bodies. Now I could see no movement at all. Gulzar believed these men had been hiding out in the building they'd just been firing from and that at night they came to the village to take potshots at the ANP at the crossing checkpoint before melting away back before morning. He was pleased with the results from the mortar. Geordie was smiling, happy with the accuracy of his shooting. He wasn't able see the bloody aftermath of his work, but through my lenses it was all too clear. Even at 400 metres I could see the visceral mess: red stains, limbs contorted at grotesque angles.

The B-1 was almost with us. Sam needed a target list. Yes, we were going to hit the village far to the east where the shooting had first started. But I was also going to drop a bomb on the spot where Geordie had already inflicted so much damage. I had made a calculation, an assessment – to me it was rational. The four enemy fighters could theoretically still be a threat, but more than that I believed the building they were operating from was a command post. I wanted to erase it, wipe it off the face of the earth. Deny the ground to any future Taliban reinforcements. And if that also meant the final obliteration of the four then so be it. It was to be a decision that haunted me from the moment I took it.

It was agreed. Initially a couple of 1,000-pounders way out to the east. Then a 500-pounder on the four bodies.

The ability to call in such destructive power was something I had been doing regularly since day one. At first it almost seemed a luxury, just another varied part of our arsenal. Now it was essential, a lifesaver. Repeatedly we had been under threat of being overwhelmed and repeatedly only the air-strikes had saved our necks. During the heat of battle there was little opportunity to wonder what it was like for the enemy to be under such onslaughts. The fact that most of the bomb runs were conducted on targets far from our position also added to the general sense of remoteness from the effects. But somehow this felt different.

'Thirty seconds and stores,' shouted Sam. I looked over to my left at the village Steve and Chipper continued to engage. There was the huge explosion we had come to expect. A minute or so later the scene was repeated. As near as damn it, direct hits. Steve and Chipper took their fingers off the triggers. There was silence. The bombardment had done its job.

'Confirm you still want target three,' said Sam.

I twisted round to look at the bodies again. Had one of them moved a few feet? I was certain it had.

I thought about what I was about to do. Use 500lbs of high explosive to destroy a small hut and in so doing finish off one man. What had happened to my compassion? Even now this victim might be thinking he still had a chance; despite his pain and injuries, a slight chance of rescue by his colleagues before it reached the point where the tide of blood pouring from his wounds could not be turned. He was clinging to life, hoping, praying he could yet return to his loved ones. Yet I had similar thoughts. I had a duty of care to the five men behind me, and the Afghans. As much as the man in front of me wanted to survive, so did they, so did I. And what about my duty to Margaret, to my children, to my father?

'Target three confirmed. Drop on it as soon as possible.'

'But, boss, there's no firing coming from there?'

'I can see movement.' Was I trying to fool myself? 'Drop on it now.'

Sixty seconds later, the B-1 cast its shadow of death over the survivor, the bomb demolishing, obliterating, the building he and the others used for shelter. Now there was no movement. Nor were there any bodies, the men either buried beneath the rubble strewn carelessly across the area or vaporised by the explosion.

Relative silence descended again.

What had I done? Had my decision been right? Was it justified? Was it legal? So many thoughts, and so many contradictory answers. My self-interrogation continued and I wasn't bearing up well under the scrutiny. I started to think I must be bad. Was I any better than the Luftwaffe pilot who strafes the helpless British aviator floating to the ground by parachute after being shot down? Better than the U-boat crew that torpedoes an Allied ship and then machine-guns defenceless sailors as they huddle in a life-raft? I couldn't say then whether I was right or wrong. I can't say now. But it doesn't stop me thinking about it.

I turned to Yasir. 'Tell Gulzar we will remain here for a while. I want him to get his men in the village to "go firm" and look out for any movement south of where they are. The team on the road I want to clear forward another fifty metres, then also go firm.'

Yasir stared at me. 'What?' he asked.

It was sometimes difficult to remember he had not grown up in the same environment as me: that English was not his mother tongue; that he didn't have the same Ulster lilt as me; that he had never completed basic training and wasn't savvy with the military lexicon. I don't think of my accent as particularly broad or difficult to understand, except perhaps when I'm excited or agitated. This was one of those times.

I jumped out of the wagon and headed towards Gulzar, Yasir at my shoulder. I went through everything again, this time more slowly, in chunks. The message got through.

Gulzar seemed content. The mission had gone to plan and his policemen had worked hard. We stood chatting for a few minutes. Then something came between us: a bullet, the round ploughing into the ground at our feet, others ripping up the dirt all about us. As I dived for the cover of the banking, another burst of fire churned up the earth where we had just been standing. It was coming from the east.

Next there was the depressingly familiar noise of a 107mm rocket. Flying safely over our heads with the familiar warbling sound of a firework, it landed a couple of hundred metres beyond us. The RPG round was rather closer, twenty metres or so away. More grenades exploded. I legged it back to my seat. Sam was shouting at me. He had seen the enemy in a tree-line slightly behind us, 250 metres to the north-east. He was shooting back with his GPMG. But I had a problem. Because we were facing south, I could not swivel my weapon far enough to join in the exchange.

Chipper had the same difficulty.

'Where are they, Sam?' I asked as I brought my rifle up to my shoulder.

'Watch my tracer.'

He was using 4B1T ammunition, so called because for every four balls (or bullets) there was a tracer round, a bullet with a phosphorus base that burns when the round is fired. I watched as the bits of deadly metal flew towards the enemy, scoring a red trail through the air.

'Seen,' I yelled back.

I was about to start shooting when I thought better of it. We needed to get the air support back and for that Sam had to get on the radio, and I needed to sort out a hit list.

'Steve, can you see where Sam is aiming?'

'Roger, boss. Do you want me to start engaging?'

'Yes, then Sam can get on the TacSat,' I explained.

It is a strange thing. When you fire your own weapon you get completely absorbed, almost obsessed with what you are doing, concentrating on acquiring and hitting targets. Making allowances for distance and the wind, focusing purely on what is in your sights, blinkered to everything else. The rest is a blur. You do not notice the enemy fire striking the ground close by or the holes being punched in the vehicle by their bullets. You just don't register how close you are to death. Perhaps it's because you don't actually see the bullets, only the damage they do. Maybe it's because they are out of sight and hence out of mind. Small, invisible. How could that innocuous fizzing noise just above my head actually kill me? Even on day three when Joe was wounded – I barely noticed when it happened and then, when I did realise, I was as much curious as scared. Oh, so that's the effect of a bullet. How peculiar. How interesting. Right, where was I? Ah yes, shooting the enemy, my rifle acting not just as an offensive weapon, but also a virtual shield. By wielding it and concentrating on it, I was making myself immune to the enemy.

How different things were now.

Curled up in my seat, map in hand, I was starting to get disturbed by the noise of the incoming fire. The whistling and cracking of supersonic chunks of lead designed to rip humans apart left me feeling unnerved. I tried hard to concentrate on sorting out another target list for the two F-18s Sam said were on their way, each armed with a 500lb bomb and six rockets. It wasn't straightforward, the possibility of an imminent, painful death easily distracting me from my task. Finally I managed to make a decision, choosing to concentrate the aerial firepower on the tree-line.

By now only Steve was hitting back at the enemy effectively with his .50-cal. Chipper was doing his best with his rifle but we still couldn't bring the other heavier weapons to bear because of the angle we were parked at. Colonel Gulzar was squatting behind my vehicle; most of his men were lying low on the track. The F-18s had arrived, but were having trouble locating the objective. Patiently Sam got back on the TacSat to try and talk them in.

Sam's job was perhaps the toughest any of us had. He was required to keep his calm whilst under intense fire and paint a picture of the battle and the topography for the pilots so they understood exactly what was going on and where everyone was. As bullets, RPGs, rockets and mortars rained down on him, he had to keep his head up so he could survey the scene and talk the pilots through what he saw. His action under fire was inspiring. Our survival over the past few days had been down to air support. And that air support was controlled by him. We owed Sam big-time.

He came through on the PRR again. 'Boss, they are offering us follow-on,' meaning that after these two F-18s had departed – having raked the wooded area with cannon fire – they would be replaced by another pair.

So far our tactics had worked pretty well. We had cleared the village by the crossing; eliminated the fighters who over the past couple of nights had been taking potshots at the ANP with such deadly results; flushed out Taliban from another settlement to the east. All together we had strengthened our position. It was time to withdraw, but it had to be orderly. We could not afford for the Taliban to believe we were running for cover with our tails between our legs. That would only embolden them. We needed a last show of strength.

'Sam, I want that follow-on.'

Seconds later: 'Boss, the incoming pilots are requesting targets.'

I asked for a repeat of the attacks on the village almost a kilometre away to the east, then the tree-line again. I slipped out of my seat to talk to Gulzar. I had to make him aware this was to be a calm pull-out and that is what it had to look like to the enemy. I would take the two WMIKs back up the road to the start point, then we would provide covering fire for the policemen. As we talked there was a huge explosion from the village as the lead F-18 delivered a bomb. As the onslaught continued Chipper carried out an eight-point turn so eventually he was facing the right way to get out of there. We did the same. I would wait till the tree-line came under attack from the air before setting off. For three hours we had been fighting; now I was anxious to return to the crossing and then the camp without any casualties.

As the F-18s came in low from the west we started to move at a leisurely pace, trying to give the impression we were the victors not the vanquished. But looking over my shoulder I saw the ANP had already started to follow us, despite my orders. Approaching the point where the track branched sharply southwards to run down the edge of the canal, I saw Shahrukh and his men already there.

Back at the crossing he started talking animatedly to Gulzar, a smile on both men's faces. I was pretty pleased, too. We had achieved our objective and I was revising my thoughts about another trip down the canal road to the 42 northing. We failed on day three, but perhaps now the time had come to try again. I gazed intently into no-man's land, wondering just how strong the enemy positions were. Had they regrouped in the wood? Were they in the building directly due south of us? What tactics would be necessary to dislodge them?

We sat there for a while before I gave the order for the WMIKs to head for home. Behind us smoke trails continued to hang listlessly in the sky above the positions hit by the F-18s. I ran over things in my mind. What would the Taliban do now? Would they pull back further south or attempt to re-occupy the ground they'd just lost? On the answers to those questions probably hung the success of any further venture down the canal road.

We progressed along Garmsir's main street, passing the bakery and a couple of teashops populated by ANA soldiers. We gave comradely waves as we went. Pulling into the base compound we met Paddy; he too had a brew in his hand, his cup the bottom half of a plastic water bottle.

'How did it go?'

'Pretty well, I think. We cleared the village by the crossing and the ANP worked well as a unit.'

'Much enemy activity?'

'A fair bit, to be honest, but it was generally a lot further away than what we have encountered so far.'

'Any idea of casualties?' he continued.

'A little,' I replied, before telling him about Geordie's success with the mortar.

I outlined the air-strikes we'd called in.

Paddy noted them all down. He would need them for his after-action report to be made when we had pulled out. Finally he asked for my recommendations on further actions the next day. I had already thought long and hard on this and persuaded myself we could achieve our ultimate objective of reaching the 42 northing. Air power would be critical. It would also require Tim to get the ANA moving south from JTAC Hill so we had a solid line of advance between the two waterways.

Paddy wasn't so certain. Yes, he wanted to reach the 42 northing. No, he was less than enthusiastic about sending troops back down the canal road. In the end someone else, back at KAF, would make the decision.

In theory the primary aim of the mission had already been achieved. We had done that on day one. The town had been taken back from the Taliban and the UK taskforce could say hand on heart no major district in Helmand was totally under enemy control. Of course that's not the same as saying every major district was under ISAF control.

We had a presence Helmand-wide but our tactical bases were in the centre of towns and villages like Gereshk, Sangin and Now Zad. Movement beyond them was not easy; in fact it was downright dangerous. We had toeholds in these semi-urban centres but little or no influence beyond them. In effect these troops were prisoners in their own fortresses. The way the taskforce attempted to take the fight to the enemy was by deploying air-manoeuvre forces and manoeuvre outreach groups, the latter conducting long-range, sustained patrols in the desert, their strength lying in their unpredictability – at least as far as the enemy saw it – and versatility. And then there was us. Initially just 17 British soldiers and 170 Afghan policemen and soldiers, responsible for liberating Garmsir, then defending it, and finally expanding the security buffer around it.

Our only advantage came from keeping the enemy guessing; using varying tactics to keep them on their toes, unsure of what was coming next, unable to properly regroup for a decisive counter-attack. But I feared the Taliban was getting wise to our methods along the canal road. We needed to open up a second front and the ANA was key to this. At least their performance on day three had finally given me some confidence in their ability to help.

Paddy still had doubts though. 'The problem I have, Doug, is that I keep firing you down that road on a daily basis and sooner or later an RPG is going to strike lucky and then we will be in big trouble.'

He was having real difficulty in backing another push forward. He carried the responsibility of his role heavily on his shoulders. He wasn't averse to risk; he'd shown that over the past few days.

But nor was he reckless. He knew we lacked real support and would be hard pushed to hold any advantage we gained. Was the potential cost of a short-lived victory too great? On the other hand if we did not maintain the initiative the Taliban would get back within rocket and mortar range of the DC, with all the consequences that entailed for the civilian population.

In the end he agreed to a fighting patrol going for the 42 northing, dependent on the say-so from KAF and agreement from the ANA. He also proposed we take the Sergeant-Major and a couple of the other OMLT members with us to make up a mortar team. Then the negotiations started. Paddy put the plan to Tim, but had no power to compel him to use the ANA soldiers under his command to support the ANP.

Tim led the OMLT members and they were in town to mentor the ANA. I was in charge of liaising with the ANP and already I was having to use one of the WMIKs Tim had lent me. He wasn't necessarily keen to extend that support, especially if that impacted on the work he was doing with the Afghan Army. We were soldiering by committee and I wasn't impressed. It left me frustrated with the OMLT. Yes Chipper, Steve and Geordie had all been fantastic, but what had the others been doing? That day for example, they'd barely left camp. They were in Garmsir to guide the ANA, yet the ANA hadn't been out. It made me angry. Weren't we all fighting the same war? I felt as if I was putting my life – together with the lives of those who came with me – on the line on a daily basis, yet the 'system' meant I couldn't rely on support from all the other British troops in Garmsir because they were answerable to a different master. Of course there were perhaps good reasons why they shouldn't have followed me anyway. Maybe Beattie was regarded as a reckless maniac, determined to get everyone killed. Why should anyone partake in his pea-brained schemes? Yet to me there was a job to be done. And as I saw it, with people trying to kill me every day, it should have been all hands to the pump. I needed more help, except it wasn't always there.

*

I took myself off to the police HQ to find Gulzar and Shahrukh. They told me General Durani had left for Lashkar Gah that morning. Annoyingly he had taken some of the ANP with him. Gulzar said they were also getting low on ammunition again. Sure, Shahrukh still retained most of his hardened troops, the ones who'd been fighting in Garmsir since day one, but there was also a fair proportion of young conscripts in the contingent, unhappy to be in the town, finding solace by smoking hash. I tried to raise their morale. I thanked Shahrukh for his repeated efforts. I was coming to realise how much I relied on his bravery and commitment, and how highly I regarded him. I was also managing to piece together his background.

When I first came across him he was dressed as a civilian; brown trousers and shirt, a heavy brown wool throw wrapped around his upper body. He was always well turned out, clean, with a bright welcoming smile. But now, upon my insistence, he was kitted out in a police uniform. It seemed rather more befitting of someone holding the rank of major. Like many of the policemen fighting in Garmsir, he originated from the Nowa district, some thirty kilometres north of the town. He wasn't a professional policeman and had completed no formal training, but rather had gained his military knowledge the hard way. In the 1980s he had fought against the Soviets in what he and many others regarded as a holy war. His efforts against the Soviet invaders meant he became known as a Jihadi and with this came honour and respect, and a title – the rank of major bestowed on him as a result of his illustrious past. For a while before the 2001 American invasion, he had even fought alongside the Taliban, his allegiance only shifting to the government as it became clear the Taliban's hold on Afghanistan was beginning to falter.

Shahrukh was a formidable character: literate, which was unusual; humorous, and exceedingly brave. Certainly the bravest man I'd come across in Afghanistan.

He and Gulzar listened carefully as I explained the plan of

attack for the next day. The difficulty for all Afghans is understanding why they should fight for a piece of ground only then to give it up? Why, they wanted to know, would we push so far south, with the intention of retreating back to the crossing by nightfall? To them it was time wasted. I tried to tell them it was about pushing the enemy back, creating a buffer between them and us; dissuading the Taliban from mounting a counter-attack. What I was saying made military sense in my eyes, but I could see the lingering doubt in theirs.

Gulzar's response when it came left me stumped. 'I need a medal and I need some whisky,' he volunteered.

Where the hell had those thoughts come from? He could have asked about the ANA, air support, ammunition, reinforcements, but instead he wanted to know about gongs and grog.

'I need a medal to show my men I am brave.' Then: 'You can get me some whisky.'

It was more a statement than a question. I noted it down.

'I'm sure Paddy can get some for you,' I promised.

I left the police station slightly bemused.

Paddy had some good news on my return. Apparently Tim had agreed with the ANA that they would push south the next day. KAF had sanctioned the plan and I would also get the mortar team. There would be no dedicated air support, though planes would be airborne over Helmand at H-hour – set for 10:00 hrs – and quick to arrive if needed. KAF had also confirmed the OMLT would be replaced the next evening; Paddy and I, the morning after.

On my roller-coaster emotional journey in Garmsir, I was back on a high, not exactly looking forward to what lay ahead, but at least certain there was an end in sight. I should have known better.

[illegible]

[illegible] things [illegible] than driving. Whatever [illegible] finally
nothing [illegible] about [illegible] all over [illegible] the hope
[illegible] will go over the [illegible] out and
more [illegible]

But what the [illegible] know of [illegible] hand
[illegible]

TWELVE
THE HORRORS OF WAR
(GARMSIR, DAY 6)

Your leg or your face?

Your foot or your hand?

Your genitals or your arm?

Which would you rather lose?

For me it was anything but my face. I was scared stiff of going home with my looks twisted and scarred by battle, perhaps burnt, maybe rearranged by bullets and shrapnel. Teeth missing, jaw shot off, eyes blinded.

If there is no dignity in death, there is certainly none in serious injury. For many soldiers the possibility of being maimed brings even greater fear than dying. With death comes finality. Nothing more to worry about. It's all over. There is the hope too that in time your family will get over their grief. Mourn and move on.

But with the loss of a limb or your sexual ability, maybe paralysis or a brain injury, perhaps incontinence, the effects last for ever. There is no escape from your past; a physical reminder of the horrors of war remains for the rest of your days, plain for all to see. And not just to see, but also to live with. Life changes for everyone. Bitterness batters at the doors of the weak-willed who, because of their injuries, all too easily get sucked down into depression, alcoholism, drug abuse, domestic violence. I had witnessed it happen. Resentment and anger lurk in the shadows ready to gain new recruits.

For the past week I had seen – all of us had seen – the ghastly consequences of what we did for a living. We were paid to fight and to wound and to kill and cow the enemy. But what if I was on the receiving end? It didn't bear thinking about. Yet I couldn't get it out of my mind. Here we were yet again; ready to take the fight to the Taliban. I had escaped so far. How long could my luck hold?

I looked around at the rest of the team. Everyone was working in silence. Finishing off their preparation. Storing the last rounds of ammunition aboard the WMIKs. Unloading and reloading their guns. Checking water supplies. Tightening their webbing. Retying their bootlaces. Going through the routines they hoped would keep them alive.

We British troops in Garmsir were a disparate bunch. From all sorts of backgrounds – inner-city Glasgow to the English home counties – with all sorts of motivations. Some of us were territorials; others, career soldiers. There were those with wives and those without. Several had children. A few had had the best education in the land, others barely a qualification to their name. People often refer to soldiers as squaddies, as if we are a generic group. It assumes a certain homogeneity, a collective psyche. But every member of the forces is different. We have varying motivations for doing what we do.

In civvy street a gathering like this would not happen. No imaginable circumstance could have thrown us together in the same place at the same time. Only the army has the power to do it. That was all we had in common, a shared uniform; that and our job for the day.

It was time to go.

'All Widow 77 call signs, this is Doug,' radio check,' I passed over the PRR.

'Chipper, check.'

'Geordie, check.'

'Sam, check.'

'Steve, check.'

'Check,' said the driver.

(To this day I cannot remember his name. I don't think I ever knew it. If I did it has been forgotten. It is the strangest thing. The heat of battle, the tactics, manoeuvres, landscape, sights, smells, sounds; they have all stayed with me – I couldn't escape them if I wanted. Yet the name of my replacement driver is a detail lost.)

I asked Sam if his TacSat was working. I spoke to Paddy over the radio. Preparations complete, we drove out of the compound in silence, on to the main street and past the baker's, the dust billowing from beneath the tyres. At the eastern checkpoint we turned right and hit the canal road, making our way back down to the southern canal crossing. There was no engagement, no sign of the enemy. Gulzar and Shahrukh were already there at the crossing to meet us. They seemed keen to get on with things, keener than us, and didn't seem to be bothered I had not brought the medals and whisky.

I had ordered Sergeant-Major Johnstone and his team not to arrive till some thirty minutes after H-hour. The last thing I wanted was to have us all sitting around at the crossing together providing a high-value target for the Taliban.

On paper the plan looked good. In principle it was a sure thing. The WMIKs would work along the road supporting the ANP. Once some progress had been made the Sergeant-Major and his men would advance to a small hill to the right of the canal road and set up their mortar position. Once we had got 600 metres forward, the wagons would stop and provide cover for the policemen to complete the assault on the building at the 42 northing on foot. Once secure the ANP would then peel off right, westwards, in the direction of the wood, then finally pull back under mortar cover. As we executed this so-called fighting patrol Tim with some of the ANA would move south along the edge of the Helmand River and set up an ANA outpost to reinforce our position in Garmsir. In some ways his was the most important task of the two. Our patrol would in effect be a diversion for him.

Everything remained calm.

The ANP stood huddled together, chatting quietly, waiting for 10:00 hrs to arrive.

One kilometre away, due south, was our ultimate goal.

The minute hand moved up to the hour mark. Then past it.

'Sandstone 78, this is Widow 77, contact south. Wait. Out.'

We weren't under attack. But I knew what I was doing. I had made up my mind the night before without telling anyone. I was sick of moving within range of the enemy, waiting for them to ambush us, and only then being allowed to call in air support. I was fed up with watching Afghans die in our name while we stuck to rules of engagement the enemy didn't have to follow. This time the planes were going to be there for the start of our operation. I would bomb the enemy positions before we moved off. Our tiny force needed all the help it could get. Six British soldiers in un-armoured Land Rovers. A dozen Afghan policemen. That was the size of the assault team, backed up by a fire-support squad comprising three Brits and five Afghan soldiers. If the enemy knew our real strength they would have laughed. I thought I heard a chuckle. I looked round.

'Sam, right now Paddy should be opening a TiC with KAF, just find out if there's any air support available and, if so, when it will arrive.'

He nodded. Crouched down in the back of the vehicle there was no way he could know whether we were being shot at or not. He took my word for it.

Was I right to take this action? Was I laying myself open to charges of operating outside the UK rules of engagement? I didn't know and at that moment I didn't really care. For me the chance of seeing my family again, even with the possibility of a court martial, seemed a far better option than running the risk of taking a bullet from some Taliban fighter who had no reason to be keeping his head down. What if I was taking aircraft other units might desperately need elsewhere in Helmand? Well, that was not my decision. KAF allocated resources in theatre, and if they were free then they would be put our way. In my mind the buck ultimately stopped in Whitehall, way above my pay scale. Military planners at the Ministry of Defence were the ones who had sent us to war without enough planes. I was just the poor sod trying to make the best of their crap decision.

A few minutes had passed.

'Boss, we have a B-1 en route. He will be with us for just ten minutes but two Harriers are scrambling to follow on.'

I got out my map.

I had seen enemy movement as we were forming up. They would become my targets. So would the wooded area where there had been so much activity on previous days. In all there were six targets. Three in the trees. One at the end of the road. And two more to the east of the canal.

The priority was the wooded area.

As we waited at the forward edge of the crossing a few rounds began to filter our way from some greenery where the movement had been. At least now I was under fire. Strange to say but in a way it was a relief. My actions were covered.

'Boss, that is us. Stores. Watch out for strike.'

A kilometre away the scenery was rearranged as a 1,000-pounder exploded. It wasn't quite where I had intended but would have given anyone nearby a serious headache. I adjusted the co-ordinates for the second strike to account for what I had just seen and passed them back to Sam.

Two minutes later and there was another mighty explosion, the wood shuddering at the force of the blast.

The enemy went quiet. I could see no movement and the firing had stopped. I gave Sam the bomb damage assessment (BDA) and called in the third attack. I told Shahrukh that, as soon as he saw the strike, he should get moving. Cover 200 metres as fast as possible, and then wait for the Harriers to arrive. When they were on station the exercise could be repeated.

At 10:30 hrs, thirty minutes after H-hour, the final blast came and the ANP got to their feet, starting to advance. They made sluggish progress compared to the way British troops cover ground, but for Afghans it was pretty reasonable.

I shouted into the PRR: 'Let's go.'

With that the Land Rovers lurched forward, keeping to the rear of the policemen. Sam was on his feet behind me, machine gun pulled tightly to his shoulder. He wasn't wearing his helmet, but there was too much for me to do to start worrying about it.

We were now being targeted by enemy fire from the east of the canal, at least 600 metres away. Bullets zipped around us, but the RPGs they were also firing were dropping a long way short, barely reaching the waterway.

'Five minutes till close air support,' confirmed Sam.

The ANP had stopped, looking for protection in the lee of the road where it dropped away into a ditch, waiting for the Harriers to arrive.

To the east some of the enemy seemed to have got a lot closer. There was now small-arms fire coming from the village just over the canal. I shot back with the GPMG, short five-round bursts, waiting for the enemy to appear in the open as they darted from one building to the next.

The Harriers arrived. I ordered Chipper to take over my targets as I turned my attention to the sites we were going to hit next away to the south-east.

The aircraft screamed in twice.

As they completed the two runs, disappearing southwards to see what was going on beyond the objective, I shouted to Shahrukh to get his men advancing again.

'Doug, this is Tommy.' The Sergeant-Major came over the radio. 'I'm beginning to move south now, 250 metres behind you and 100 metres out from the road.'

'Don't get too close and don't go up the hill till we have cleared the ground around it.'

'Boss, the pilots have seen vehicles moving some three kilometres to the south-east, beyond those villages,' Sam said, pointing way into the distance.

'Can they engage them?' I asked, already knowing what the answer would be.

'You know Harriers can't self-designate, and anyway they can't identify them as the enemy.'

I felt pissed off but I knew the speed and operating height of Harriers was such that they would never be able to clearly identify the vehicles as enemy or friendly.

'For fuck's sake, that means the enemy can just roll up our east flank and hit us as we withdraw.'

'That's if it is the enemy,' Sam warned.

Of course it was enemy. No civilians would be this close to the fighting. Those who had not returned to Garmsir from the north would be way out in the desert. Any who did stay within the area were forced to pay the penalty, the Taliban commandeering their vehicles and press-ganging the young men into fighting with them. Added to that, Gulzar had warned us to expect Taliban reinforcements from the south; his intelligence was that up to thirteen vehicles were moving our way, carrying some 100 extra fighters. And so far his information had been pretty good.

The shooting around us intensified. That from the east was being matched with heavy gunfire from directly down the road. The Taliban in the wood had also gathered their wits about them and were joining in. The ANP dived for cover in the drainage ditch.

We needed more bomb runs to get us out of our rut.

Colonel Gulzar crept his way to the front of my vehicle.

Through Yasir he said he had intercepted some Taliban radio traffic.

'What are they saying?'

'The commanders are warning the men that if they turn and run, then they will shoot them.'

I wanted to believe what Gulzar said. But there was the chance of a trap. The message might just have been put out by the Taliban to lull us into a false sense of security, knowing we monitored their chat.

A Harrier swept in from my left, dropping another bomb to the east of the canal. The firing from there stopped. Then the second Harrier came in, low, from the same direction as the first, the pilot releasing his weapon due south of us, before pulling up sharply to put some clear air between him and the Taliban. This was only a 500lb bomb, but the resultant explosion was as shocking as anything I had seen since arriving in Garmsir. Perhaps the effect was due to the hard surface of the road. Instead of a tight plume of smoke and debris billowing straight up into the air, the resultant cloud of debris swept out horizontally, engulfing everything in its path for perhaps fifty metres. It was the perfect opportunity for our next tactical leap.

'Any BDA?' queried Sam.

'Sam, I can't see a fucking thing.'

'I can't tell them that, boss.'

'Say good strike, and ask them to strafe the trees.'

We moved again. With the ground clear to our right Tommy Johnstone led his team up the hill to establish the 51mm mortar.

'Tommy, don't do anything yet, but take a look at the wooded area 600 metres to the south-west.'

Sam told me there was time for just one more gun run from the Harriers before they disappeared north. Their replacements, A-10s, would not arrive for another fifteen minutes. Shit. The time gap concerned me. I was fearful the Taliban would seize the opportunity to try and destroy us on the road. This was a chance for Tommy and his team to earn their keep with support fire into the wood where I believed the Taliban command centre to be. Chipper and Steve would keep engaging east. Then the ANP would push south once more.

I needed to be sure Tommy was looking at the same spot as me in the woods. The foolproof way of ensuring that meant being by his side as he fired. I told the crews my plan and slipped out of the WMIK, starting to run back towards the hill. Puffs of dirt erupted around me as I went. In my mind every Taliban fighter in the area had Beattie in his sights. I only slowed when I got behind the hill, putting it between the enemy and me. I started to walk, trying to catch my breath. I was sweating, beads of moisture slipping down my back, my chest, my face. But so what was new? If one thing had been constant in Garmsir, it was the heat.

I glanced back at the two vehicles. It was shocking. The amount of ordnance zipping under, over, around, even through them was astonishing. Viewed from here, I could not understand how we had so far managed to survive. I started the climb up the mound; in fact it was another ancient hill fort. Just as I reached the brow of it the PRR burst in to life.

'Doug, this is Chipper. We are desperately short of ammo. Steve is down to his last 400. I've only got 600.'

We'd now been in contact for an hour – perhaps it wasn't so surprising we were getting through bullets as if there was no tomorrow.

I called through to Sam and told him to get hold of Paddy on the radio to see if he could send any more down to us.

I turned my attention back to Tommy and the wood.

'I need some accurate fire on those trees,' I explained before talking him in to the target. 'If you follow the wood line south you'll see a prominent step that moves away from us in a westerly direction.'

'I see it.'

'Well, in the apex of that step I need you to drop some HE.'

'OK. I'm going to send in some smoke first so you can confirm I've the right spot.'

Tommy's crew rapidly made their adjustments and within a minute a smoke bomb was on its way. I squinted in the sun, looking for the landing spot.

The round landed short. The mortar was tweaked again. Boom. Seconds later a puff of smoke at the impact point. Closer this time, much closer.

'That'll do, Tommy. On my call I want high explosive on that location. No more than five rounds over six to eight minutes. Until then keep those bloody Afghans from being so trigger-happy, will you,' I said pointing to the Afghans lying prone just beyond him.

As if to make my point for me a pair of ANA soldiers who had crept down to the hill from the crossing fired their RPGs almost simultaneously at nothing much in particular. What a waste of ammunition.

I slid back down the hill, the earth giving way as I tried to dig my heels in.

Sam was on the radio again, telling me the Harriers had gone.

'Tommy, did you hear that? I want that fire mission to start in sixty seconds.'

I took a deep breath and started sprinting back to the WMIKs. It was strange to be heading towards danger rather than away from it. If anything the amount of fire the vehicles were attracting was on the increase. I didn't try to dodge or weave. You can't side-step bullets. You just focus on your destination, and run. And pray.

The praying paid off. I made it. But there was no respite. The ammunition situation was critical. Time to speak to Paddy again.

'Sandstone 78, we are now 500 metres along the road, taking fire from four enemy positions. We need the re-supply.'

'Roger. Estonian call signs now on their way to you. Air support too.'

The enemy firing intensified even further.

'Tommy, rapid fire into the wood.'

He redoubled his efforts. Sam and I tried to take up the slack where Chipper and Steve had eased off to conserve rounds.

I kept risking a peek over my shoulder back up to the crossing. At last I caught a glimpse of two Estonian trucks heading our way, top gunners shooting eastwards. They pulled up behind us. Everyone except Sam stopped what they were doing, jumped out and began transferring boxes of ammo. The Estonians were not alone. I was taken aback to see Sean Langan handing over supplies whilst at the same time trying to find out what was going on.

'Sean, what the fuck are you doing here?' I asked, but didn't give him time to answer. 'Doesn't matter, just get yourself in that ditch and keep your head down. You can film what you like from there.'

A few moments later and we had got everything the Estonians had to offer. They didn't hang about, U-turning and racing back the way they had come. Sean stayed on.

I clambered back into my seat just as the first A-10 began an attack run with its guns along the trees. What marks these aircraft out is their ability to fly so slowly, giving them time over targets. Normally this would be a problem for planes because they'd be vulnerable to fire from the ground. Less so with the A-10s. Their bellies are heavily armoured, greatly increasing the amount of punishment they can take before being downed. For the hapless souls beneath them, this apparent invincibility just adds to the shock.

Shahrukh and his men were taking another step forward in our protracted, staggered assault on the 42 northing. He had taken the decision to push two policemen somewhat further ahead than the rest to tease out and engage any Taliban waiting in ambush.

My intention had been to stop at 600 metres but with the support coming from the A-10s and Tommy Johnstone I pushed on further. We had now reached 700 metres. And still we didn't stop. Centimetre by centimetre we descended on the objective, keeping just behind the ANP men.

Seven hundred and fifty metres.

Sam shouted that we were down to our last A-10 run. We would have to make the most of it. Combined with rapid fire from Tommy this would be the ANP's best chance to cover the final 250 metres. I watched in fascination as the A-10 came in from the east to deliver its deadly cargo. It opened up, heavy-calibre cannon rounds spitting out, raining down on the building at the objective, tearing up the walls, churning up the earth around it. Thump, thump, thump. Thump, thump, thump. The building started to disintegrate.

'Move now!' I yelled at Gulzar.

'Fire now!' I screamed at Tommy.

The ANA on the hill opened up with their rifles. Tommy directed mortar bombs on to the building just hit by the A-10.

Eight hundred metres.

Rounds started to land about us from yet another position to the east of the canal. I didn't dare go any further. We would have to support Shahrukh from here. Chipper brought his wagon up in line with ours. I ordered Steve to try and suppress the attention we were getting from this new enemy location. I tried to talk him in but he just couldn't see what I was seeing. I told him to put some tracer rounds through his .50-cal. I watched as they landed 100 metres short and perhaps two knuckles too far left. He fired again. This time he had the correct building in his sights but was hitting it on the wrong side. Just then the enemy appeared out in the open to the right of the structure. He didn't need further instruction. He got the message and started pumping round after round into the area. Chipper joined in, too, one taking over from the other as each had to reload or clear a jam. The constant engagement gave the Taliban no time to think or act.

In front of me the ANP were almost there. Nine hundred and fifty metres from the start point, just fifty metres from the end of the rainbow. Now they were also using RPGs to blast the Taliban out of the building. It was working. From where I was I could make out enemy fighters slipping out of the back, taking off down the road. I lined up my GPMG and pulled the trigger. A short burst flew past the ANP at the fleeing Taliban. I don't know if I hit the enemy but I managed to drop almost all of the ANP. Policemen dived for cover, thinking for a moment they had been ambushed from behind.

Gulzar ran up to me.

'Beattie, there are Taliban in the cornfield immediately behind the building.'

This was one for the mortar team.

'Tommy, I need you to fire over the heads of the ANP in depth to support their move.'

'Doug, I only have five HE rounds left.'

'I know. Give me a smoke round first. I don't want you hitting the ANP.'

I slumped down in my seat and waited, binos hard against my eyes. I heard the mortar go off. Then saw a puff of smoke. The round had landed way, way short; by about 350 metres. A brief lull and then another thud. Another smoke round was on its way. This time it was close enough.

'That'll do. Two rounds of HE. Go.'

There was another cloud of smoke, but this wouldn't have been the tame affair the last two were, shrapnel having been sent spinning out to a radius of twenty to thirty metres, perhaps even more because of the hard ground, a ripple of death expanding out from the impact point.

As the bomb exploded, finally – after six brutal days of advancing, fighting and retreating – the ANP got to where they were going. No matter that the aim had initially been to seize this point just twenty-four hours after the operation started. The policemen were in the objective building on the canal road. This was the 42 northing and just after midday on day six it was ours.

What they had achieved was nothing short of miraculous. This was a disparate band of men, seriously outnumbered, almost fatally under-trained, embarrassingly low on resources, yet they had achieved their goal. We had helped them, of course.

With air-strikes, mentoring (kicking them up the arse), our own exploits on the ground. But this was really an achievement for the ANP, and to a lesser extent the ANA. It was against all the odds.

I got on the radio to tell Paddy the news. He was happy for the Afghans, as I was. But we both knew it was a hollow victory. We wouldn't be holding this ground, couldn't hold it even if we wanted to. As so many times in the past week we would withdraw.

I could hear Shahrukh's men continue to fire as they went from room to room. The fire concentrated on us had ebbed away, the Taliban now more concerned with the ANP's exploits. We had become an afterthought.

I got back on the net to Paddy. 'Have you managed to get us any more air cover?'

'No. Has Sam?'

Sam had tried but the cupboard was bare. We had had all we were going to get and now we would be alone in clearing the area and getting out in one piece.

'Colonel, I need your men to work along that tree-line for about 200 metres and then go firm while I sort out an extraction plan,' I said to Gulzar.

I wanted to press home our advantage. I hoped that by clearing along the row of trees towards the wood the Taliban would get caught between the ANP and the Sergeant-Major's team on the hill. My hope was the enemy would retreat westwards towards the village of Jugroom, their supposed stronghold.

But how to get out of here?

The ANP was the most vulnerable part of our little expeditionary force, now way ahead of us. The policemen would have to move back first, under covering fire from the WMIKs and the hill. Then we would pull back, repeatedly leapfrogging Sergeant-Major Johnstone as we went; covering, withdrawing, covering, withdrawing, till we reached the crossing.

But there were complications.

Gulzar shouted out to me, 'I've got two casualties. One dead, one injured. And I have just heard the Taliban are moving up our eastern flank behind the villages in the distance.'

This would threaten our pull-out, not just as far as our start point for the day but maybe all the way back to the town centre.

Not for the first time I felt extended and exposed. It would take only one bad spin of the dice and we would be in real shit. Time to go.

I could see movement down in the drainage ditch to my right. Two ANP were struggling to carry their wounded comrade, sweating not just from the effort of carrying the dead weight in the blazing heat, but from trying to hang on to their weapons so as not to drop them and leave them behind for the Taliban.

Tommy Johnstone fired his last three HE rounds on the wood, before laying down as much smoke as he had remaining.

Shahrukh and some of his men came past me. For the first time that day I saw them moving quickly. I ordered Tommy and his contingent to get going. There was a last flurry of gunfire from the ANA, then silence as Tommy's team packed up and headed out.

Was that everybody? No. What about Sean? Where was he? Had he left with the ANP? I couldn't see him. I called Chipper on the PRR. It was OK. Sean was in the back of his vehicle. Now it was our turn to go. The enemy fire picked up as we left, Steve giving as good as he got. Sam too. We raced full pelt back to the crossing.

I looked around, making sure everyone was present and correct. They were.

As I dismounted I saw a commotion going on by one of the HESCOs, a huddle of Afghans including Gulzar and Shahrukh with raised voices and gesturing limbs.

'Yasir, what is going on?'

'The policemen are complaining that the body of their colleague who was killed has been left out there. The Major says he is going to go and get it.'

'You have got to be kidding.'

I was incredulous. What were they thinking of? I wandered closer to the argument.

'We don't have any support for this. It's madness.'

Gulzar replied for Shahrukh, who had run off with a couple of the others. 'It is for the honour of the dead man's family. The ANA are also going forward to collect their commander.'

He was talking about the soldier killed during the assault on the woods led by Tim on the third day. Although I knew the Afghans had a deep-felt sense of duty to their dead, I was appalled they would even consider such a move now. I tried to remonstrate with Gulzar but to no avail. Even as we spoke, an ANP truck roared up to us, Shahrukh in the front with a driver, two more of his men in the back. Barely slowing they rounded the HESCOs and raced off down the canal road. At the same time a second group of ANA soldiers and ANP moved towards the hill, and then the wood, to try and get the other body.

I was rooted to the spot. I could see the ANP truck progressing down the track, the only disturbance around it a cloud of dust thrown up by its wheels. There wasn't a round fired at it. Nothing. All day we had been shot at, harassed from all sides, but this mercy mission continued on its own serene way. I gazed in amazement as the truck swerved to a halt, the extraction party jumped out and manhandled the lifeless body into the back. The journey back started. It was to be as peaceful as the outward leg.

How had they got away with it? Had Gulzar brokered a deal with the local Taliban leader to allow Shahrukh to move with impunity? It wasn't beyond the realms of possibility. I had heard of similar things happening elsewhere in Helmand. Or had the enemy been as dumbfounded as I was by this suicidal mission? Too incredulous to react? To this day I do not know the answer. And it appeared as if the Afghan soldiers were so far having similar luck. They were now beyond the hill, in the open ground between it and the trees. But I wasn't going to hang about to watch this spectacle play out. There was still the worry that the Taliban would cut us off as we continued our withdrawal.

As our small British convoy headed north the peace was broken by small-arms fire and the explosions of RPGs. We weren't the targets. The noise was coming from far behind us. The ANA's fortune had taken a turn for the worse. I was glad we were on our way back to the camp.

Your leg or your face?
Your foot or your hand?
Your genitals or your arm?
Which would you rather lose?

A group of trucks came spinning into our compound, the Colonel's pickup leading the party; the peace broken by revving engines, screeching brakes, doors being opened, doors being slammed shut, Gulzar shouting orders. We all stopped what we were doing. I put down my brew and dragged my thoughts away from our earlier close encounters. Walking towards the vehicles it became clear I would have been better dwelling on the past rather than succumbing to my curiosity.

In one of the pickups I could see a couple of Afghan soldiers crouching down in the back, their faces ashen. I made the mistake of heading towards it.

I tried to count how many men were there on the floor of the vehicle. I thought I counted five. But it was so hard to say, for this wasn't a group of individuals, this was a jumble of body parts. Legs were intermingled, arms intertwined, limbs contorted in hideous positions. Not all were attached to their owners. The flesh had been cut, slashed, hacked, ripped, torn, punctured, gouged and seared. Chunks of muscle and skin hung by threads. Bits of bone stuck out everywhere. Femurs, fingers, knees, knuckles, skulls, ribs; some still covered in sinews, tendons, veins; others brilliant white, shining in the late-afternoon sun. Someone had been through this lot with a butcher's knife, and not very expertly at that. Blood continued to pump from gaping wounds, seeping, oozing across the floor of the truck, giving everything a deep crimson sheen as it went. The smell of it went to the back of my throat, coppery, invasive. But there were other scents, too. Piss. Shit. Vomit. Two, perhaps three, of the injured were screaming, moaning. The others were silent, the life already almost out of them.

Yasir had reached his limit. He turned away and threw up. I stood there aghast, my brain trying to work out what I was looking at. I was shoved to one side. Thank God. Tony Cowley moved into action.

One by one the men – I was right, there were five of them – were lifted out and laid under the cover of the concrete awning along the front of the college building, next to the policeman brought in just twenty minutes earlier. I watched the Afghans struggle to move the casualties without causing them more harm. As the bodies were disentangled, the injuries became even more shockingly obvious. I couldn't take my eyes off one man who had a bloodied stump instead of a hand, a single digit remaining where a full set of fingers should have been, giving a macabre thumbs-up. The men from the OMLT got to work under the Corporal's direction. Sean Langan was there, too. Not filming but helping. He was holding on to a leg. This one was still attached, just. Sean was trying to elevate it to stem the bleeding, without pulling the whole damn thing away from the torso.

I left the dreadful scene behind me and persuaded Yasir to come with me to talk to Gulzar. He was standing some distance away, seemingly disinterested in the plight of his men.

'What the hell happened?' I asked him.

'It was while my men and the ANA soldiers were trying to get the commander back. One of the policemen fired an RPG. It exploded even before it left the barrel.' He shrugged his shoulders. 'The operator died instantly, these others were wounded.'

Not for the first time I saw a man who seemed to have little interest in the suffering of those under his command. It was strange. There was this honour amongst the Afghans of caring for the dead, but what of the living? Or the barely alive? Where was the humanity then? I was full of fury. I wanted to stick my fist in his face and mark time on his head. Instead I walked away. As I did so, more ANA vehicles arrived. They had another body with them, that of their commander. So they had achieved the goal.

There were now some thirty ANA soldiers standing about talking. Something didn't add up. If we had twenty more soldiers at the western outpost the ANA had reached that afternoon whilst we were on the eastern edge of our territory, then who was manning JTAC Hill? Who was at the northern canal crossing? Probably no one. The ANA must all have abandoned their posts on hearing the news about the commander and the RPG accident. If the enemy decided to counter-attack now, well, it didn't bear thinking about.

'Yasir, tell these men to get back to their posts.'

The trouble with interpreters is that more often than not they translate what you say, but not the way you say it. I was giving an order. Yasir made it sound more like a polite request: if you wouldn't mind, if you have time, when you are ready. The soldiers ignored me completely. I wanted the OMLT to get involved; after all, they were in charge of mentoring the ANA, but they were all busy with the wounded. Through Yasir I tried ordering them again. Still nothing. Things were falling apart. I started shouting, gesturing, pointing. To the ANA soldiers it was as if I wasn't there. Then I began to push them one by one away from the compound building and towards their vehicles. I now had my pistol in my right hand, hanging down at the side of my leg so they could see it. It was clear to me. They were disobeying a direct order and if we, the British, didn't regain some sort of discipline, we were going to be faced with an armed mob, intent on doing just what on earth they liked.

Slowly the soldiers started to move back, away from the injured. Just in time Tim also arrived on the scene, having returned from setting up the newly captured western outpost.

What would I have done if one of the ANA had raised his gun to me? Would I have done the same? Would it have come down to brinkmanship? A deadly game of chicken? Heaven only knows. Once again I had put myself in a vulnerable position. Once again I had got away with it. What I did know was that I didn't trust the ANA. Perhaps it was because I had done all my fighting with the ANP. I was also annoyed with the OMLT. Yes, they had casualties to treat, but that was only one part of their job. Their prime role was to oversee the actions of the ANA.

I hoped that within the next few hours all of this would become academic. The re-supply from Bastion was due at 19:00 hrs, hopefully to include not just ammunition but also fuel for our pull-out the next day.

Paddy was talking on the radio. He looked troubled, but then a lot had been happening. I didn't really give it any thought.

Ten minutes later he came over. 'Doug, we've been ordered to pull out.'

I didn't really get the point of what he was saying. I already knew that.

'What, before we hand the situation over to the new ANA force?'

'There isn't going to be a relief force. We're all leaving with the ANA tomorrow and that's that.'

Paddy must have made a mistake. This couldn't be right. No way would HQ be abandoning the ANP to hold Garmsir on their own. It would never work. They couldn't do it. Probably wouldn't do it. Were our bosses mad? Or just stupid?

'You have got to be kidding, right?' I said in disbelief, directing my anger towards Paddy. 'We pull out and the ANP will be hot on our heels and the last six days will have been for absolutely nothing.'

'I know, but that is what KAF is telling me. I need you to go to Gulzar and explain the situation. I'll get on to Lash and see if they can apply any pressure on KAF.'

I turned away without answering. My conversation with Gulzar was short and to the point. Gulzar was clear on what he would do if no relief were forthcoming. He'd follow us straight out of town. This time I couldn't blame him. Indeed, if I were an Afghan and had just been told that news I wouldn't have hung around waiting for the next day. I would have gone there and then. ISAF could not be trusted, so why play their game any longer? The Taliban had been stirred up and were bringing in fighters from across the border. The Pathfinders had already gone. The Brits and Estonians were going, along with the ANA. What could a handful of Afghan National Policemen achieve on their own?

Sean sensed something was up. He came over to find me. I didn't do anything to hide just how pissed off I was as I answered his questions. He wanted to know if I would do an interview. Try and stop me. This was the lowest point of my campaign so far. He filmed me as I spoke, not needing to prompt me at all. I knew what I wanted to say. When we finished he was gracious enough to ask me whether I had said anything I might regret and that he would wipe the tape. I declined his offer. Through him I wanted the British public to understand what we had done and how finally defeat came not at the hands of our enemy, but at those of our own commanders.

I sat alone as the OMLT and ANA prepared to leave. Sam and the driver knew we were just waiting for confirmation from KAF on the ANP situation before we too readied for the drive back north.

Half an hour later and Paddy had the update. 'The pull-out continues as planned,' he said. 'Except that we stay.'

'What?' was all I could manage as I met his gaze.

'The OMLT and half the ANA will leave at 08:00 hrs tomorrow. You, me and Sam will remain, together with thirty of the Afghan soldiers. Lash will try and get help to us from 21 Battery but that's unlikely to arrive for at least another twenty-four hours.'

It was simple enough. By keeping the three of us in place, British HQ could say they were providing a mentoring role to the ANA, on the basis of which we could retain some of their men. That way we might still be able to hold the northern canal crossing and the new western outpost. But now I had to go back to Gulzar and explain the U-turn and get him to stay with us, committing his men to the southern crossing, JTAC Hill and the eastern checkpoint at the end of the main street.

'What made them change their minds?' I asked.

'I told them we would lose the town by mid-afternoon if they didn't. As for us, well, I explained we had all volunteered to stay.'

THIRTEEN

OUT OF SIGHT, OUT OF MIND

(GARMSIR, DAYS 7 & 8)

They wouldn't believe you if you told them.

There are around 165,000 service personnel in the British armed forces, 200,000 if you include reservists.

In September 2006, about 5,000 were in Afghanistan.

But the defence of Garmsir now fell on the shoulders of just three: Paddy, Sam and myself.

'Do you want a brew, boss?' Sam said. He didn't really need to have asked.

'That would be great, Sam,' came Paddy's reply.

It was the first time I had heard Paddy refer to Sam by his first name. Normally it was Bombadier New or JTAC. In the military it's generally frowned upon to get too close to your men: 'familiarity breeds contempt', that sort of thing. It's seen as an erosion of the boundaries, an undermining of the command structure. I have never seen things in quite the same way, believing that in certain circumstances it's reasonable to inject a bit more humanity into your dealings with subordinates. And if this wasn't 'certain circumstances' then I didn't have a clue what would be. I had some sympathy with Paddy's choice of words.

*

We had watched the others leave at about midday. There wasn't much said as they mounted up for departure. I shook hands with Tim. He looked a shadow of his former self. His eyes were tired and sunken, big black bags surrounding them. The face wasn't that of the fresh-faced, enthusiastic young officer who had left Lash just a week earlier. It was haggard, weathered, covered in a beard. There was no doubting the tough times Tim had been through both physically and mentally. He had been in charge of the OMLT, and through that the ANA. It was a big task and he had done his duty, but at some personal cost.

There were brief goodbyes with Chipper, Steve and Geordie. It was strange. We had been through so much, yet I still knew very little about them. There hadn't been much opportunity for small talk, and even when we had a moment to ourselves, there always seemed to be better things to do with those precious minutes: eat, drink, clean, sleep. But a bond had been formed between us. Not friendship as such – we didn't know each other well enough to be described as friends – but certainly an understanding. We had been thrown together in adversity. We had helped each other out. And we had all come through to the other side. At least, so far. I was sorry to see them go.

The convoy snaked away into the distance: fourteen British soldiers and forty-five ANA troops, their time done. We were the rump – three men who were supposed to be mentoring; a handful of Estonians who weren't there to fight; thirty ANA members who didn't want to fight; and fifty policemen who mainly didn't know how to fight, most of the Afghan veterans in Garmsir already having been replaced by young conscripts.

The plan was that the OMLT would drive back to Lash and on arrival transfer the vehicles over to troops of 21 Battery Royal Artillery. In the short term they would come down to make up the numbers before KAF finally figured out how to reinforce us in a more lasting manner.

Not for the first time did I have my doubts about the supply chain. How was it 21 Battery didn't have their own vehicles? For

Bombardier Sam New, the JTAC in Garmsir, with interpreter Yasir. The Afghan's face has been obscured to protect his identity.

Me about to mount-up before another trip down the canal road.

Tim Illingworth.

Jay Frost, Paddy Williams and I share a rare moment of humour at the agricultural college in Garmsir.

Joe Cummings waiting to be casevaced after being shot on Garmsir day three.

Paddy Williams squats down to talk to Tim Illingworth who has found some welcome shade.

JTAC Hill in Garmsir.

Anthony Cowley, our medic in Garmsir, treats a badly wounded Afghan soldier.

Just minutes after we escaped the ambush on Garmsir day nine. Note the tall, dense crops – perfect cover for a surprise attack.

Jay Frost contemplates the ambush on our safe arrival back at JTAC Hill.

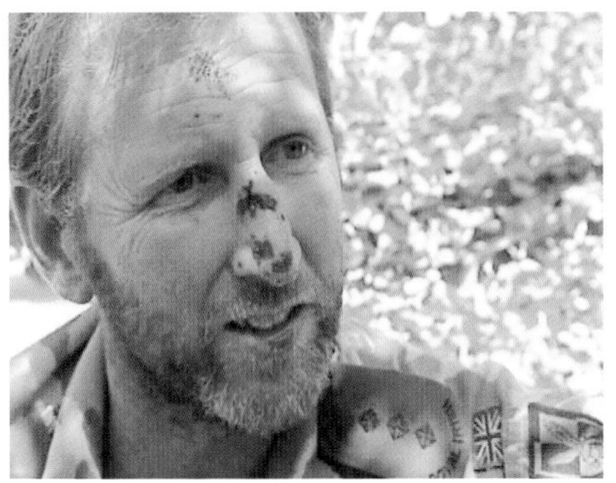

My battered and bruised face just after my return trip to Garmsir.

Smile. The opening of a new PSCC centre in Lashkar Gah in December 2006.

The view over Tangye near Kajaki to the hills beyond.

Members of the Afghan National Police being briefed in Kajaki in January 2007.

Some of the Afghans who fought with me in Afghanistan.

A Chinook about to land in the Afghan desert.

Me with my Military Cross after being presented with it by the Queen at Buckingham Palace.

that matter, why were there no other frontline soldiers who could have come to our aid? What the public failed to understand and no one in authority was ever in a rush to explain was just how few of those in Afghanistan were for combat. Perhaps only 1,500 out of the 5,000 total were fighting men. The rest offered logistical support. Engineers, cooks, quartermasters, signallers, clerks and so on and so forth. All necessary roles, but why no more infantry to do the job at the sharp end?

Tim and the others disappeared from view, first them, then their vehicles, finally the accompanying cloud of dust. What to do now other than drink tea? Making a brew was about the only thing we had the resources to do, and yes, it did make things seem better. The morning passed slowly. We gathered together bits of kit, sorting out the ammunition, fuel and food left by the ANA and OMLT.

By early afternoon I was getting bored. Sam and I decided to go for a drive to survey our territory. At the northern canal crossing we found things in pretty good order. The defensive positions were robust and looked at least semi-permanent. Ten Afghan soldiers were there holding the fort. Then we headed back south. At the eastern checkpoint, at the junction with the main street, we were greeted with a bizarre sight. Three Afghans under a blanket, doing what Afghan men under a blanket do. At least they had found the time in between their male bonding to improve security. A Soviet Dushka 12.7mm heavy machine gun had been mounted on the roof of a building.

On we went, down to the southern crossing, only to be met by a rabble; fifteen ANP in a sorry state, and far from alert, not least because of the drugs they had been taking. By the side of a wall lay the telltale signs: a pile of stripped poppy heads.

However, before I could start berating them for their behaviour a number of ANP trucks pulled up alongside us. Out of the first one jumped Shahrukh. Without pausing to say hello he marched off to the front of the checkpoint, followed closely by three of his subordinates. In their wake, struggling to keep up, came a fat man carrying a video camera. I stood bemused.

'Do you know what's going on?' I asked Yasir, who was chatting to a couple of the other policemen.

'The man with the camera is from Afghan TV news in Kabul. He's here to film the capture of Garmsir from the Taliban.'

My bemusement grew.

The journalist, sweating profusely, set up his equipment, locking the camera on to the tripod; then Shahrukh took centre stage. On cue, and at no one in particular, he fired an RPG. The reporter flinched but kept recording. Then Shahrukh fired another RPG. Then another. He turned and grinned at the lens.

My first thought was, what a waste of ammunition. For a week the ANP had bemoaned their lack of equipment and here they were blowing it all for TV. Then I thought about what a contrived report this was going to be.

Yasir explained the recapture of the town had already made the national news and now the people wanted to see pictures to prove to themselves they weren't being lied to by the government. Well, they would see the pictures; if only they knew what they were showing.

I decided to leave before the enemy decided to start shooting back.

We drove back to the town, along the main street, to the western end of our domain. Next stop was the bridge over the river. There were just two policemen there, not only guarding it, but also showing an entrepreneurial streak, exacting tolls from users. Apart from these two the checkpoint was there in little more than name only. A couple of HESCOs stood empty, no one having bothered to fill these wire and cloth cubes with the dirt and rock that would provide at least some ballistic protection during attack, and for that matter would stop them blowing away in a stiff breeze.

Then it was on to JTAC Hill. Along with the southern canal crossing this was probably the most important bit of ground under our control. I struggled to the top to join the ten policemen posted there. I looked out at the commanding view to the south.

From the elevated position I could see for about five kilometres, the ground mainly a mix of ploughed fields and crops of corn the height of a man and seemingly ready to harvest. Dotted about the area were numerous buildings of varying sizes, but almost all surrounded by a wall. Breaking up the scene were regular criss-crossings of hedgerows and small copses, irrigation ditches and streams.

Then I studied the landscape much closer to home.

The hill itself was shabby and squalid. Human waste littered one side of the mound. Empty ration cartons, ammunition boxes and shell cases were strewn everywhere. Plates lay about with half-eaten meals still on them. But I wasn't about to give them a lesson on personal hygiene. At least they were there, not just in body, but also in mind; thankfully there was no sign of the drug-taking some of their colleagues were engaging in.

My eyes returned to the broader picture. I followed a sandy track winding away from the hill, following the line of the Helmand River until it reached a series of buildings and fields perhaps a kilometre away and disappeared from view. From my map I knew that 500 metres or so further on was yet another set of buildings, a hamlet perhaps. Further still was the Taliban stronghold of Jugroom. Between these two bits of habitation was the ANA outpost set up just the day before by the soldiers under Tim's leadership, whilst I battled away down the canal road. The twenty soldiers there were coming under repeated attack as the Taliban tried to dislodge them. There was nothing I could do to help. Paddy wasn't about to agree to Sam and me going on a two-man one-vehicle fighting patrol to relieve them. Not that I was in the mood to do so.

We headed back to the agricultural college, where Paddy was waiting for us. Crouching down around the radio we talked about what we had seen. The ANA position must be the priority.

As soon as the men from 21 Battery arrived we would attempt to reach the Afghan soldiers with much-needed food, ammunition and moral support; if they hadn't capitulated beforehand.

Finally we had the time and inclination to find out a bit more about each other's circumstances. Sam was nearing the end of his six-month tour, but he wasn't expecting to be shipped out any time soon. JTACs were in short supply and realistically he would be required to stay on. He was resigned to at least another month in Helmand, probably much of it in Garmsir if a relief force ever turned up. To him it didn't make much difference where he was. And with Garmsir it was at least a case of better the devil you know.

Compared with Sam's veteran status, Paddy was a raw recruit when it came to Afghanistan. He had been in the country for just three weeks. Having finished a posting in the UK, he volunteered to come to Lashkar Gah to briefly work at the PSCC. Given that prior to his arrival I was the only one manning the PSCC, he doubled our strength overnight. Should he get out of this scrape unscathed, the plan was to be back to Britain by the end of September, meaning a tour of just five weeks.

Someone was calling us over the radio with welcome news. The OMLT had arrived back safely and passed their vehicles to 21 Battery. But a full briefing of the situation in Garmsir was going to take a bit longer and our support was not going to leave until at least first light the next morning. All being well they would arrive with us by noon.

That night sleep was as elusive as it had been all week. My mind constantly returned to Shahrukh acting up for the camera earlier that day. It made me think about Sean, and how my opinion of him had changed over the past days. He had been brave, determined, straightforward, helpful. Not one of us in military terms, but part of the group, sharing experiences. What a shame he was no longer with us. It had been good to have a witness there to record events, though I was curious about how his film would be edited. How would each character come across? How would I come across? Bitter, angry, mad, bad, brave, reckless? It could be all or none of those things.* One thought quickly segued into another. How were things at home? What were Luke, Leigh and Margaret up to? Were they concerned they hadn't heard from me?

Thank God I was leaving the army. It was a decision made even before I came to Afghanistan. I vowed to put the military firmly behind me if only I was allowed to escape with my life. Stuck in Garmsir, I was more certain than ever it was the right thing to be doing. But would my luck hold? They say fortune favours the bold, but what about the foolhardy? Would I be punished for my cavalier approach? Punished for the deaths of Afghan comrades killed following my orders? And how about the enemy? The four men I had mortared and then bombed. The Talib I shot on the first day. The enemy fighter I had bayoneted. Was my conscience clear when it came to the way they met their ends? I finally drifted off, the thoughts merely replaced by dreams, nightmares.

It only took a gentle nudge to wake me, to get me jumping to my feet in a panic, pistol raised.

Paddy was standing next to me. I stared at him.

'Doug, your turn on radio stag.'

12:00 hrs came and went. So did 13:00 hrs. It was not till 14:00 hrs that the first, faint trace of a sand and dust cloud appeared on the horizon, out to the west of the town. It was several minutes later before the vehicles kicking up the storm came into view: 21 Battery was on its way. I reached for the binoculars round my neck, except they weren't there. I cursed, now remembering I had let Gulzar borrow them. And my other, larger pair was in the Land Rover. I had to make do with the four-times magnification provided by my rifle sight.

---

* Sean's film, 'Fighting the Taliban', was eventually shown on Channel 4 as part of the *Dispatches* series. The programme was nominated for a BAFTA in 2008.

Paddy shouted up to my position on the roof. 'Doug, do you want to get out there to meet them and lead them in?'

'Yep, sure.'

Any excuse to actually do something. It had been a slow morning. More admin, a chat with the Colonel, who wandered over to our compound to make sure we hadn't abandoned him during the night. That was about it.

I did the driving, Yasir next to me, Sam in the back. We crossed the bridge and ended up west of the river. I glanced again at a village I had seen from the roof off to my left. Studying it earlier I was surprised by two things. One was how many people I could actually see busying themselves about the place; the other was that none of them were young men. Old men, yes. Women and children, yes. But no males of working, productive age. I asked Yasir about it, already half-knowing what the answer would be.

'They are either fighting for the Taliban, as ordered by the village elders, or fighting for the government, as ordered by the village elders.'

We slowed, then stopped, to await the arrival of the battery. I was expecting to see some faces I knew from my time at the PSCC. They had helped ferry us about Lashkar Gah. I wondered what they would make of us: our filthy clothes, caked in blood, sweat and dirt; faces burnt red and peeling from the sun; the Land Rover leaking like a sieve from the pummelling it had taken from enemy fire. I wondered whether they would also pick up on the more subtle signs. Would they see in Sam and me what we had seen in Tim? The anguish, the stress, the doubt, the responsibility, the exhaustion, the fear? The blessed relief at their arrival?

The first person I recognised was the sergeant in the lead vehicle that pulled up next to us. I had no idea of his name, but at that moment he was like a long-lost relative. He smiled as I went over to shake his hand.

I walked on to the second vehicle. In the left-hand seat was Simon, the battery commander, whom I knew well from Lash. Then I saw who was behind him: Steve.

'What the fuck are you doing here?'

'They needed a gunner.' He shrugged with a wry grin.

I grinned back. I wasn't about to look a gift horse in the mouth.

After a few more hellos I pointed out to Simon some of the tourist attractions in this part of our patch. Then we were off again, me in the lead, heading for the college. It wasn't quite on the same scale as the liberation of Berlin; there were only six vehicles behind me. But they contained nineteen men, and when you had been just three, well, it seemed like salvation.

Amongst the rest of those who had arrived were Zemar, a new interpreter, and another replacement driver for me – Lieutenant Jay Frost, of the Royal Logistics Corps, who was with the OMLT in Lash and was responsible for the ANA contingent there. He had wanted to come on the original mission but couldn't be spared. This time he made it because he was qualified as a driver and drivers were in short supply. Not exactly the sort of task a lieutenant might have expected to find himself doing but at least it got him out of the office.

21 Battery's day job was as an air defence unit attached to 16 Air Assault Brigade. But in Afghanistan they had been re-rolled as an infantry company, tasked with holding ground already taken.

Paddy was as pleased to see 21 Battery as I was. After a warm welcome he continued the briefing where I had left off. Once the theory was over with we decided to do the tour: the northern canal crossing; the eastern checkpoint; the southern canal crossing. Simon and his sidekicks got to see it all. Then we introduced him to the ANP. As a major, Simon was nominally the highest-ranking British officer in Garmsir and so I thought it right he should make the acquaintance of the senior Afghans. It didn't take long till I regretted the move. From the moment they met, Gulzar complained: complained about his boss General Durani; complained that the British weren't as professional as the Canadians and Americans he had previously worked with; complained that the British failed to use aircraft and artillery as effectively as our coalition colleagues. The conversation became more animated still when Simon let on that he knew something about artillery because he was an artillery officer. Gulzar couldn't believe his luck. He thought that would be the end of all his problems and the Taliban would now be bombarded into submission.

As I sat and listened I became increasingly bored by the man, my dislike of him intensifying. The way I saw it he blamed everyone but himself. And I detested how he seemed so dismissive of the fate of his own men, several of whom looked far too young to be fighting and dying.

Silently I was hoping we would not have too much more to do with Gulzar. 21 Battery were only due to be with us for a maximum of forty-eight hours and during that time our priority was to shore up ANA positions to the west, leaving the ANP to consolidate what they had already achieved.

The intention was to relieve the ANA southern outpost the next day. But there was preparation work we could do that afternoon before dark. The idea was to get out across the river and into the village I had studied earlier. From there we would move southwards along the western bank until we reached yet another hill fort, perhaps the largest in the area. This would afford us a great view of the ANA position and also show us where the Taliban strongholds and ambush points might be.

Shortly before 16:00 hrs we got under way. I was in the lead WMIK; the sergeant I knew from Lash commanded the one that followed, supplied by Simon. One of my biggest worries was getting blown up by a mine. We had no intelligence on, or experience of, this part of our territory. And it was not just weapons laid by the Taliban that worried me. The Soviets had left a legacy of unmapped munitions that wait patiently to catch out the unwary.*

---

* On 6 September 2006, in one of the worst such incidents, Corporal Mark Wright of 3 PARA died from injuries sustained after his patrol strayed into a minefield. Several of his colleagues were badly hurt.

The move through the village was tactically straightforward. I would advance and stop, then provide cover for the sergeant's Land Rover. He would bound ahead and then cover me as I leapt past him again. But we hadn't done this as a team before so I checked and double-checked he knew the procedures before we headed out.

We reached the other end of the village without incident. Beyond the houses lay agricultural land. More than one field contained a poppy crop. As we drove along, I saw an old man tilling the soil. He looked up as he heard us approach, stopping what he was doing. Putting down his tool, he stepped towards us. I ordered a halt and jumped out followed by Yasir. The farmer told a familiar tale.

He said that for six months the village had been targeted by insurgents. Repeatedly it was mortared, then pillaged, the Taliban seizing food and taking away the young men at gunpoint to fight for them. Any of the elders who tried to resist were subjected to a beating or worse.

His view of the Taliban was interesting. Apart from those locals press-ganged into service, he believed the majority were foreign, coming from Pakistan and Saudi Arabia, Iran, even Bosnia.

'Yasir, ask him how he earns a living.'

'I grow crops,' he replied.

I wanted to hear him admit the full story. 'What sort of crops? Poppies?'

'Of course,' he said as a matter of fact. 'Poppies grow well and sell well. I can get two crops a year. I have a wife and four children to feed. What do you expect?'

'Why not grow corn?' I persisted. 'The government will buy it off you.'

He gave me a world-weary smile. 'It doesn't yield the same as poppies and anyway every twelve months I'd get only one corn harvest.'

There was so much more I wanted to ask. Are you aware your poppy crop gets turned into drugs? Do you know most of the heroin sold in the UK comes from Afghanistan? Do you appreciate the social, emotional and physical harm those drugs do to our population? But I knew it was a waste of time. He didn't have the slightest clue about how we in the West lived our lives, just as I didn't really understand the pressures on him. It was a case of complete mutual misunderstanding.

We pressed on, leaving the old man to his subsistence existence, and made a beeline for the hill fort. The view from the top was as good as I had hoped. Looking due south, there was another village about 1.5 kilometres away on our side of the river, the west. We could see people moving between this and the Taliban stronghold of Jugroom on the other side of the watercourse.

Before our deployment we had been told the village we were now observing south of us was allied to the Taliban and was providing the enemy with food and water. Whether this was a forced union or based on more principled grounds we didn't know.

I scanned anticlockwise across the river. Jugroom came and went from view, then when I was looking pretty much due east my eyes came to rest on the ANA position. It was in one of those ever-present walled compounds, dominating the track that ran down from JTAC Hill. I could understand why the Taliban would want to clear the soldiers out of there.

'Boss, what is that movement in the tree-line just south of where the ANA are?'

I refocused my binoculars on the spot Sam was pointing out. The enemy were easy to see; several fighters crouched in the greenery clutching their AK47s, no doubt ready for another harassing raid on the nervous soldiers. They were well out of range. Our only chance was to call in air support, but even as Sam got on the TacSat I knew we wouldn't get it till the Taliban actually attacked. I was right.

We sat there on the lip of the hill, wondering what to do next. The answer was duck. A round whistled past, no more than a metre above my head. I threw myself to the ground, arms and legs flailing. Head in the dirt, I listened to the sniggers. I didn't see the funny side of it. A stray bullet can kill just as easily as a well-aimed one. Indignantly I clambered to my feet and fired my SA80 in the general direction of Jugroom. It was never going to bother anyone. Used individually the SA80 has an effective range of around 300 metres; a skilled marksman should hit something at 400 metres. As part of concentrated and concerted fire from a section then it is effective to 600 metres. My target was twice that far away.

But my frustrated fusillade did have one effect. It gave the ANA early warning of the Taliban approach. They couldn't quite see where the enemy was, but it put them on their guard and they joined in the random shooting.

It was time for us to leave. Our location was compromised and I didn't want to be caught so far from home without help.

That evening we chatted about the next day. Simon was concerned. He had more intelligence that some members of the ANP were playing both sides, nominally fighting for the government but actually passing on operational details to the Taliban. I knew this wasn't an idle rumour. Before Garmsir I had spent some time in Sangin, my job to run an investigation into collusion between policemen and the insurgents. But before things got fully under way it all became academic. The ANP capitulated to the Taliban, handing over their equipment, weapons and vehicles in the process. I had come to trust Shahrukh with my life. The others I couldn't vouch for. H-hour was to be 09:30 hrs. The ANP wouldn't find that out till just before.

FOURTEEN

AMBUSH

(GARMSIR, DAY 9)

The last of the ammunition and food had been loaded into the Land Rovers.

Everything checked and double-checked.

I was actually feeling pretty relaxed.

In Garmsir terms I was expecting day nine to be something of a picnic. Our task was straightforward, each step already mapped out. Move some 600 metres south past JTAC Hill along the rough sandy track running down the east of the Helmand River, keeping the fifteen-strong contingent of ANP I had secured from the Colonel earlier that morning over a cup of tea just ahead of us. Go firm while the policemen cleared the ground beyond a blind bend. Then nose forward to a point where the ANA outpost would be visible. Make sure the Afghan soldiers realised it was us approaching – and not the Taliban trying to sneak up on them – before proceeding in an orderly fashion to their position to be welcomed as liberators as we handed out the scoff, ammo and cigarettes. Easy. What could possibly go wrong?

I turned round to look at Jay. He was sitting perfectly still, staring straight at me, an impression of worry etched onto his sunburnt face, brow furrowed with deep trenches, beads of sweat glistening in the already scorching sunshine.

'Fuck me, Doug, are you OK?'

'Sure. How are you?' I shouted back over the cacophony of gunfire.

'Yeah, great, but I thought you had been hit.'

'Me? I thought YOU had been fucking hit!'

I could still see a thin puff of smoke rising from just behind Jay's left ear. The wisp curled gently into the air and disappeared. It was coming from a bullet hole in his headrest. A large-calibre round had missed smashing his skull, pulping his brain, by no more than an inch. I pointed it out to him.

'I thought I felt something come past.' He looked back towards me. Then the direction of his gaze changed just slightly.

'Look,' he said, nodding his head at my seat. I glanced to my right. In the ballistic matting, against which I had been leaning just moments earlier, there were two similar holes, slightly smaller than the one next to Jay's head, but equally well formed.

We had got away with it, again, but for how much longer? We were caught in a Taliban ambush and in serious trouble. Some bloody picnic.

It had all happened so quickly. As planned the ANP had disappeared round the corner to secure the area ahead of us. My Land Rover – followed by the one from 21 Battery that was accompanying me – had driven slowly through a shallow stream that fed the river. We had continued perhaps thirty metres along the narrow road, leaving behind the tree-line that had offered some cover from prying eyes, low earth banks to either side of us.

It was then that the mayhem had started. It seemed to come out of nowhere. My vehicle had shaken violently as the first volley of bullets struck the near-side wing. It was a pair of these that had come so close to prematurely ending my tour of Afghanistan, not to mention my life.

The blast of an RPG reminded Jay and me that just because

we had survived one fusillade we were far from out of danger. In fact things were deteriorating rapidly.

All four of our small team's machine guns – two in my vehicle, two in the one behind – were now raining down fire on the enemy no more than 100 metres away to our left.

Not that this seemed to be affecting the consistency of their shooting. My WMIK was hit repeatedly. Metal striking metal. The various sounds of impact making themselves heard above the chatter of our weapons. Thwacks, pings, hollow tinny noises. Round after round penetrated the un-armoured skin of our vehicle.

'Throw smoke!' I ordered Jay as Taliban fighters revealed themselves one by one and started to advance on us. They could sense we were in trouble and they wanted our scalps, all too literally I feared.

We had to get out of the killing zone. It was getting frantic.

'Car two, car two! When the phos grenade goes off I will cover your withdrawal back to the other side of the stream.'

As I shouted my instructions, more shooting started up, this time from our front, coming from the edge of a field. Why hadn't the ANP cleared it? For that matter, where the hell was the bloody ANP? Why weren't they coming to our rescue?

I pulled at the empty ammo box attached to my GPMG and flung it out of the vehicle, before fumbling about for the fresh supply I knew was somewhere at my feet.

'Throw that bloody smoke!' I repeated to Jay. What the fuck was he doing?

I turned towards him as the visibility remained depressingly crystal clear. He was struggling to get the pin out of the grenade. Whether from nerves or because his mind was still otherwise occupied analysing his recent brush with death, he seemed to have forgotten how the British red-phos grenade works. The pin needs to be twisted ninety degrees before it can be pulled out. I grabbed it from his hands, removed the pin and hurled it towards the enemy.

It detonated with a dull thud, sparks of phosphorus fizzing out of a cloud of dense white smoke, which quickly obscured us from the enemy. But we kept firing, rounds disappearing into the pall at a phenomenal rate.

'Car two. Move. Now!'

Half a minute later I was out of bullets again and doing another reload.

'Boss, they're having trouble behind us,' screamed Sam.

I hardly dared to look. The other WMIK was sitting helplessly, half in, half out of the stream, bogged down in a deep pool, one of the rear wheels up to the axle in the clear water bubbling around it. Worst of all, because the track was so narrow, car two now seemed to be blocking our own escape route. I could see the driver frantically trying to get himself out of trouble, selecting and deselecting gears, but going nowhere.

'Fuck it. Fuck it. Sam, keep firing.'

'Roger, boss.'

There was a sliver of good news. Paddy had called in air support, having watched the whole drama unfold from JTAC Hill.

Unfortunately I doubted it would reach us in time. We were trapped, with the enemy both to the side of us and ahead of us. We were pouring fire towards them, but they were still advancing metre by metre. It was time to make some decisions before we were annihilated. There were only two real choices. Either abandon the vehicles and retreat on foot, torching the WMIKs as we went with high-explosive grenades, or try and get the stuck Land Rover out of the mire.

Option two was by far the more risky thing to do. I was determined to give it a go.

It had been drummed into us that a vehicle is a bullet magnet. It attracts lead, like flies to shit. In an ambush you want to get as far away from the machinery as possible, at the same time destroying as much equipment as you can so it doesn't fall into enemy hands. Many of the burning British vehicles seen in Iraq and elsewhere by the UK public on their TV sets are not ablaze as the result of enemy action but as a result of UK forces carrying out so-called 'Op Deny'.

We were in a difficult position, but then we were paid to be in difficult positions. There had to be a way out of this that would save the vehicles. And this wasn't just a matter of foolish pride. They were about the only tactical advantage we had on the ground in Garmsir and I refused to be the one giving that away.

More bullets struck the Land Rover.

The battle was so fierce I hadn't even had a chance to put in a contact report to Paddy, though it was barely necessary, given his grandstand view.

'Doug, what if I back up and try and shunt him out?' asked Jay.

Worth a try.

'Go on, then. I will talk you back.'

I stood up in my commander's seat as Jay engaged reverse and we started a backward crawl. What a sight we must have been. One wizened old soldier standing to his full height, clutching the gun turret, under intense enemy fire, trying to direct the young driver to ensure he didn't stuff us into a sand trap.

As we got closer, I could see there was just a chance we could squeeze past car two and get behind it before perhaps trying to bump it forward. 'Jay. Plan B. I'm going to get out and see if we can get you past so you can push the Land Rover out forwards, otherwise I'm worried we'll just shove it further into the shit.'

Out of the corner of my eye I caught a glimpse of a blur coming our way. The RPG slammed into the earth between the two WMIKs and exploded. Half-anticipating the blast, half-reacting to it, I dived out of my seat on to the ground. As shards of shrapnel flew past, other lighter debris fell on and around the vehicle. I glanced up, covered in dust and soil. Not for the first time, I started imagining the carnage that would ensue if one of the grenades found its target. The high explosive in the weapon itself. The ammo on board the Land Rover. The fuel. All exploding and on fire. It would be hellish. I was certain of that. I had seen it repeatedly in my dreams.

Every instinct told me to stay down low, safe against the dirt, head out of sight, and crawl out of the danger zone. But I couldn't. I needed to stand up so Jay could see me. I had to imagine myself bullet-proof. Legs shaking, I got to my feet, forcing myself to stand straight and get myself in a position where I could guide Jay back.

I waved my arms in the air, shouting out directions. 'Left a bit, steady, right hand down, bit more. STOP!'

Thank God Jay's skills extended beyond a basic knowledge of road signs and the theory test. Deftly, swiftly, he manoeuvred the car past the obstacle.

It's funny how the mind works. From focusing on the deaths of my men, I was now suddenly worried about the Land Rover's paintwork. 'Jay, please don't put too big a dent into our wagon,' I said to myself. Would the cost of the re-spray come out of my wages?

'Jay, take it easy,' I cried out.

He gave me a 'fuck you' look and slipped the clutch, jumping forward.

The two vehicles shuddered as he brought them together. Twice he rammed the stricken WMIK. Twice it failed to budge free, our efforts merely pushing it further into trouble, our angle of attack too oblique. So much for my plan B.

The shooting around us continued. The enemy was getting braver. Getting closer.

It was time to revert to plan A, or at least a rehashed version of it.

'Jay, get in front of car two again,' I screamed, jumping once more into my seat. Without answering Jay squeezed round the chicane and back to the point we had started from, back towards the storm of bullets. From our side, Sam had already put 1,000 rounds through his barrel. I had fired over 600. It would have been many more if I hadn't been spending so much time directing traffic.

'OK, this time we are going to hitch the two wagons together and drag the WMIK free,' I said to Jay as calmly as I could, trying to exude confidence.

As I spoke I attempted to fire with my rifle. As if to encourage me two Taliban rushed out from behind a small single-storey building, heading for the shelter of a second one some seventy metres away. They never made it, cut down by 7.62mm rounds from three GPMGs and two SA80s. Plainly I wasn't the only one who had seen them.

Slinging my weapon over my shoulder I slipped out of the WMIK. Up down. In out. It was like musical-bloody-chairs.

At the front of each Land Rover there is a tow rope, tied on and ready for use. The commander of the other vehicle and I turned our attention away from the enemy and uncoiled the line attached to his car. We pulled it a few metres across the sand and clipped it to the back of my wagon.

'Go, Jay, go!'

Without bothering to take up the slack, Jay floored the throttle and let out the clutch. The wheels slipped in the loose gravel, before finding purchase. There was some forward movement before they started spinning again, the WMIK shuddering to a halt as the other vehicle acted as an anchor.

'Have another go!'

Jay backed up a few feet and repeated the action. The engine revs increased sharply, then died off as the clutch started to bite. This time luck was on our side; the rope became taut, then with barely any resistance car two was on the move, free of the water. We unhooked ourselves and I got back to the job of killing the enemy, having ordered the other commander to reverse out of the mayhem . . . this time keeping it on the hard stuff.

I tried to work out how long the engagement had been going on? I didn't have a clue. Was it five minutes? Ten minutes? Thirty? I couldn't tell. So much had happened.

The B-1 was now only a few moments away but Sam hadn't had a chance to give the pilot a detailed description of the lay of the land because he was too busy manning his GPMG. For the third time I loaded a new belt of ammo into my own machine gun.

By now car two had managed to get back beyond the stream and was some forty metres the other side of it, out of view of most of the attackers. Good for him, shit for us. We were now the sole focus of Taliban attention. At least three of the enemy had advanced to within sixty metres. I needed Sam to start communicating with the B-1 crew pretty damn quick. I plotted the grid reference of the spot the enemy was occupying; then I plotted it again. I couldn't afford to get it even slightly wrong.

'Boss, the pilot wants to know the initials of your name.'

'What? Why?'

'Because they're going to be hitting a target so close to us there is a fucking good chance we are going to get caught up in the explosion. They want to get your details to cover their arses when it all goes wrong.'

'Tell him Delta Romeo Bravo.'

The B-1 would be dropping a 500lb bomb.

'Thirty seconds and stores.'

I was petrified. Half a minute is plenty of time to ask a lot of 'What ifs?'. What if the co-ordinates are wrong? What if the pilot has finger trouble and puts in the wrong digits? What if the bomb goes rogue? I also wondered whether I should be putting my head as far down under the dashboard as I could or trying to look up to gauge the effectiveness of the strike. The others had already made up their minds. Sam was huddled in the back, braced hard against the bulkhead. Yasir was with him. Jay was crouching on the track, beside the vehicle, head in his hands, trying to put two tonnes of British steel between him and the impending blast. I decided to join him, but had left it too late. Even as I was about to move the bomb exploded – right on target. Unlike other detonations I'd experienced, the sound and vision reached me at virtually the same instant. I felt the shock wave as it washed out over us; debris started to rain down, human remains almost certainly amongst it. The firing had stopped the moment the bomb impacted. Some of my confidence returned.

'Sam, same again.'

As we waited for the repeat strike, Jay unfurled himself and reoccupied his seat, then snatched reverse and put a few metres between us and the enemy.

The second bomb exploded. It was bigger – a 1,000-pounder – and noisier, but the damage wrought seemed to be less, probably because it had been swallowed up by softer ground than the first one, which absorbed much of the impact.

We used the strike to inch away from trouble. The shooting had died down and now we too had reached some sort of safety back round the bend. Continuing in reverse I was about to count my blessings when Colonel Gulzar's white four-wheel-drive came bowling towards us. We were at another impasse. He was trying to go forward and we were desperate to go back, and on the narrow track each was stopping the other from achieving their goal.

'What has happened to my men?' demanded the Colonel.

I wasn't completely sure. I hadn't seen them since the attack began. I assumed they had made it down to the ANA compound.

'They should be safe with the soldiers,' I suggested, before describing the ambush. I kept to myself my certainty that it had been an inside job, with one of the Afghan policemen having tipped off the Taliban about our plans.

I persuaded Gulzar to return to JTAC Hill with the rest of us. But he wasn't content with doing it the easy way. Instead of reversing up as we were doing, he insisted on trying to do a U-turn – with predictable results. I cursed as his car became stuck across our line of retreat. I sat there fuming as his men had to dismount and manhandle the vehicle out of trouble. All the while I had visions of the enemy regrouping and charging down the track with a vengeance, seeking retribution for their comrades killed by the B-1.

*

Back at the hill I sat down in the shadow of a low rampart and undid my body armour. My shirt, dark with sweat, soaked through, was stuck to my chest. I looked down. My breathing was still heavy, my body still trying to get over the physical and mental exertion of the ambush. As I caught my breath I drank greedily from a bottle of water, no matter that it was at about forty degrees. I told Paddy what had happened and explained my suspicion about how it had happened. It seemed clear that any future progress along this road would not be made using vehicles. The ANA still needed to be relieved but it would be done the next day and it would be done on foot. We just couldn't afford to lose the WMIKs.

Almost nostalgically I asked how Simon was getting on down the canal road. Better than us it seemed. Looking south from the southern crossing they had seen two Taliban vehicles on the road close to the 42 northing. Simon and his crew had opened up with .50-cals and GPMGs. Before long one of the enemy vehicles was ablaze. So was the local countryside, a reed bed ignited by tracer rounds. Simon was certain they had killed the vehicle's occupants.

I glanced at my watch. It seemed the last contact had lasted for no more than half an hour. It was possibly the shortest I had been part of since arriving in Garmsir, but we had got through huge amounts of ammo. Sam had fired at least 1,200 rounds from his GPMG. I wasn't far behind.

The other men were still on a real high from the firefight, adrenalin coursing through their veins, talking ten to the dozen, exchanging war stories, enthusiastically pointing out the newly made holes on the wagons, recounting their near misses. The blah, blah, blah, a nervous reaction to what had taken place. They weren't shell-shocked, more exhilarated by what they had been confronted with and endured. And more importantly, escaped from unscathed. Finally the excitement started to wear off and they began to come down from their highs. Brews were made. One by one Jay and the others slipped into contemplative moods.

Later that afternoon I was sitting with Simon and Paddy, arguing about how to relieve the ANA. We were faced with our perennial problem: lack of British muscle. 21 Battery were due to leave at first light, bound for Lash, leaving the three usual suspects holding the fort. Once again KAF had failed to muster a suitable replacement, the idea now was that we would receive some support from a troop of soldiers from the Danish reconnaissance squadron, equivalent in size to a British platoon, some twenty-five men.

'We will still need to get through to the ANA,' I urged Paddy. 'We can't leave them.'

'I know that, but we still have to see what rules of engagement the Danes will be operating under.'

It was a bizarre situation. And a source of endless frustration. We were a multinational force, all on the same side, faced with a common foe, yet the way soldiers from each country did their job was unique, all with national quirks and caveats. It was no good planning a joint op without knowing what your brothers-in-arms could and could not do.

'Is there something we can achieve tonight?' asked Simon, an eagerness in his voice. 'Push through to the ANA under cover of darkness?'

Simon was desperate to help, but he was under orders, and those orders were to return to Lashkar Gah in the morning, sharpish.

'I'm not sure about that,' replied Paddy. 'We don't have night-vision aids and while we might be able to do without them, the Afghans certainly won't. I'm not risking friendly-fire casualties just because our trigger-happy allies can't see in the dark.'

We were interrupted by Gulzar's vehicle swinging into our compound. As he came to a halt I went to meet him; not out of politeness, but because I didn't want him to see all the supplies that were piled up behind us, brought in courtesy of 21 Battery. He would only demand a share of our bounty and, by threatening the removal of the ANP's co-operation, hold us to ransom till he got his way.

Gulzar could barely contain his excitement. 'The Talib are coming north up the track, to collect their dead and wounded. If we head down the western side of the river we will be able to hit them while they are still on the move.'

'How many of them are there?' I enquired.

'Twenty-five, possibly thirty.' Which in Afghan-speak probably meant a dozen or so.

I told the Colonel to wait where he was.

'Paddy, what do you think of the idea?'

'It is worth looking at, but I am not going to let you go out with just the two vehicles again.'

Simon was like the cat that had got the cream. He had been looking for a way to help and now he'd found it.

'Paddy, let me go, too. I'll take my three crews with Doug.'

The deal was done.

'Doug, I have senior rank here, but as far as I am concerned you're in charge.'

'Thanks, Simon. Can you relay to the others that their call signs for this trip are the positions they assume in the convoy as we head out.'

Men scrambled around, gathering ammo and wolfing down their scoff. Someone threw the last of the rounds for the 84mm anti-tank weapon – our equivalent of the RPGs the Afghans were using – into the back of a wagon.

We formed up. I looked back. For the first time in nine days I was leading a contingent of more than a brace of cars and six men. Indeed, my little squad had swollen in size, almost tripled. There were five WMIKs, each with three soldiers and, amongst the machine guns, a trio of .50-cals.

We trundled out along the main street and across the bridge to where Gulzar was waiting. We didn't slow down as he pulled out, immediately trying to overtake us and lead the column. It didn't take long for the enemy to get annoyed with our presence. We were perhaps halfway between the village I had driven through the previous day and the hill fort when firing started from the other side of the river. In retaliation we opened up with a broadside, all five top gunners simultaneously pouring fire across the watercourse. I couldn't resist a small smile. Come on, then, you bastards, do your worst.

I could clearly see three Taliban sprinting along the river back towards a small stone building. I shot at them but was too slow, the rounds impacting just behind them, throwing up dust as they did so. Some of my colleagues had also seen the enemy and had joined the chase. But they were no quicker than I had been and the men reached what they must have thought was refuge.

It was to be the death of them.

Ten rapid-fire weapons, a mix of 7.62mm and .50-cal, saturated the simple mud structure with fire, blasting it to pieces. There was no return fire from the enemy. I could picture the scene, the three of them grimly, hopelessly, scrabbling about on the floor, trying to keep low, looking for any sort of shelter but already knowing they were doomed. I wondered what it must be like for the last of them left alive waiting to die, the others already cut to pieces. Maybe he had pulled what was left of his comrades' bodies up against him in a vain attempt to escape the bullets. He must have been left petrified by the sound of the impacts, all too aware that his meagre protection was disintegrating around him, his fate inescapable. What were his last thoughts? Fear? Helplessness? Loneliness? Horror? Anger that his last decision on earth, to enter the building, had been the wrong decision?

I stopped shooting to change my ammo box. It gave me the chance to scan the rest of the ground across the river. I saw more of the enemy. Several were still moving northwards, at the edge of a cornfield. Others must have been waiting in reserve as we were also getting shot at from a tree-line way south of the now-shattered building.

I needed to allocate specific targets for each gun. I shouted out the arcs of fire to each of the vehicles through the open PRR mic, the firing quickly taking on a more controlled form as the gunners each focused on their own area of responsibility.

Boom. There was a loud explosion from behind us, perhaps sixty metres away, clearly audible over the small-arms fire. We kept engaging.

Boom. There it was again. I was at a loss to understand what was causing it.

Experience told me it wasn't a mortar round. Nor did it have the warbling sound of the 107mm rockets.

There was another explosion. I started to worry they might be rounds from a recoilless rifle (RCL). Not, as it might sound, a weapon spewing out your common or garden 7.62mm bullets, but a piece of kit firing much larger-calibre rounds that, because of the way it worked, was relatively compact and usually mounted on the back of a vehicle. Instead of all the blast being contained in the breech, an RCL allows some of the explosive gases out through the back of the weapon, offsetting the recoil and reducing the kick. The weapons are often used in an anti-tank role. Now I feared they were being used against us.

'I think it must be an RCL,' I shouted to Sam.

'I don't know what it is, but it's getting fucking close.'

A fourth explosion sent up a chunk of road some forty metres in front of us.

There had been some intelligence the Taliban had gained access to recoilless technology. It seemed that info might just be right.

Our contact was visually stunning. Fire and flame was visible, coming from one end of the cornfield. Tracer zipped across the lazy blue river in red dotted lines. Rounds from our underslung grenade launchers were doing damage to a lush green tree-line directly opposite us and all along the enemy positions verdant foliage was spinning into the air, shredded by bullets passing through it.

The small building where we had targeted the three Taliban lay in ruins and was about to become a funeral pyre, a small fire having started in one corner of the shattered shell, flashes of red visible through gaps in the debris.

I estimated we had killed or wounded at least nine of the

enemy. Certainly all fire had stopped from the cornfield and building; our main opposition now came from the south-east.

There was yet another big explosion. We had to go.

It was role reversal. We had been at the head of the column, now we were fifth and last, Sam covering our arses as we pulled out.

I was pretty certain Paddy would be interested in the RCL and so he was.

'Why do you think they're doing this now?' he asked back at the camp, wanting to get my thoughts on the Taliban's use of what appeared to be heavier weapons.

'Well, we haven't been able to dominate the ground in front of our positions since days five and six,' I said, referring to the forays we had made down to the 42 northing. 'The ANP replacements are raw and reluctant to fight, and this morning was a disaster. I think they know we're up against it and want to pile on the pressure.'

My greatest worry was that by using the RCL, the Taliban was now in striking range of the town centre, a position they had not been in for over a week.

Paddy looked serious. 'OK, I had better get on to KAF and tell them the latest good news.'

As he traipsed off to the radio, I headed back to the wagons. Time to count the remaining ammo and redistribute it equally. I checked my GPMG. There was a belt of fifty rounds left in the box. I detached it and slung it in the back. It was Yasir's job to gather together the ammunition odds and sods and clip them together to form a new single belt.

Paddy called out for me.

'What did they say?'

'They want to know where the RCL was being fired from.'

I wasn't completely sure. I took my map from my jacket and, unfolding it, laid it on the ground. I scanned the lines and symbols and pointed out an area to the west of the village of Jugroom. It was my best guess.

'Any other news from KAF?'

'There's information the enemy are sending in reinforcements.'

'Where from? Laki or Koshta?' I named two Taliban strongholds, both about 20 km south of Garmsir.

'Neither. From across the Pakistan border, they think.'

Sod it. Heavy weapons, reinforcements, 21 Battery returning to Lashkar Gah the next morning, us left to hold the baby yet again. Come on the Danes.

As we mulled over this latest twist of fate, Colonel Gulzar appeared in his white jeep – yet again. My heart sank. What on earth did he want now? I wondered. As he stopped and got out, Paddy walked over. I was happy to leave him to it; I had had enough of speaking to Gulzar. Their conversation didn't last long, Gulzar getting back in to his vehicle and Paddy going off to talk to Claus the Estonian, our mechanic.

'Gulzar has found an IED, just over the bridge. Claus says he'll take a look.'

Paddy filled me in as Claus climbed aboard Gulzar's wagon and the pair headed off west.

'Why doesn't Gulzar just do what his colleagues did at the canal crossing? Pick it up and throw it in the river?' I mused.

'Maybe that's what Claus will end up doing,' Paddy replied.

We both had a chuckle. There hadn't been many of those. Not that this was really a good reason to laugh. We had been using the bridge since the day we arrived and only an hour or so ago we must have travelled over the device Claus was now on his way to assess. Perhaps we should have been more careful. Laying mines and booby traps as they withdraw is a favoured Taliban tactic. As at the southern crossing we had been lucky not to be victims of it.

A quarter of an hour later Claus was back, having priced up the job. It was clearly one for him. He started to drag himself into his heavy blast-suit, as Paddy got on the TacSat radio back to KAF to tell the EOD head-shed what was going on. What Claus had found was a device similar to that on the canal road, though on a rather larger scale; six anti-tank mines piled on top of each other, instead of just two. Only the bottom mine was linked to the command wire, but when that went off so would the others. The damage inflicted on anyone travelling past that spot at the time didn't bear thinking about. The explosion wouldn't have dropped the bridge – but would have prevented any vehicles getting across it.

Oddly Paddy received a 'Wait, out' from KAF, meaning they had gone away to think about what we were doing. I couldn't quite understand why. Claus was a bomb-disposal expert and here was a bomb that needed disposing of. QED. He didn't hang about for KAF's answer. A couple of minutes later and he was off, back to the bridge. Another couple of minutes after that and KAF was on the radio again.

'KAF are sending a team down to clear the mines,' Paddy told me.

I looked at him quizzically.

'They say the Estonians don't have the right training for this sort of operation.'

'Well, they had better get here bloody quick because Claus is already on his way and I'm not going to be the one to chase after him and say he isn't up to the job.'

I stalked off, not for the first time baffled by the system. Was this someone just being precious about their job, worried about losing their specialist pay if any old soldier from a former Soviet-bloc country could do the task just as well? I wasn't in the mood to be charitable.

Claus eventually returned, job done, the mines separated and then blown up in a controlled explosion. But he couldn't guarantee there weren't more devices out there. So that was that – the bridge became out of bounds to ISAF troops; we'd have to use a ford in the river some 200 metres further north. Not that this applied to the Afghans. They were not unduly concerned about the possible presence of more devices and continued to race across the bridge in both directions.

KAF was furious about what had happened. When they asked why Claus hadn't been stopped, Paddy explained the Estonian was already on his way before the order came in and, given the nature of the terrain and presence of the enemy, it wasn't practical or safe to go after him. A slight massaging of the facts perhaps, but isn't there a saying that truth is the first casualty of war?

FIFTEEN

THAT WAS CLOSE

(GARMSIR, DAY 10)

It couldn't have been more than forty metres away: a 500lb bomb designed for the enemy almost destined for us.

Lying flat on the roof of the ANA compound, my head in my hands, my body shoved up hard against the low parapet, I had been expecting a near thing, but that was close, much too close.

A tremendous explosion had filled the air and the shock wave reverberated out. The whole building started to shake. I could feel myself lifted into the air, rising in unison with the roof beneath me, before settling back down. The blast took my breath away; there was a ringing noise in my ears. Clumps of soil – some complete with grass and stems of corn still attached – began to rain down on me. So too did a sprinkling of metal; thin shards, ragged chunks, penny-sized pieces of bomb casing jumbled together with bits the size of my hand. There was a pitter-patter as the smaller debris landed around me, punctuated with the heavy thuds of larger items bouncing off the masonry.

I tried to bury myself deeper into the wall, as the dust and dirt covered me.

For more than a week I had been wondering what it would be like to get caught up on the wrong side of one of our air-strikes, scared stiff that it might actually happen. Now I knew as much as I ever wanted to know.

Through the continuous tone ricocheting around my head, I heard Sam shouting into the radio.

'Stop! Stop!' he yelled.

Slowly I raised my head. 'What the fuck happened?' I asked him.

Looking over the wall, I saw the crater made by the bomb. It seemed so close that I felt as if I could have reached out and touched it.

Sam didn't answer me but continued talking to the Harrier pilots.

I shouted down to the Danes and Afghans to see if they were all right. OK, came back the answer. Now there was a voice in my ear, battling to be heard above the ringing. It was Paddy on the radio, real concern coming through. He thought we had been hit. He wasn't far wrong. I told him I would get back to him when I knew more about what had happened.

I was now kneeling on the roof. It had changed somehow. Where it had been flat, it was now completely bowed in the middle.

'Boss,' Sam started. 'The pilot says he had a rogue bomb. The fins didn't deploy correctly. Do you want a repeat mission?'

What a question. The pilots had already levelled one building to the south of us where the Taliban were taking shelter. The bomb that had just gone AWOL – and nearly ended our war – was supposed to have destroyed a second similar house just across the track from the first.

Did I want them to try again? If the pilot was posing the question then he must have been confident the problem was not going to reoccur. I wanted to believe him, but it would be my wife widowed, my children left orphaned, if things went wrong again, not his.

I was losing my nerve. 'I'm not sure, Sam. That was bloody close.'

'Well, they haven't got long on task. Perhaps we should go for target three?'

It didn't take long for me to make up my mind.

'Target three it is.'

'The Harriers have airburst munitions which would be the most effective in the tree-line.'

'Go for it,' I said, glad the decision had effectively been taken out of my hands.

I lay back down to try and calm myself.

Something attracted my attention. Out of the corner of my eye, within arm's reach, I could see a contorted scrap of military hardware. I made a grab for it, and instantly regretted the decision. Silently I shouted out, wincing in pain as the still red-hot fragment burnt a hole first in my glove, and then in my hand. I gritted my teeth, determined not to let Sam know just what an idiot I had been trying to pick it up. There was movement above me.

Two distant arrowheads in the sky.

The Harriers were streaking in on another bombing run. I felt slightly more relaxed. The target was some 300 metres away. They couldn't get this wrong, could they? Sam and I looked out across the lush landscape, down the track, past the buildings, over cornfields, to the trees in the middle distance, verdant because of the Helmand River running nearby, surviving, indeed thriving, despite the desert that extended out beyond them.

Suddenly the tops of the trees shattered in front of us. It was as if the whole canopy was made of glass and someone had thrown a huge rock at it. There was a flash and then fragments of green and brown exploded in all directions from the epicentre of the blast with enormous speed, pursued by smoke. Then they began to slow, before falling idly to the ground.

Sam didn't ask me for my opinion but spoke reassuringly to the pilots. 'Good strike.'

The Harriers had gone. But minutes later their replacements were on station. Two F-16s of the Dutch airforce. It was the first time we had seen the Dutch since arriving in Garmsir. As Sam directed them in I was back on the radio listening to Paddy at JTAC Hill.

'Colonel Gulzar has told me that the local Taliban commander has been killed by your last bomb,' he said. 'He also claims ten of the commander's bodyguards died. The Taliban have been ordered to move back from your location at the ANA outpost and towards the village of Jugroom to set up a new defensive line.'

I noted that according to Gulzar we were now responsible for killing three area commanders since the operation began. Pretty good going, I thought to myself, before reflecting this was like striking off the Hydra's head only to see more appear in its place. Where would it all end?

Before long the Dutch pilots had done their job and gone. It was our turn now. Get out of the compound and clear up.

I went down to the courtyard and spoke to the contingent of Danish soldiers who had advanced to the outpost with me, the Danes who had arrived in Garmsir a few hours previously.

First thing that morning Simon had had to leave, taking with him the men from 21 Battery, plus Steve, as well as the Estonians. Yasir went too, his duty more than done. Simon waited as long as he could but at 09:00 hrs they were off.

21 Battery had only been with us for thirty-six hours but they had made a big difference. Knowing their time was limited they went all-out to shore up our position, even undertaking vehicle patrols the previous night whilst Paddy, Sam and I tried to catch up on some sleep.

Nor was their presence just about a show of numbers. They also appeared to have inflicted a lot of damage. According to Gulzar's – albeit dubious – figures, some thirty Taliban fighters had been killed over the previous two days and four of their vehicles destroyed. We had also pushed the Taliban further south along the river. There was no way of verifying the numbers but without doubt Simon and his men had taken the fight to the enemy.

I shook his hand before he mounted up, thanking him for his support over the past couple of days. Then Claus came up to me. I shook his hand, too. Then Yasir's.

Paddy was concerned 21 Battery's departure would give the Taliban an excuse to go on the offensive. When I heard gunfire from the south I feared he might be right. But this was no attack, more like the Taliban reminding us they were still around.

As the others headed off, Paddy, Sam and I sat where we had spent so much time over the past few days; under the concrete awning of the college. I gazed around and observed a picture of relative calm, but it was all too easy to remember the misery played out in the camp. Over there – the concrete step with the dark stains – was the place a British medic had dealt with critically wounded Afghans, treating them with a whole lot more tenderness and skill than they would have ever received from their countrymen. This was the site where a group of mainly young, impressionable and enthusiastic soldiers had witnessed the grisly horrors of war and become increasingly aware of their vulnerability and remoteness. They hadn't been abandoned by the chain of command, but that didn't stop them sometimes feeling they were off the map, as far as HQ was concerned.

At the far end of the compound the bonfire still smouldered, patches of red glowed amongst the growing pile of cinders; it was our attempt to destroy the evidence of what had happened around us, an attempt to cleanse our environment. But there was no simple way of sanitising our minds. The memories and experiences were there. Fixed. For good.

It was strange though; we had created a routine amongst the misery and squalor. Oh so quickly had the rituals of preparing for battle and fighting for our lives, of coping with terror and exhaustion, hunger and uncertainty, become the framework of our world. None of it had yet taken on an air of the mundane or banal but it had become regular, each day starting and ending in similar ways. And at that moment there was no sign of a break in the pattern. Not that I could very easily imagine going back to my old view of normality – having a pint, watching the footy, reading the paper. What I had once regarded as the usual signs of a normal life now appeared so far away as to be unreachable.

I turned to Paddy, to the familiarity of conflict.

'I think I should try again to get down to the ANA outpost but this time on foot.'

'What will you need?'

'Well, at least five of the Danes when they arrive. Sam with his radio, of course. And Zemar.'

'I'll speak to the Danes when they arrive to see what they can do for us,' Paddy said. 'Are you going to take any Afghans with you?'

I thought it over for a few seconds. 'No, not on this one. I'm still nervous about what took place yesterday. I don't trust them. If Shahrukh were here, then perhaps yes. But I don't think he's back from his village yet.'

Paddy nodded and went off to speak to KAF and Lash to clear the mission.

The Danes rolled into town just after 10:00 hrs, six vehicles in their convoy: four smaller ones, lightly armoured, known as Eagles, and two larger trucks: one carrying supplies, the other housing a medical facility the like of which I had never seen.

It was an emergency room on wheels and seemed a far cry from the stretcher and medical bag Corporal Cowley and the Estonians had had to make do with.

The Danish commander who came looking for Paddy was the spitting image of Harry Potter: small round glasses, young, earnest-looking; a real wizard superstar.

My first impression was he didn't want to be in Garmsir. He and his men were due to leave Afghanistan within the week and it sounded as if he would rather be in Camp Bastion, preparing to do a handover before departing.

I walked away disheartened, leaving Paddy to play the diplomat, soothing Harry's ego and reassuring him they would be on their way sooner rather than later. He then took the commander on the standard patrol of our territory.

While they were gone Gulzar arrived. He was on his own fact-finding mission and wanted to know who had arrived and what they had brought. I was reluctant to enter into conversation with him, knowing from bitter experience that he took any engagement as a signal to stay. But the Danes knew no better. One of them offered Gulzar a Coke, which he gleefully accepted and promptly sat down. He couldn't keep his eyes off the medical wagon. He wanted to know if the facility would be made available to his men should they get hurt.

'Of course,' said the Danish doctor.

Gulzar's face lit up and he gestured for the doctor to give him a tour.

I remained with the other new arrivals as Gulzar was introduced to stethoscopes, defibrillators, syringes and more drugs than you could shake a stick at. The ANP leader was still with us when Paddy returned nearly an hour later. He came to join us, but it was only after Gulzar eventually tired of our company that Paddy was prepared to tell me how he had got on. He was impressed with the Danes and said although they were not under his command, they recognised they were there to support us and Harry was therefore happy for us to have four of his men.

Nor were the Danes the novices in Afghanistan I might have thought. They had spent time in the north of Helmand in the town of Musa Qala during some of the worst fighting there, trying to defend the DC. It emerged the JTAC had had a lucky escape. An RPG had destroyed the command post he was manning on a perimeter wall and he had tumbled out of the compound. Concussed and slightly wounded he lay hidden amongst the rubble whilst the attackers were fended off.

Our stroll finally got under way at 14:00 hrs. Gentlemen's hours.

The group was split into two fire teams. Myself, Zemar, Sam and a Danish medic comprised one. The other was all Danish, led by a young black sergeant. Luckily comms wasn't going to be an issue. They used the same PRR as we did. I ordered the men to travel light, carrying as much water and ammunition for personal use as they could, but little else. This was not about a full-scale re-supply of the ANA, just an attempt to break the siege and perhaps push the Taliban a little further south.

In the full heat of the day we headed off from the bottom of JTAC Hill. After a hundred metres or so I looked back over my shoulder. Both Paddy and Harry Potter stood tall atop the mound surveying the scene, looking every inch like Roman emperors watching as their champions entered the Colosseum. I hoped we weren't marching to our deaths, but I had made sure everyone was prepared for trouble. The Danes were under instruction to fire first and ask questions later if they found themselves in a tight spot. And they weren't just to rattle off a few rounds, but saturate the area with lead so as to put us on the offensive and give me a little time to call in air support if needed.

I gave Paddy the thumbs-up.

For several hundred metres we moved easily, almost relaxed, but after every step the stream – just beyond which we were ambushed the day before – got that bit closer. I felt my chest tighten and my hands begin to sweat.

As we reached the watercourse I held up my arm. The patrol stopped behind me. I gestured for the Danish sergeant to stay with me. I told him to put his team out in an extended line to our left. Then I started to give him ground indications. The point of this was simple. It established landmarks that everyone would recognise and easily relate to. For example: the slightly bent silver birch in the middle distance around 400 metres away became 'tree'. Not only did this pinpoint a specific object, it also, equally importantly, gave its range. Then I explained how we would push forward. One fire team at a time. Either leap-frogging as we went, or concertinaing together and then stretching apart, but without altering which group was in front. This latter movement has the appropriate military name caterpillar.

We moved off.

The butt of my SA80 was in my shoulder, the selector lever in the automatic position. If we were engaged I would point the weapon in the general direction of the enemy and pull the trigger, holding it down until the magazine was empty some four seconds later.

Our progress continued unhindered.

We came up to some buildings. The Danes cleared the first one. Then we jumped past them, making a dash for the second. I wasn't first to reach the door. Getting slow in my old age, I thought, though perhaps that was just the half of it. Maybe I had made an unconscious decision not to be first. I knew I had done well enough in the face of the enemy during my time in Garmsir. I wasn't a brave man but nor was I a coward, and I had not let any of the others do things I wasn't ready to do myself. But was that changing? Was the instinct of self-preservation taking hold? I wanted desperately to leave Garmsir in one piece. Was my hesitation a sign of that wish? If so it was in competition with another emotion. I also had a burning desire to finish the campaign with honour. A quote I had heard, goodness knows where, gnawed away at me. 'A thousand years cannot repair a moment's loss of honour.'

The Danish medic booted his way through the opening, unhinging the woodwork. Everything went quiet. There was no shooting. I followed him in with Zemar. Sam remained outside to inspect a hole in the wall probably caused by one of the air-strikes he had called in.

The room was bare except for a few cooking pots, some straw matting and a couple of multicoloured blankets. There was also something in the corner. Peering into the gloom I could make out an AK47, covered in what seemed to be congealed blood. The mechanism of the rifle looked healthy enough and the barrel was straight. It would probably have worked. But the fold-away metal stock was buckled and split. Looking at the blood it appeared as if the weapon's owner had had his hands on it when the damage was done.

Back outside, a number of well-worn tracks disappeared off into the cornfields around the building. There was little doubt that this was an observation point for the enemy, easily accessible and out of sight of anyone on JTAC Hill. Maybe this explained how the ambush had come about.

I allowed myself to relax again. We were now just 400 metres north-east of the ANA compound and had not been jumped. In my mind the immediate danger had passed – it looked as if the enemy had pulled back.

We continued along the track. With fifty metres to go, the compound was in clear view. There was only one building within it and it was on top of this that an ANA guard was posted. Zemar was wary about standing in the open and shouting at him for fear the guard would respond with a nervous, trigger-happy burst of gunfire. I encouraged my interpreter to make contact by yanking him out into the middle of the road by his shoulder. Another man had joined the sentry on the roof. After a few moments of study he shouted down to Zemar, instructing us to go to the compound's gate. Luckily it was on our side of the perimeter wall. As we approached, it opened, and an Afghan soldier beckoned us in.

The compound and its inhabitants were in a sorry state. The ANA troops were tired and dirty. They were all living in the single room of the single building we had seen from the outside. This was where they slept and ate, and where the commander had his control post. On its roof was the sentry position, made up of a few sandbags and bits of rubble. The ruins of an adjoining wall were the only way to climb up to and down from the vantage point. In another part of the wall a blanket hung limply, hiding a big hole. It was through this that the ANA did their business; I couldn't help thinking the chances of a Taliban round up your arse would prevent you lingering too long reading the *Garmsir Gazette*. In the centre of the courtyard was a small well with a hand pump. Beside it was a pile of poppy heads. It was clear what the soldiers did in their spare moments.

The soldiers started to crowd around us as if we were the answer to their prayers. We weren't. The best we could manage was to offer a little moral support, lend an ear and perhaps mount a patrol forward of their position in a show of strength – or, at least, hopeless optimism.

A gap formed in the closed ranks and a couple more soldiers stepped through. They were holding cups of tea. It would be a bit strong to say I was moved by their hospitality but the brew was certainly very welcome. But their despondency was soon to show through. If Paddy, Sam and I were disillusioned by our own isolation, so too were these ANA soldiers. They resented the rest of their force being pulled out with the OMLT. And there was no doubt they would have gone too if they had had the vehicles, and the confidence they could get back to Garmsir DC without casualties.

I went up on to the roof with the ANA commander. He pointed out where all the trouble lay. The track we had used to get to the ANA compound snaked southwards, through a tree-line that crossed it at right angles just seventy to eighty metres away. Another few metres beyond this were a handful of dwellings, clustered together on both sides of the track. I was told these were being used by the Taliban on a regular basis as forward positions. Further on still were yet more cornfields and then a wood. Behind all of this was the Taliban stronghold of Jugroom.

I asked Sam if he would be happy calling in air support on the buildings immediately in front of us.

'Only if everyone is back here at the compound. And we

would have to be on the roof to assess the attack. It is close but we should be able to do it with the pilots properly briefed.'

That was it, then. We'd go out and put some pressure on anyone who might still be in the huts.

We inched away from the compound; my team to the left of the track, the Danes to the right, led by the sergeant.

I was hunched over, my head pulled down into my shoulders in a vain attempt to make myself smaller, less vulnerable, less visible to prying eyes. The sweat had reappeared in force. For any soldier, moments like these are the worst. Walking towards possible trouble, not knowing exactly who or what is out there, not knowing which one of you the enemy have in their sights. As we came level with some cultivated land, we dropped off the track and down to the edge of the crops.

We came to a slight left-hand bend. The enemy positions were now no more than thirty or forty metres away, but because of the curve I could barely see them. On their side of the road, the Danes had a much clearer view.

'Delta fire team, go firm and cover me as I go forward,' I said over the PRR in a sort of stage whisper.

My progress was snail-like. One slow, slow step after another. My hunched position had morphed into a crouch.

As more and more of the buildings slipped into view I ordered the Danes to start moving again.

Almost imperceptibly I covered the ground, one size nine after another. My back was drenched, my palms moist, my weapon clenched in gloved hands that gave me a degree of grip.

Slowly did it. Easy. Easy.

Then the inevitable.

The silence was broken by a burst of fire from the first building on the left, which was still only just emerging into view. The earth in front of the Danish sergeant erupted into little fountains of dust. Then more bullets came my way, zipping and fizzing through the air, scything through the crops. Instinctively I ducked even lower and pulled my trigger, spewing ammunition towards our attackers. I could hear the Danes doing the same. Within moments my SA80 went silent, the cocking handle stopped at the rear of the weapon, the thirty-round magazine empty.

'Moving!' I yelled, turning to run the way I had just come, allowing those behind me, who couldn't engage because I had been blocking their line of fire, to open up. As I ran I snapped home another full mag.

The exchange had quickly become pretty intense. It was time to decide what to do. Press home our advance or withdraw to the compound and call in the planes. I chose the latter. With five foreign nationals fighting alongside us there was just too much chance of confusion if we went on.

'Delta, this is Charlie. When I throw smoke I want you to withdraw back across the track to me.'

As the phos grenade exploded, the enemy fire increased, the Taliban probably thinking this was a screen for an attack rather than a retreat.

The Danes scrambled across the road in pairs. When they were safely over I gave the order for a withdrawal, fire team by fire team. As I spoke enemy bullets continued cutting through the field, sending bits of corncob, leaf and stalk flying around us. The pullback was one of the scariest things I had done. We were blundering through crops without being able to see our destination. We were going in roughly the right direction but it was still unnerving. The lack of visibility also made it impossible for either fire team to effectively cover the other for fear of shooting them rather than the enemy. We only had forty or so metres to go through the field but it felt more like four hundred. Finally we broke out into the open and made the final sprint back to the compound, the metal door held open for us as we dived through it.

Even as I counted everyone in, the Danes headed straight for the firing ports in the compound walls to support the ANA in case there was any Taliban follow-up assault. I was impressed with how the Danes had acted. They were disciplined and enthusiastic. The sergeant had led well.

I clambered up the wall leading to the roof and our vantage point. Sam was already here. He said two Harriers were overhead but having difficulty pinpointing our position.

'Would it help if I threw smoke?' I asked.

Via Sam the pilots agreed that it would. Whilst the aircraft repositioned for a run south, I dropped off the roof and ran to the metal door, yanking at a spade that had been wedged against the handle to keep it shut. I looked up at Sam.

'Now,' he shouted.

I pulled the door open, removed the pin from the grenade and lobbed it out. A few moments later and it had done the trick.

'Boss, they've got us.'

I headed back to the roof to wait for the bombs.

'We're going back out,' I said to the Danes as the air-strikes ended. 'To see what damage has been done to the buildings.'

This time though we would advance through the crops and not down the track. Our initial objective was the building struck on the first bomb run. The Danes were to check the compound around it for signs of the enemy, whilst my team crossed over and dealt with the building that was the target for the second bomb, which had in fact so nearly done for us.

There was no hanging around. We were out of the door and over to the crops in no time. Once in cover we rushed on, forcing a way through the jungle of stalks. It wasn't stealthy but it did get us out the other side double-quick and meant we could actually see again. Emerging from the field we were almost at the tree-line. A stream ran along it, left to right, heading for a pile of rubble by the track; a pile of rubble that just a short while ago had been offering shelter to the Taliban.

As the Danes peeled off to start their part of the clearance work, we passed the shattered remains of the dwelling on our way across the track. I could see body parts protruding crazily from the bricks and mud; a leg here, an arm there. Was that a piece of skull? It was difficult to work out what belonged to what. Totting up the limbs I reckoned there were two dead. The more the better.

Also interesting was a series of trenches dug under the trees, each big enough to accommodate a couple of men. It dawned on me that they were part of the enemy's front line and the point from which they must have been launching attacks on the western side of the town.

As Sam took up a covering position the Danish medic and I moved down the track, heading for the first building complex on the right. We stopped at a door. One, two, three, I kicked it in. As it gave way we dived inside and found ourselves in a small courtyard. There were two outbuildings. A quick inspection revealed them to be empty. Then our attention turned to a larger longer building, a house or barn.

The Danish medic took out a HE grenade but I shook my head and pointed to the red phos bomb he was also carrying.

He was right – normal practice was to lob in an HE round, then follow it up with gunfire room by room. But we weren't in a normal situation. We didn't have much ammo and almost no support. If there were any enemy inside, then I decided we were going to smoke them out, shooting them as they exited trying to find fresh air.

I took up position by the door; the medic was underneath a small window set high in the wall. On my command we both threw our grenades in and dashed back to a wall by one of the outbuildings to await the results. There were two explosions, almost simultaneous, then sparks flew out of the openings followed by thick white smoke. But nothing else. No sign of the enemy. After two or three minutes the air began to clear and we went back over, entering the house cautiously, not firing but scanning all the corners with our rifles. There was no one there, just a few cooking pots and blankets.

Back outside I reported to Sam. 'Building clear.'

Then there was the sound of gunfire.

'Delta, this is Charlie, what have you got?'

'Enemy moving in the wooded area to the south of us.'

'OK, go firm. Is your building clear?'

'Yes, clear, three enemy dead.'

'Roger, we are now moving forward.'

I covered Sam as he inched along the wall of the next compound. I knelt down as he got to a door and booted it in, before chucking in a grenade and following it up with a burst of fire from his rifle. It turned out to be only a courtyard. There were no dwellings.

Then things hotted up.

Rounds struck the wall close to the door Sam had just gone through. An RPG detonated nearby. The shooting increased, both from the enemy and the Danes.

'Charlie, this is Delta.'

'Send, Delta.'

'We have ten to fifteen enemy moving through the woods in our direction. There are a further ten or so in the cornfield directly south along the track.'

The sergeant was speaking with a high-pitched voice, the sign of someone under pressure. Another RPG detonated, this time close to the Danes. Suddenly Sam came running out of the courtyard door and flung his rifle to the ground, yanking at the straps of his TacSat radio, trying desperately to get it off his back. Seemingly oblivious to the Taliban rounds hitting the ground around him, he ran across the road before taking shelter behind a wall, his arms flailing madly about his head. I couldn't understand what had happened.

'Sam, Sam. Are you OK? What's going on?' I shouted at him.

Furiously he continued to bat the air.

'Sam, for fuck's sake, what is it?'

Finally he replied. 'Fucking hornets, big fucking nest of them. Bastards stung my neck.'

He started to calm down, cautiously moving back to pick up his equipment. I laughed out loud. Here we were in the middle of a major counter-attack, bullets and bombs whizzing all about, and Sam's priority was getting away from some insects. I didn't laugh for long. Things were now getting pretty tight and I could hear the Danes shouting urgently to each other, the enemy making steady progress towards them. And there was nothing in reserve. There was no air cover available. No mortars. And there were only seven of us, Zemar having ducked down out of harm's way, his hands firmly planted over his ears.

I came to the end of yet another magazine. I pulled it out and stuffed it down the front of my jacket before slamming a fresh one home. I released the bolt and it flew forward, collecting another round and feeding it into the breech. The enemy were now within fifty metres of the Danes, a couple even closer than that, almost within grenade-throwing range.

We would have to withdraw.

I looked round to check our line of retreat only to be met with the strangest of sights. Hurrying down the road towards us was a group of ten Afghans all dressed in civilian clothes. Had I not known the man leading them I would have thought the enemy had outflanked us and was attacking from the rear – it was Shahrukh, brown robe flowing about him (what had happened to that bloody police uniform I insisted he wore?), an RPG launcher on his shoulder, a smile on his face.

As he reached me, he dropped to one knee in the sand. Without any proper sort of aim, he fired a grenade in the general direction of the Taliban. His men rushed past.

Then he asked the question I was just about to ask him. 'What are you doing here?' Not for the first time he added, 'This is my fight, not yours. Do not fight again without me.'

It sounded like an order. I briefed him on what was happening as his men excitedly joined the fray. Their firing wasn't accurate but it was extremely heavy and started to turn the tide in our favour. The Talibs who had got so close to the Danes were starting to pull back. As the incoming fire reduced Shahrukh told me I should get my men out. He said he would give us cover before following. I was happy to oblige.

Happy to be rescued by the Afghan I admired most.

I didn't even know he was due back, and I wasn't sure whether he had decided to come to our aid under orders from Gulzar or through his own initiative. Either way I sure was glad to see him.

Back at the compound I promised the ANA commander we would be back the next day with supplies. Then it was straight back to JTAC Hill. I tried to remain vigilant but the adrenalin was wearing off and I started to feel the full weight of the radio and other equipment on my back. Exhaustion came over me in a wave. I began to feel disconsolate. Once again we had been in heavy combat and once again we had gained ground only to give it up.

At last we got back to our starting point. We had only been gone for four hours, but it seemed many times that. The Danish commander came down the hill to speak to his men, but I did not hang around. I jumped into the driving seat of the WMIK, urging Sam and Zemar to follow. We drove the short distance back to the college. I had only one thing on my mind. A cup of tea.

Suitably refreshed I waited for Paddy to turn up. When he did I went through the action. I also told him about the defensive positions we had found and the Taliban's willingness to counter-attack to retake the ground. This seemed to be their line in the sand, the point beyond which they would not retreat. If ever I had any doubt, now it was gone – a very large ISAF force would be required to shift the Taliban and hold Garmsir for any length of time. From what I had seen there was no guarantee it would materialise. As for us, we were only scrapping with the enemy, trying to dominate an area increasingly being dominated by them, making slight progress at the margins, if that. It all seemed so bloody futile.

SIXTEEN

GOING UNDER

(GARMSIR, DAYS 11 & 12)

The morning of day eleven came early in Garmsir. The sound of a 107mm rocket exploding not more than a quarter of a mile away in the town centre shook me and the others from our slumber. In the darkness and only half awake I struggled to find my helmet and body armour; then struggled again to put them on.

For the first time in ten days the Taliban had got close enough to the DC to target it with indirect fire. It was a depressing moment. Most of all I was worried that the members of the local population who had started to return over the past few days would now retrace their steps and abandon the town, unconvinced that either ISAF or the Afghan police and army could guarantee their safety.

Over the next two hours six more rockets landed around us, the closest just a hundred metres away. Keeping our heads down inside the agricultural college we weren't able to locate the source from which the rockets were being launched.

The 107s eventually gave way to mortar fire, groups of three bombs landing followed by a brief lull, then the process repeated. Gulzar had already told me this was the Taliban way of doing things prior to the initial loss of the town on 9 September.

Things seemed as bad as at any time since we had arrived.

Being stretched so thinly I had not had a chance over the previous few days to get to the east of the town and reassess the situation there. I was not even sure how many members of the ANA and ANP were now in the area. My best guess was twenty-five Afghan soldiers spread between the northern canal crossing and the southern outpost we had been at the day before. I reckoned there were about fifty policemen manning positions at the eastern and southern canal crossings, JTAC Hill, the bridge over the river and serving as Gulzar's private bodyguard.

But I was about to have to do a recalculation. An ANP pickup swung into the college grounds, followed by Gulzar's vehicle. They both barrelled over to the Danish medical truck. In the back of the lead vehicle was a policeman who had been shot in the leg at the southern canal crossing. He screamed in pain as the Danish doctor and medic manhandled him towards their mobile surgery. The doctor reached for a syringe and jabbed it, stabbed it, into the man's other leg. Within moments the morphine worked its magic, the patient quickly quietening down.

I watched the goings-on from a small wall, the medic writing down details to pass to Paddy so he could send his nine-liner back to KAF. The doctor categorised the policeman as a T1 casualty, giving him the highest priority for evacuation. The victim had been shot in the thigh, the bullet exiting just below his buttock. He was losing a lot of blood.

As the medical drama unfolded in front of me I took the chance to speak to Gulzar, and asked him for the loan of some trucks that afternoon to help with the re-supply of the ANA southern checkpoint.

'Why don't the ANA use their own vehicles? I have no fuel,' he complained.

Fucking people, here we go again. Bargaining, bartering, haggling, when they should have been offering. Weren't we all supposed to be on the same bloody side?

'I will give you some fuel, but you know the ANA vehicles are all up at the northern canal crossing.'

Gulzar gave me a quizzical look. 'Will they send a helicopter to get my man out?'

'Of course they will, so what about the vehicles?'

Reluctantly Gulzar finally agreed to the loan of one truck that he would send down to us at 14:00 hrs.

As we finished our bit of business Paddy walked over to the medical facility.

'Doctor, KAF want you to explain the casualty's injuries and why you have categorised him T1,' he said, looking embarrassed at having to make such a request.

The robustness of the doctor's response took us both by surprise.

'I will not explain to them,' he said unhappily. 'I am a doctor and I have made my diagnosis. If we don't get the Immediate Response Team here soon this man will lose his leg. If they take any length of time at all then he will die from loss of blood and I will make a formal complaint to my HQ.'

He turned his back on Paddy to continue work on the injured man. Paddy had no choice but to go back to the radio and pass on the message.

I could hear the doctor mumble to the medic, 'How dare they question my ability and judgement? I am the one with the patient in front of me, not them. Let them come and live in this shit hole and maybe they'll have a different view on how things work here.'

I couldn't help but think he was right. There were too many people further up the chain trying to control things without listening to what the ground commander was saying. It reminded me of my time serving in Northern Ireland. Back then it was the job of those in the Ops Room to give advice when an incident occurred but not to question the decisions being made at the scene.

Paddy came back over with news of the IRT. 'They will be

lifting within ten minutes and should be here within half an hour.'

Next he spoke to Harry Potter and asked if the Danes could deal with the casevac as he didn't have enough of us to do the job properly. Besides, we had to prepare the re-supply of the ANA. Harry agreed.

The Apaches arrived first, taking up positions over the town while they waited for the Chinook. On board that would be the medical team, normally one doctor and a couple of paramedics. Also on board – half a platoon from the QRF. They'd have the job of securing the landing-zone perimeter whilst the casualty was loaded.

The Chinook loomed into view, dropping out of the sky towards the ground. From where I was watching I could see a huge dust cloud rise up to meet the aircraft as it descended. The nose reared up as it came in to land, the helicopter crouching on its haunches before the front also settled, the whole grey/green monster disappearing into the blanket of sand thrown up by the tremendous double set of rotors. No more than three or four minutes later and the helicopter lumbered into the sky, turning to point back the way it had just come. High above, the attack helicopters took their cue and also turned for home, keeping the mother ship safely between them, covering her trip back to Camp Bastion.

The day drifted on and we heard more news over the radio of the RIP ('Relief in Place') where the new arrivals of 3 Commando Brigade were taking over from the soldiers of 16 Air Assault Brigade. It was this complex changeover, so the bosses had us believe, that had prevented us being adequately supported. Finally the topic of conversation turned to us and Paddy was told when our replacement would take place.

'Doug, the new OMLT is made up of 3 Commando and is due to leave for Garmsir in the morning. They hope to be with us by last light.'

'What about us?'

'Not sure yet, they haven't decided how long we need to stay on.'

The reality was it would probably be days rather than hours. There was quite a handover to give. As for the Danes, their squadron commander out in the desert west of Garmsir wanted to see his men depart the next day, but we were not keen on that. It would leave us with only the men from the OMLT, who would be unfamiliar not just with the town, but also Afghanistan, and would have no experience of working with either the ANA or the ANP.

I left Paddy to mull over the permutations. The ANP truck had arrived and with Zemar's help I filled it with fuel, before transferring the ammo, food and water for the ANA. Standing watching were the two policemen who came with the vehicle, cigarettes lolling in their mouths.

'Zemar,' I yelled. 'Tell these men that if they don't start helping I will speak to my good friend General Durani and get him to cut off their hands.'

The effect was as good as I could have hoped for. I had been half-joking but it seemed the men took the threat seriously. The cigarettes dropped to the ground and they began shoving equipment and supplies into the back of the Land Cruiser. Perhaps Durani's reputation for ruthlessness wasn't just an urban myth.

With Paddy briefed, it was not long before our two-vehicle convoy was ready to go – me driving the WMIK in front, with Sam up top manning the machine gun, and Zemar in the commander's seat. We stopped for a few moments at JTAC Hill to tell the policemen they were not to fire south under any circumstances for fear of shooting us in the back. I was fairly confident our route would be trouble-free. I couldn't see that the Taliban would have moved back this far north since the skirmish the day before, and anyway ANA runners had been going up and down the track all day without incident.

I was proved right. After ten uneventful minutes we reached the ANA position. A sentry out on the track shouted to his colleague on the roof of the compound building, warning of our arrival. We got directed to the north perimeter wall where I reversed the WMIK up against it, the ANP doing the same with their vehicle. Soldiers came out to offload what we had brought. They still looked haggard, tired and dirty, but at least the supplies brought a little smile to their faces.

The ANA commander appeared. He explained that things had been pretty quiet since we left. There had been the odd bit of shooting from the wood, but no RPG attacks. Patrols he had been sending out seemed to have prevented the Taliban getting back to the tree-line and occupying the trenches.

As we stood talking, a vile pungent smell got up my nose. At first I ungraciously put the blame on the man standing next to me, but I soon realised I was wrong. The odour was that of rotting flesh, coming from the bodies of those we had killed twenty-four hours previously and that the sun had gone to work on since, putrefying them with its heat.

Just before my mind wandered off, imagining bloated corpses and pecked-out eye sockets, there came the all too familiar sound of gunfire. Incoming gunfire. Rounds landing close by.

The commander and I dived for cover behind the compound wall, Sam not far behind.

'I don't believe this, Sam. Here we go again.'

'You know what, boss, I'll be happy when you leave Garmsir. You're a fucking bullet magnet.'

We both started laughing before making a dash for the WMIK. Him to get on the TacSat to call in air support. Me to man my machine gun.

I didn't think this was a proper assault, just harassment, but I decided a show of strength would reassure the ANA and convince them we were taking their predicament seriously.

Sam began to draw up a target list as I engaged the enemy through a cornfield, expending 200 rounds just like that.

The F-16s did their job. After two bomb runs, hitting positions along the tree-line where the trenches were, the jets screamed southwards to hit buildings closer to the village of Jugroom. I wanted the Taliban to see we could also cut off their line of retreat and so encourage them to get out of the area while they still could. It seemed to work. The incoming fire slowed to a trickle and then dried up.

'You know what, Sam. When I get out of here I am going to get some simple sort of job. Be a milkman perhaps or a postie.'

'I can't see it, boss. I don't think you will leave the army. I can see you coming back here again sometime.'

We said our goodbyes to the commander and promised to come back again the next day. He asked us to bring some bread. We said we would. The ride back to JTAC Hill and then the college passed smoothly enough. Back at base Paddy was trying to work out how our own RIP would work.

'Doug, I've now got some sort of plan from KAF.'

'So what is it? Are we flying or driving out?'

'Once the OMLT gets here tomorrow evening we are to give them a handover as best we can. Then the next morning we head out with the Danes to meet the rest of their squadron before driving north to Lash. When we are nearby, a patrol from 21 Battery will come out and pick us up, leaving the Danes to continue to Bastion. Got it?'

Well, it was a plan, though it wouldn't leave much time for the OMLT to become familiar with the ground before they were on their own.

'Are we all leaving, then?' I asked, already knowing the answer.

'No. Sam stays.'

Paddy could see the disappointment in my eyes. 'You know how valuable JTACs are. He'll have to remain for another three or four days until it's time for him to leave theatre.'

It wasn't my fault he was being left behind but it might as well have been, given the way I felt. Sam had shared every experience with me. For the past twelve days he had done everything asked of him, not once complaining. He was as good a serviceman as you will find anywhere. We had survived countless dicey moments and now I was abandoning him – or so it seemed to me.

After Paddy finished the briefing, I went over to break the news to Sam. He seemed pretty sanguine about the whole thing.

'Don't worry about it, boss. If I wasn't here then I would be somewhere else,' was all he said.

The day ended as it had started. More rocket attacks and more mortars. Also heavy firing from the direction of the southern canal crossing. It appeared that because of our success in the west the Taliban were concentrating their efforts in the east. Twenty-four hours later and we'd find out just how dear this would cost us.

Hurry up and wait. That was what most of day twelve had been like. The Taliban did their best to keep us on our toes with more mortars and rockets, but for most of the time I sat around in the sun, listening to the radio over which we heard regular updates on the progress of our relief.

Their route was similar to the one we had followed almost two weeks before and the problems they were encountering were similar too. Vehicles bogged down in the sand, mechanical faults. At one stage the Pinz with most of their supplies in broke down. The OMLT asked if they could abandon their attempt to reach us till it was fixed. The request was denied, running repairs were made and they soldiered on. This made for painfully slow progress.

Last light had now passed and we continued our vigil by the radio, waiting for word that the convoy was almost with us. Finally it came. They were within five kilometres of the DC.

'Doug, could you go out and see them in?' asked Paddy.

'No problem,' I instinctively answered, though after a few moments consideration I decided I was not particularly happy to be driving out into the desert with just the one vehicle. Too late now though.

I heaved myself to my feet and called out, 'Sam, mount up.'

I shouted for Zemar too. He looked far from eager, dragging his heels, talking to the Danes.

'Zemar, whenever you're ready, please.'

We melted into the darkness of the unlit town with just our convoy lights on so as not to give away our movement to too many prying eyes. I could see just about nothing. I attempted to follow what I thought was the middle of the road on the assumption that at least there I was unlikely to hit anything or anyone. The night was clear and the stars out, but the moon was not giving us any ambient light.

We got to the eastern checkpoint and turned left. I jumped out to talk to a policeman before we continued north, warning him that an ISAF and ANA convoy would be coming his way in the next hour or so.

The canal road was treacherous. To the right was a steep drop down to the water; on the left, an only slightly shallower slope down into fields. I was scared stiff of coming off the road so I turned on the sidelights – bugger the tactical implications, I wasn't going to end my time in Garmsir upside-down in a ditch waiting to drown as others had done before me. During the invasion of Iraq in 2003 a Household Cavalry Regiment vehicle left the road and rolled over into some water – the driver and commander both died. Not a glorious way to go. What a waste.

It took us about a quarter of an hour to get to the northern checkpoint, before pulling in beside the ANA command post. Sitting in the darkness I allowed myself a few moments to think about what had gone before. It seemed an age since we first assaulted this crossing, me with my machine gun firing wildly. Then there was the Talib I shot as he came out of the cornfield, a cornfield we must have just passed but that I failed to notice in the inky night. I wondered if he had had a proper burial? I hoped he had, wished his body hadn't become the stinking rotten mess we had experienced the previous day.

My melancholic contemplation was broken by Paddy's voice on the radio. The OMLT were now only about a kilometre away but unsure as to which track would lead them to our position. Could I set up a signal to guide them in?

I drove over the crossing and out beyond the checkpoint. There was no way I could use sidelights here so progress along the rutted track was painfully slow. After about 400 metres I decided we had gone far enough. Sam agreed. I radioed Paddy and told him we had gone firm and would light a firefly to guide the others towards us. A firefly is a strobe-light which is commonly used for calling in aircraft at night. When fitted with an infrared cover it is only visible through night-vision goggles. That's what the OMLT would need.

I strained to hear the sounds of vehicle engines. The night was peaceful; a slight breeze brought a refreshing change from the harsh heat of the day.

We sat in the darkness for a while, me holding the light up at arm's length. After several minutes I handed the baton over to Sam and turned the WMIK round to face the way we had just come. For some reason we couldn't get comms with the OMLT even though they could only have been a couple of hundred metres away. It was left to Paddy to tell me they had seen the firefly and were closing in on it. I peered out into the night but still couldn't see anything. I couldn't hear much either. I didn't want a meeting out here in the middle of no-man's land so I started to drive slowly – given the terrain it wasn't going to be any other way – back towards the crossing. At the checkpoint I pulled up once again and waited to see what happened.

Finally I made out our relief. First of all I saw the silhouette of a British Land Rover, and then the detail on it started to appear. Beyond it more vehicles slowly materialised. I turned off the light as a young captain came over to say hello. I shook the hand he offered but there wasn't really the time for pleasantries. I wanted to get us safely into town, dropping the ANA off at a pre-designated bit of hard standing, by a derelict petrol station, on the way. There were twenty vehicles in the convoy. This time any inability on my part to stay on the straight and narrow would be compounded many-fold. I put the sidelights back on. Not that my halogens were the only thing illuminating the darkness. Some six kilometres south I could see the telltale streaks of tracer; incoming fire aimed at the ANP position, marking the night sky. By the volume of it the policemen were having a torrid time.

I called Paddy. 'Sandstone 78, this is Widow 77.'

'Send, over.'

'We have a lot of fire in the area of the southern crossing.'

'Roger, Widow 77, there's also heavy fire aimed at the ANA southerly compound.'

This was something we hadn't seen before – a sustained attack on both sides of our southern front line. We came to the point where we needed to turn right down the main street. I halted the convoy, got out of the driver's seat, and jogged back to speak to the Commando captain. I ordered him not to fire south as we had friendly forces down there and I didn't want a blue-on-green incident. I went back to my vehicle and we moved off again. At the very same moment some of the tracer we witnessed far off to our left started to land in the DC, rounds striking buildings to our right.

'Sandstone, this is Widow. Contact. Wait. Out.'

I needed Paddy to open a TiC. More than likely we were going to need air support. Paddy responded saying rounds were also now landing on the agricultural college. JTAC Hill was also being hit. The counter-attack could not have come at a worse time. We were in no position to send OMLT forces to either of the besieged locations and the Afghans manning them were at their lowest ebb, weak and demoralised from not having been properly supported or relieved for more than seventy-two hours. And, without other troops operating in the south of Helmand, the Taliban had had free rein to bring in their own supplies and reinforcements for this offensive.

Halfway down the main street I glanced over my shoulder, but couldn't see the OMLT. Where the fuck had they got to? I stopped abruptly and ran back to try and find them. After a hundred metres or so I came across the captain. He explained one of the ANA vehicles had crashed and the convoy had split in two. Not good news.

'Look, just leave it and we will come back tomorrow. Just get your column re-formed and get moving.'

We set off again, trying to keep tight against the buildings on the left to protect us from the incoming from the south. Further ahead there was a big gap in the buildings where several had been demolished. Through the opening, enemy tracer was zipping into the DC. I was pretty certain this was by accident rather than design. The Taliban were probably aiming at JTAC Hill or the ground to the south of the town but their aim was in all probability so poor that much of it was ending up here. I raised Paddy on the radio. He reported fire was still heavy at the college and that he would call us back when there was a lull.

We sat and waited. Finally the all-clear came through – as did news from Sam.

'Boss, a B-1 should be overhead anytime now. Got any targets for him?'

'Not yet. I need to speak to Paddy back at base and find out exactly what is going on.'

Once more we crept forward, directing the ANA to their overnight lie-up as we went. Back at the college Paddy greeted the OMLT and showed them where to park. I was just about to climb on to the roof of the college when I got caught in the full beam of a pair of headlights. Gulzar was back.

'Zemar, go and tell him to turn the bloody things off.'

Gulzar barged past Zemar, leaving the interpreter to talk to the driver, and made straight for me, talking furiously, his arms waving madly. I didn't have a clue what he was on about.

'Zemar, over here.'

He hurried back and translated matter-of-factly. 'Colonel Gulzar says the southern crossing has fallen. There are now no Afghan policemen there, just Talib.'

There was more.

'All the ANP have now pulled back to the eastern crossing, which the Taliban are now advancing on. Everything south of this is lost.'

I didn't know what to say. It was a bloody disaster. It had taken two days to seize the southern crossing and for another ten days we had grimly held on to it. Now, just as we were about to get more forces, the Taliban had seized their opportunity and recaptured it. We were back to square one. What a waste of time.

'Colonel, confirm that you have no forces at the southern crossing?'

'No ANP, just Talib.'

At least that gave me my target for the B-1.

I gave Sam the grid reference for the crossing to pass on to the pilot a mile above us, telling him I wanted a 2,000lb bomb dropped on the bastards. There was just time to get on the roof to view the ground south before Sam shouted, 'Stores.'

I couldn't see the crossing itself but I knew in which general direction to look. I gazed out, not wanting to blink, reluctant to miss anything. There was a huge flash that illuminated the ground for hundreds of metres around. Two or three seconds later and the noise of the explosion rolled over us. Paddy and the members of the OMLT had stopped talking and were looking towards the source of the blast.

'Good strike,' I shouted to Sam, calling for a repeat mission.

This time several of the OMLT joined me on the roof. For most if not all it was the first time they had seen something as destructive as this. The second strike was just as mesmerising. All our good work building defensive positions had just gone up in smoke – with more than a few of the enemy too I hoped.

I called in two more attacks, this time on buildings close to the crossing. After the final one, all firing from that direction seemed to stop, as did the shooting from the south-west.

The B-1 had reminded the Taliban fighters of their mortality. They slipped away into the blackness. But there was no doubting who would be happier with the evening's events and it was not us.

For the OMLT and the ANA it had been a harsh introduction to the realities of Garmsir and I doubted things would appear much better when daylight arrived. The new arrivals would have to pick up the pieces, trying to retake the ground to the south and east. If it wasn't done soon, then the crossing at the end of the main street would be liable to fall too and then the whole town would follow. I didn't want to think about that.

It was only 21:00 hrs and it promised to be a long night, waiting for further enemy attacks. I was exhausted. For two weeks we had soldiered on, first gaining, but then losing, ground. I had nothing left to give. The fight was going out of me. I resigned myself to a wretched journey back to Lash.

Paddy did his best to offer some help to the new arrivals and asked KAF if we and the Danes could be allowed to stay for another twenty-four hours to help shore up the defences. The answer was a blunt no.

I lay in my sleeping bag, turning things over and over in my head. What if I had been braver? What if I had been more measured? What if we had had more resources? What if I had been more competent? What if? What if? What if? There was no end to it and I kept coming back to my own perceived failings. I couldn't shake off a feeling of guilt. Guilt at leaving when there was still work to be done. Guilt at leaving the Afghans when I, we, had promised them so much. For them there was no escape. Where could they run to? This was their territory, their home. They would be left to clean up any mess long after I was on a plane home. 'Inshallah' – 'God's will'. It was a phrase the Afghans used endlessly to philosophically explain the twists and turns of their difficult lives. But I couldn't help thinking God had abandoned Garmsir and the Afghan defenders a long time ago. All I had done was give them hope – when there was none. I drifted off into a fitful sleep; would it be my last in Garmsir?

SEVENTEEN

PULLING OUT, GOING BACK

(GARMSIR, DAY 13)

Shahrukh wrapped his arms around me in one of those infamous Afghan bear hugs. He clapped me on the back, then released me, the usual broad grin fixed across his face. Through Zemar I was reminded once more that this was his fight and not mine. I was not to go getting into trouble again.

What was there left to say? Of all the Afghans I had come across, Shahrukh stood head and shoulders above the rest. Brave, loyal, fierce, honourable, entertaining. I wished him well. It was as if I had known him for a lifetime. Indeed, the past fortnight in Garmsir seemed almost that.

I also got a hug from Colonel Gulzar.

His parting words were a reminder, too: 'Don't forget to get General Durani to send more supplies and men.'

I nodded.

'Oh, and my medal.'

The pair of them walked away, and I turned my attention to the WMIK. What a state it was in – covered with ragged puncture marks, the result of shrapnel strikes. Dotted between them were signs of the damage done by bullets. I studied the commander's seat, my eyes dwelling on the headrest and the two innocent-looking holes caused by the rounds that could just as easily, back on day nine, have taken off my head had I not been leaning forward to fire the GPMG. On such brief moments does one's fate rest. Stepping back I saw all the antennae had long gone, shot off by the enemy, yet the Land Rover was still serviceable. If only she could survive one last journey and get me back to Lash.

I climbed into the seat on the driver's side. Paddy did the same on the passenger side. Zemar had already clambered into the back where Sam would usually have been, the machine gun normally mounted there removed for the trip home. We waved at Harry Potter to say we were all set for departure. A red smoke signal went off on the far side of the bridge across the Helmand River where the rest of the Danish squadron was waiting for us. In reply Harry set off a green smoke grenade and we pulled out of the college for the last time. Quite why all this manoeuvring couldn't have been arranged by a few words on the radio was beyond me. Talk about advertising your presence. And quite why the rest of the Danes needed to display themselves by the bridge at all, rather than remain a few kilometres out in the desert, was another mystery. We had shown our hand to anyone who happened to be watching. This wasn't a surreptitious withdrawal, rather an invitation to the enemy to come out and cheer.

As we headed out into the emptiness, leaving behind the blue of the water and green of the vegetation, there wasn't much talking going on in our wagon. Paddy* and I had both become lost in our own thoughts, not worried about navigation, happy to follow the tyre tracks of the vehicle in front. For a while I dwelt on whether what we had done in Garmsir should be judged a

---

* Paddy Williams of the Blues and Royals quite deservedly received a Military Cross for his time in Afghanistan. Tommy Johnstone was mentioned in dispatches. But to my great disappointment our JTAC Sam New was never recognised for his magnificent efforts in Garmsir. If one person showed the utmost calm and professionalism under fire, on a daily and sustained basis, then it was him.

success or failure, but the further away we got from the town the more I started to think of the future. I was looking forward to my R&R, just seven days away. As we trundled away from trouble I began to relax, something I had not done for almost a fortnight.

The General stood in front of Colonel Charlie Knaggs's desk. It was forty-eight hours since I had left Garmsir and Durani had arrived with the news I feared.

'Now we only hold JTAC Hill and the eastern crossing. The OMLT refuse to stay in the centre of the town and instead have made the northern crossing their base.'

And there was worse. Colonel Gulzar had threatened to withdraw unless more reinforcements were sent; and the relationship between the ANA and the ANP was at rock bottom, the former believing members of the latter murdered one of their number whilst out on a patrol.

The General believed there was a simple solution: 'Send Beattie back. He understands how to fight the Talib. He's brave and knows how to work with Gulzar and Shahrukh.'

I was in demand and I didn't like it.

Charlie Knaggs wasn't keen either but he recognised something had to be done if we weren't to lose the town completely. He wanted to know if I would be willing to return to Garmsir for two days. Willing wasn't quite the right word. I asked Paddy's advice and he was adamant – I shouldn't go. But I ignored him. Against my better judgement I said yes. It was an offer I could not in reality refuse. Did they understand the guilt and responsibility I was carrying for what had happened in that town? There was no way I could really decline. They had tapped a raw nerve whether they knew it or not. I wondered what Margaret would think if only she knew?

The next day started early with a flight out of Lashkar Gah by Chinook, headed not north to Bastion or east to Kandahar, but back south to Garmsir. I wasn't alone. Travelling with me were twenty-five Afghan National Army soldiers, replacements for the world-weary ANA troops I had been trying to cajole and encourage just a few days earlier, who would now make the return trip to their base at Shorabak, near Camp Bastion.

The landing zone we touched down at lay close to the northern canal crossing. A driver in a pickup truck was already waiting for me. I jumped in beside him and we made the short, bumpy journey to the checkpoint. There to greet me was a two-man welcoming committee comprising the young OMLT captain I had led through the darkness upon his arrival, and Sam.

Matter-of-factly the captain gave me a quick rundown on how things had deteriorated even further since our departure. As we spoke it became clear he was not happy to see me. He was brusque to the point of rudeness and wouldn't look me in the eye. I could tell he didn't regard me as a saviour but rather as a sign of his own inability to have regained the initiative. As far as I was concerned, the situation was no reflection on him, but that wasn't how it looked from where he was standing. What else came through though was the OMLT's distrust of the ANP in general and Colonel Gulzar in particular. It did not bode well for the immediate future. To a degree I understood the captain's reservations. Indeed I had some, too. But without some form of working relationship between the parties the whole thing was going to turn to dust.

In silence we drove to the DC. The main street was like a ghost town. It was as if all life had been snuffed out. No bakery, no teashop, not a civilian in sight, not even a dog or cat. It wasn't that the town was more badly damaged than when I left – it was in ruins then – but devoid of people it was a shapeless heap of bricks and rubble, rather than the focus of human activity it had once been. The remaining buildings looked lost and mournful.

It was a completely depressing sight.

As we got closer to the agricultural college my hopes were briefly raised as I saw a group of Afghans standing beside the road. Were these the locals I was looking for? They weren't.

They were policemen. My disappointment eased however when I recognised the man in the middle of the huddle. Shahrukh. As we passed I waved and he grinned back.

In the shadow of the college overhang I talked tactics with the OMLT captain. In my mind it was clear we needed a military success to boost morale. I suggested I lead an attack the next day to try and take back the southern crossing. I wanted to take Sam and two more of the OMLT troops with me, plus a handful of the ANP. He agreed to the plan. So did Gulzar. This time we would not drive to our target, careering down the canal road. We'd be going on foot.

An ANP pickup dropped us off halfway down the main street and we worked our way through gaps in the buildings till we had sight of open country. Shahrukh was in the lead with eight policemen; I was behind them with Sam. In the distance I could already see our first objective, the small U-shaped farm complex we had withdrawn to for lunch on the second day and from which point we then launched our chaotic charge on to the canal crossing, my WMIK in front, Chipper's behind.

It was a strange, very uncomfortable feeling, being about to fight for the same ground once more. So much hard work had already gone into securing these positions, and what for? The less than welcome chance to do it all over again. I hated the thought. Had we not already used up our share of Lady Luck? Would the gods smile on us so favourably again?

The answer quickly came.

No more than twenty metres out from the DC, heading south, and the enemy opened up on us from the far side of the canal. I looked around for cover. There was a wall away to my right, not that high. I ran at it and tried to vault over. As I did so the mud started to crumble and the whole thing gave way. I collapsed with it, tumbling, plunging into a deep dry drainage ditch on the other side – head first. I lay there winded, staring up at the sky. My right hand throbbed in pain. I struggled to catch my breath and raised my arm to assess the damage. Two of my fingers jutted out at chaotic angles, still straight, but clearly dislocated. I tried to focus in on my nose, only to go cross-eyed as I looked down it. Even so there was no doubting that it too was bent, blood streaming from it. I could feel a range of cuts and scrapes across my cheeks and forehead. My chin ached, as if someone had just caught me with a perfect uppercut. On top of it all I felt dazed, confused and nauseous, probably from concussion. It was all pretty minor stuff, embarrassingly minor, but it seemed as if my war was over at least for the time being.

I sat where I was, trying to regain my senses. I didn't protest when Sam and Shahrukh slid down the bank to haul me out. What would I have done without this pair to look after me?

They led me back to the shelter of the buildings on the edge of the town and less than ten minutes after clambering out of an ANP pickup, I was helped back into one. I was annoyed at myself; and ashamed. My triumphant return to Garmsir had come to a shuddering halt and now I had to leave my colleagues to get on and do a job I had suggested and should have been sharing.

On our return to the college the Estonian doctor sauntered over to assess my wounds. He decided to put the fingers back in place there and then. While a soldier sat on my legs as I lay on the ground, he grabbed hold of one of my fingers and gave it a sharp tug, before letting it spring back into its proper position. Before I was able to protest, he had done the same with the second. Then he splinted them together with a small bit of wood that looked like a lollipop stick. Next he examined my nose. It was sitting at a strange angle – even more crooked than the time I had broken it as a youth – and refused to stop bleeding. Kneeling in front of me he grasped it with his hand and gave it a yank. As he guided it back into place, my eyes started to water and a squeal of pain escaped my lips.

'There you go,' he said. 'Much more handsome now.'

Well, that's what I wanted to believe he was saying, though as the words were in his native tongue I didn't have a clue.

All he had left to do was a bit of cleaning up. He dabbed at the abrasions with disinfectant. The patching-up done, I sat back and waited to be evacuated out. Because of the concussion I was classified a T3 casualty. But I felt a fraud. For almost two weeks I had watched day in, day out, as any number of injured Afghans were brought to the base, many with horrific injuries. Several would die, most would be horribly maimed. Where did I measure on their scale of suffering? Absolutely nowhere, that's where.

Two hours later I was told a helicopter from the IRT was inbound and I needed to be moved to the LZ (landing zone). I wondered whether I would be the only one flown out. As I waited for the aircraft an Estonian vehicle charged up, an Afghan policeman laid out in the back. He had been shot in the face; there was blood pouring from his mouth and down his chin. He struggled to breathe. I knew who he was. Shahrukh's bodyguard.

'What happened?' I asked one of the Estonians, not really wanting to hear the answer. But it came anyway.

'Two ANP killed and this one wounded.'

A strap tightened across my chest.

A moment or two later and Colonel Gulzar arrived to oversee the evacuation of his man. I wandered over to him. There was no Zemar on hand to translate but I knew he knew what I was after.

I stretched out my arms, palms raised, a quizzical frightened look on my face. 'What happened?' I mouthed Shahrukh's name.

He replied with the same word before shaking his head, a sadness in his eyes. There was nothing more to be said, at least nothing either of us would have understood.

Later I found out what had happened. Shahrukh had been killed during an assault on a building overlooking the canal crossing.

I just couldn't believe it. The one Afghan I had truly come to admire, dead doing the task I had set for him; a task I should have been sharing except for that fucking wall. I wanted to cry.

Stress and frustration welled up in me. The emotion was ready to burst. For two weeks he and I had shared the hairiest of moments. Now, right at the very end, when I was not there, unable to help, he had died doing what he always did – leading by example, from the front. I felt like a child in need of comforting, as if I had lost a relative. But there was no one to turn to; I was left alone with my thoughts and my anguish. I swallowed back my tears.

On the flight to Bastion the medical team worked furiously to keep the policeman alive. There was nothing else for me to do but sit and watch. Watching too were a dozen men from 3 PARA who made up the QRF. They also glanced in my direction, plainly wondering just what was wrong with me, comparing the few cuts and bruises on my face to the bullet hole in the Afghan. I didn't want to return their gaze. I tried not to meet their eyes. Whatever good I might have done in Garmsir over the previous two weeks, whatever progress we'd made, whatever bravery I might have shown, it had all been eclipsed by the death of Shahrukh. For me it was as personal as it could get. Christ, I had always known war was bad. Terrible things happen. But why now? Why him? Why not me? They are the same basic questions all soldiers ask themselves. And are never able to answer.

EIGHTEEN

GOING HOME, GOING TO THE PALACE, GOING BACK AGAIN

On 13 January 2007 I completed my last mission in Afghanistan.

On 14 January I left Kajaki in the north of Helmand.

On the 15th I left the province.

A day afterwards I left the country.

Another twenty-four hours beyond that and I was in my living room with Margaret, drinking a glass of wine, about to begin four weeks' leave. And that was it. From the front to home in a blink of an eye.

For me there had been no decompression stop-off in Cyprus as there was for the boys from 3 PARA. No chance to drink beer on the beach, to lark about with my mates, to vent my emotions by scrapping with the others. There were no lectures on combat stress, no information on post-traumatic stress disorder, no one to talk to about shared experiences. I was on my own. Except for my family.

And how could I tell them about bayoneting a man in the neck? About living with perpetual fear? About calling in airstrikes on men you know are probably already mortally wounded? What would they say?

I was terrified of Margaret's reaction. I could see she was

desperate to know what I had been through, eager to share my trauma, and through that joint burden to ease my suffering. But would she be so accommodating when she found out the reality? When she discovered not only that I had had to kill, but also the way I had done it? I wasn't sure and it scared me.

So after the initial euphoria of returning to my loved ones, the guilt and the worthlessness, the shame and the embarrassment soon returned. Being an older soldier I knew there were places I could go and get help – over the years I had advised other people to do the same – and yet when it came to it I didn't seek out that help for myself.

I had been a soldier for more than a quarter of a century. I had served in other conflict zones. I had been an RSM and was now a late-entry officer. I was supposedly mature enough and ugly enough to look after myself. PTSD? Not me. Call in the professionals? No way. Often I tried to speak to Margaret but could never really get to where I wanted to go, my nervousness of her opinion, her judgement of me, always blocking progress.

What if she saw in me a man completely at odds with the one she married? What if after all this time she decided the real me was not one she wanted to be around? What if telling her the truth about Afghanistan drove a wedge between us, rather than brought us together? As the days passed it became harder and harder to break down the barrier, but the trouble was I needed some sort of emotional outlet more than ever.

Nights were becoming an endless stream of battles. Time and again I found myself charging up and down the drainage ditches that dissected the landscape around Garmsir. As I ran I encountered countless bodies. Lifeless and bloody. They were dressed as Afghans. But it was when I looked into the faces of these people that the real horror surged through me. I recognised them. Not as people I had fought alongside but as my wife and children, my relatives and friends. The cycle of death would only be broken by Margaret shaking me awake, as I shouted out in my fitful sleep.

The strange thing was I didn't really mind this mental anguish. Just as all those years ago I had regarded the beatings I received during basic training as some sort of retribution for shooting Raymond and being a bad son, so now these nightmares I viewed as the price to be paid for surviving unscathed. For leaving Shahrukh dead on the battlefield. For walking away from Afghanistan when so many others had not, could not.

At the same time as I remembered my actions, I also tried to analyse them and in doing so I necessarily did what I feared my wife would do – I judged them and hence myself. Some say that soldiers are unthinking people, without conscience or care. My experience of others, certainly my knowledge of myself, is that the opposite is true. Everything I did in Afghanistan I laid open to scrutiny and I was not afraid of being critical. The truth is I went to Lashkar Gah because I wanted to. I could have stayed behind a desk at KAF, but I chose not to. The same with Garmsir. I happily accepted the challenge. I wanted the chance of some glory, the opportunity to take the fight to the enemy.

Time and again in Garmsir I had to react as incidents happened around me. There were no long periods of time to mull over things, to weigh up the pros and cons, to consider the ethical dimensions of the job. War does not allow for that. You are faced with split-second life-and-death decisions time and again, and you have to get on with it. React. React. React. Did I get everything right? Perhaps not. Did I break some rules? Probably yes. But at least I made my choices. In the heat of the battle, when I was consumed by fear, when all I wanted to do was turn away, I made my choices and I got the job done. But what I didn't know at the start of the operation, as we headed south through the desert, couldn't fully appreciate, was what the final cost of my ambition would be. On me. And on others.

It was an absolute miracle that no British soldier was killed. For all my impetuousness I was at least able to bring my colleagues out alive. Save for Joe and the wound to his arm, save for my bust nose and bent fingers, we had escaped physically unscathed. Not so the enemy I had wrought death on. Not so the Afghans who fought by my side. Many had died, doing what I had bid them do, Shahrukh amongst them. His death continued to hit me hard, far harder than I expected. He lost his life on my mission, leading my patrol. And I wasn't there to share the burden of authority. I had left the scene. Yet he had taken up the baton and kept going; as always, showing his men the way. As always, refusing to let Beattie down. Amidst the myriad images that haunted me, it was the face of Shahrukh that kept pushing its way to the fore.

A friend once told me that he found the easiest way of getting things off his chest was to write them down, and in doing so he also managed to make others aware of his fears and foibles.

With time on my hands and no sign of another way out of the grinding memories I tried it for myself. Mostly I wrote when I was alone and the house was empty. It was easy to conjure up the sights, sounds and smells of Afghanistan. I couldn't have forgotten them if I had wanted to. On numerous occasions Margaret asked if she could read what I had written, but I would find some excuse for not letting her. It was stupid, because the whole idea of writing had been to communicate. Instead I was now reliving Afghanistan both day and night and drifting further from my family. I had to break the cycle and I was running out of time. If I didn't show her something soon then the damage between us would be done anyway. At last I gave her a few pages to read – an account of my second day in Garmsir. I sat in silence and watched as she slowly, carefully leafed through the work. As she read, she started to cry, the realisation of what I had been asked to do and hence what I had done hitting home. I kept watching, looking for a reaction. Revulsion, anger, incomprehension, fear, disappointment. I waited for the incredulity. None came. When she reached the end her tears flowed more freely and we hugged. And I sighed with relief.

Over the next fortnight I wrote and wrote and wrote, and this time Margaret got to see every last word I committed to paper.

The more I remembered, the more saddened I became about the plight of the Afghans. This was not just my story and that of my British colleagues, it was also a testament to the native population with whom we fought. And they were paying a huge price; dying in their droves. Over the six months 3 PARA were in Afghanistan during 2006, the battlegroup lost some sixteen killed in action, and around thirty were seriously wounded. However during my time in Garmsir alone, at least twelve Afghans died and a further twenty-seven were injured. And yet these casualty figures were barely mentioned in the British media. I understood why. The UK public had a natural interest in 'our' boys. Many would have had relatives in the military or known someone who did. And the soldiers were there at the behest of our politicians so it was right those back home should know what they were doing – and what they were suffering – in the name of the British people. Yet to fully grasp what was going on, one also needed to be presented with the context of the war in Afghanistan. After all we were supposedly there to help the country. Yet is it a country worth saving? In fact is it a country at all? There are at least five different ethnic groups in Afghanistan and scores of tribes. More than thirty languages are spoken. Perhaps the only thing they have in common is their Muslim religion.

Few of the Afghans I met felt any great allegiance to the Kabul government of President Hamid Karzai. Not many had any great love for democracy. What they were fighting for were loyalties and obligations on a much smaller scale. It was about the family, the village, the tribe. People they knew and respected. In that sense they were actually not much different from me. In Afghanistan I wasn't really fighting for Queen and country. I was there for my regiment, for my colleagues, for my friends. And increasingly, despite the difficulties and general wariness, some of the Afghans had become my friends. Perhaps that was why I found it so hard to put them out of my mind. Perhaps I felt we Brits had an obligation. We had started the job and now we needed to finish it.

*

Margaret and I showed our invitation and identification to the policeman on duty at the gate and were quickly ushered through.

Side by side we strolled across the forecourt towards the building, the gravel scrunching under our feet as we went. We stared up at the magnificent façade, the imposing stonework, row upon row of windows, and the Union flag flying from the flagpole.

Buckingham Palace looked magnificent.

I smiled at Margaret and we went inside. It was as grand as I could ever have imagined. The high painted ceilings, the portraits on the walls, the luxurious carpets, gold seemingly everywhere. I'm sure my jaw must have dropped. I know Margaret's did.

It was time to go our separate ways. My wife was shown through to the hall where the ceremony would take place. I was directed to a waiting area where many of the others also to be decorated that day, early in March 2007, had already congregated. There would be ninety of us in total. Most of those around me were civilians. One or two I thought I recognised – were they celebrities? – the majority I did not. I looked around wondering what they had done to warrant being there. For the umpteenth time I asked what I had done. Of the small group of military personnel I was the only one getting an award for work in Helmand, though a second officer from the Royal Irish would be getting an MBE for his time spent in Kabul. I was told I would be in the last group of five to be presented with their awards.

An aide ran through the protocol for the event. How we should approach, how we should greet, how we should speak to . . . the Queen. The Queen! This was not what I had expected. I remembered that Colonel Collins had received his OBE from Prince Charles, so all along I had been expecting some more minor royal to officiate here. But Her Majesty. I could not have been more humbled, yet the whole sense of experience and honour was at odds with that old emotional companion of mine, guilt. Guilt that, despite the writing, despite the passing of time, would not leave me alone. I wanted to be excited about the day, but guilt was doing its best not to let me, constantly reminding me that I had left dead friends and colleagues on the fields, plains and mountains of southern Afghanistan.

Finally it was my turn. I moved to the final holding area and on a nod started to walk forwards, across the ballroom, towards the Queen. At last my thoughts of Afghanistan were banished – by Rowan Atkinson. The closer I got to her the more I thought about the sketch in which his character Mr Bean meets the Queen and bows, only to head-butt her and knock her out. Where do these most abstract of thoughts come from? I didn't really care. It had lightened my mood and made me smile and that was no bad thing.

I stopped and looked at our sovereign. She was absolutely immaculate. She had a formal dress and jacket on, topped off with a large rimmed hat. She was as small as I had imagined, and slightly plump, but this suited her down to a T. Her face didn't hide her age, yet it was without real blemish. She had the sort of expression you might expect from your grandmother, warm and reassuring.

Quickly and without fuss she pinned the Military Cross on my chest before congratulating me and asking me about my time in Afghanistan. She seemed amazingly well briefed. She wanted to know about my impression of the country, what it was like working side by side with the Afghans, how I had found the culture, and whether it was a difficult job. Given my nervousness I am sure my answers did little to enlighten her.

Then Her Majesty looked me straight in the eye. 'So,' she said. 'Just what did your wife think when she found out you weren't sitting behind a desk in Kandahar?'

Good question, Ma'am. Bloody good question.

She took my hand and from that I knew it was my cue to leave. We had only talked for three minutes, perhaps four at the outside, but it felt as if she spent more time with me than with anyone else. Of course she hadn't.

I stepped back, still facing her, before I bowed, without incident, turned to my left and walked out of the hall. Immediately my medal was taken away, put into a box and then returned to me. I went off to have my photo taken.

I had made up my mind and this time it was final. In July 2007 I would leave the army. I had done my bit. They had got all they were going to get out of Doug Beattie and now I was going to devote myself to Margaret. After all those years of marriage I determined to put her and the children first. I also hoped leaving would offer me an escape route from the past. I started to go on courses to help my transition to civvy street. Margaret and I made plans for our future. And for the first time in many weeks I began to look forwards, and not back to my experiences in Afghanistan.

Things were looking up. But then in early spring I heard the news. 1 R IRISH had been warned off about another deployment in March of the following year – the regiment was going back to Afghanistan. My heart sank, but I remained resolute. I thought I could manage to avoid all of the preparation and emotion associated with the announcement. I was based at the Infantry Training Centre (ITC) in Catterick in North Yorkshire. The rest of the battalion was in Inverness and from there they would be going to Ternhill in Shropshire. Our paths wouldn't cross. There was no chance of being reunited before I finally handed in my weapon.

Except fate conspired otherwise.

Early in June I received word that the CO, Lt-Col Mike McGovern, would be visiting the ITC within the month, and as part of the trip he wanted to see me.

The day arrived and I walked into the office he was using and sat down in front of him. At his shoulder was the current RSM, John Millar.

The Colonel congratulated me on my MC and then came to the point. 'Would you be willing to stay on for an extra eighteen months to help train the battalion for deployment?'

'Does that mean I will then deploy with the rest of the guys?' I asked.

'You will.'

I glanced at John and then focused on the Colonel again.

'Of course I will stay on, sir.'

I could have hesitated, could have asked for time to think about it, could just have said no. But I didn't have any choice in my answer. What was I supposed to say? Young men – some not much more than boys – in my regiment were about to go to Afghanistan and face heaven knows what. Young men, many of whom I knew, some of whom I hoped looked up to me and respected me. How could I let them go without me? How could I sit at home as a civilian and watch their progress on the news, perhaps hearing of the battalion taking casualties, thinking that maybe had I been there I might have been able to do something to help? How then would I ever live with myself?

And there was something more. Although I had done my bit for the army over all those years, it had also done its bit for me. It had looked after me, supported me, paid me, motivated me, given me a career and a vocation. The regiment had taken me in and made something of my life. I owed it. It was a question of loyalty. Anyway, what on earth would I do if I left? I wasn't trained for anything else. I wasn't suited to 'normal' life. Who would employ someone like me? Soldiering was what I did and what I knew. It was in my blood. I had always been a soldier, plain and simple. No more, no less. A soldier. An ordinary soldier.

I stood up and left the room. There was something I had to tell Margaret.

CITATION

CAPT D. R. BEATTIE MC, ROYAL IRISH REGIMENT

Captain Beattie commissioned into the Royal Irish Regiment on 29 April 2005, having previously served as Regimental Sergeant Major of his 1st Battalion. He was posted to Afghanistan on 24 July 2006 as the Operations Officer in the embryonic Joint Security Co-ordination Centre, working closely with Afghan national Security Forces in Lashkar Gah. His overall exemplary performance has been cited separately.

On 10 September 2006 Captain Beattie volunteered to be a Liaison Officer with seventy Afghan National Police (ANP), part of a larger Afghan/ISAF force to recapture the town of Garmsir from the Taliban – a vital role. Heavy fighting began on 11 September with an assault on a canal bridge and it soon became apparent that whilst individual policemen were prepared to fight, they lacked leadership, training and organisation. Under pressure, committed to the fight and temporarily stalled, the police looked to Captain Beattie for help. There was no option for him but to take responsibility and, through an interpreter, he set about reorganising, teaching assaulting skills and conducting house clearances on the job, by personal example and under fire. For the next ten days his inspiration and example gave moral and physical resolve to the Afghans and was absolutely key to the eventual success of the operation. From 11th to 23rd September, Captain Beattie was in close combat and under heavy fire every day. In the initial phase he personally led the fight and guided police in an advance over 1.5 kilometres, outflanking Taliban positions and unhinging their defences. He helped clear compounds and houses, often on his own, and seized the District Centre. He then organised the town defences against enemy counter-attack.

Captain Beattie committed many acts of bravery on this operation that were witnessed by the Chief of Police, two British Officers and a British journalist, but one occasion stands apart. On 18th September he led a joint Afghan Army and Afghan Police patrol to reinforce exposed police checkpoints under enemy fire. The patrol was ambushed by Taliban who allowed the leading vehicles to pass through the killing zone before springing the ambush on Captain Beattie's two vehicles – his own vehicle taking several direct hits. He immediately fought back with his commander's machine gun and began extraction drills. The second vehicle in his patrol became bogged in and Captain Beattie stopped under heavy fire to hitch it up so it could be towed out of danger. At the same time he continued to suppress the enemy with his weapons and called for close air support. The enemy being just 100 metres away, he had to call in a series of extremely close air support strikes on Taliban positions. This gave the Afghans a chance to regain the initiative and drive the Taliban away.

Captain Beattie's conduct throughout this twelve-day operation was above and beyond the call of duty. His role was to pass information, not to fight. But in order for the mission to succeed, he calculated seizing of the initiative was essential. Throughout the action he placed himself selflessly in positions of extreme danger and how his clear-thinking and robust leadership inspired an Afghan success is exemplified in his calm extraction of a vehicle and crew under enemy fire. His outstanding courage, leadership and selfless action under constant enemy fire turned the tide of events in Garmsir. He is deserving of the highest recognition.

Doug Beattie was awarded the Military Cross in December 2006.

[illegible]

[illegible] operations [illegible]

[illegible] Security and Assist[illegible]

organization for [illegible]

[illegible] was [illegible] in [illegible]

Taliban were ousted from power [illegible]

[illegible] not [illegible]

GLOSSARY

AH	Attack Helicopters – US-designed AH-64 Apaches.
AK47	Soviet-designed 7.62mm–calibre assault rifle. Over 100 million have been manufactured. Cheap, robust and simple to use.
ANA	Afghan National Army
ANP	Afghan National Police
BDA	Bomb Damage Assessment
CQMS	Company Quartermaster-Sergeant
EOD	Explosive Ordnance Disposal
GPMG	General Purpose Machine Gun. 7.62mm-calibre machine gun that can be used on a bipod, tripod or else mounted on a vehicle or in an aircraft. Rate of fire: 750 rounds per minute.
HE	High Explosive
IRT	Incident Response Team, the group of medics and soldiers on constant standby at Camp Bastion to carry out medical evacuations across Helmand Province.
ISAF	International Security and Assistance Force. The umbrella organisation for international intervention in Afghanistan, it was created in December 2001 after the Taliban were ousted from power by Operation Enduring Freedom. It is not a United Nations force but is deployed under the authority of a UN Security Council mandate. Since August 2003 ISAF has been led by NATO.

JTAC	Joint Tactical Air Controller. JTACs manage the movement of aircraft within their areas of responsibility. This responsibility ranges from the safe movement of helicopters delivering supplies, through surveillance operations, to calling for, or clearing the use of, air-delivered munitions in support of ground forces.
KAF	Kandahar Airfield
NDS	National Directorate of Security. Afghanistan's internal security service.
OMLT	Operational Mentoring and Liaison Team. Made up of British soldiers, the OMLT helps train the Afghan Army and supports them on missions.
PEP	Poppy Eradication Programme
PRR	Personal Role Radio. Range: 500 metres.
PRT	Provincial Reconstruction Team. PRTs are part of the ISAF mission in Afghanistan and are a combination of international military and civilian personnel based in provincial areas of the country, extending the authority of the Afghan government, supporting reform of the security sector, and facilitating development and reconstruction.
PSCC	Provincial Security and Co-ordination Centre. Established to bring together the ANA, ANP and NDS on matters of joint working. I was there to mentor representatives of each and show how they could operate together.
QRF	Quick Reaction Force. Its members either work as a single unit responding to security incidents or as part of the IRT where they have the job of securing the Helicopter Landing Zone when an aircraft is sent to extract battlefield casualties.
SA80	The British Army's standard individual rifle. 5.56mm–calibre.
TacSat	Tactical Satellite communications equipment. Sam

New used this radio equipment to speak directly to the pilots sent to help us.

TiC — Troops in Contact – a situation where British troops are under fire from the enemy.

WMIK — A Land Rover fitted with a Weapons Mount Installation Kit that allows it to become a platform for a variety of armaments. In Garmsir my WMIK was equipped with a .50-calibre heavy machine gun and GPMG.

PICTURE CREDITS

Courtesy of the author: 1, 2, 3, 4, 8, 11, 12, 16, 17, 18, 19, 24, 26, 27, 29, 30, 31, 34
© British Crown Copyright/MoD. Reproduced with the permission of the Controller of Her Majesty's Stationery Office: 5, 6, 7
Corbis: 9, 33
© Philip Gomm: 10, 14, 15
Rex Features: 13
© Tim Illingworth: 20
© Sean Langan: 21, 23, 25, 32
© Jay Frost: 22
© ITV: 28

INDEX

(The initials DB in subentries stand for Doug Beattie. Digits beginning names are indexed as if spelled out.)

Afghan National Army (ANA), 7, 69, 84, 92, 94, 96–7, 102–5, 112, 126, 127, 132, 133, 134–5, 144–5, 149, 151, 155–7, 160–1, 163, 178, 193, 194–5, 197, 208, 210, 212, 213–20, 230, 232–3, 235, 244, 272, 275, 282–3, 279–82 *passim*, 284, 288
  ANP's deteriorating relationship with, 287
  DB's distrust of, 218
  death of commander of, 161, 163, 214–16, 217
  relief mission to southern outpost of, 230–3, 235–43, 260–70, 275–7
  RPG accident kills members of, 215–17
  partial pull-out of, 219, 222
Afghan National Police (ANP), 7, 69, 77–9, *passim*, 80–2, 84, 87, 88–107 *passim*, 109, 110–11, 112, 114, 116–27 *passim*, 131–3 *passim*, 135, 136, 141, 144–6, 148, 151, 154–5, 157, 160, 163, 164, 178, 179, 185, 186, 191–6 *passim*, 201–2, 204, 205, 207, 210–16, 218–19, 230, 235, 249, 275–6, 283
  ANA's deteriorating relationship with, 287
  casualties among, 213–14, 216
  Danes treat wounded member of, 272
  drug-taking among, 223, 224
  OMLT's distrust of, 288
  operational details passed to Taliban by, 233
  Taliban ambush and, 237, 243
Afghanistan:
  Afghan TV news in, 224
  bloody history of, 71
  British Helmand Task Force in, 74, 194
  Camp Bastion in, 14, 74, 76, 165*n*, 274, 288
  'chai boys' (rent boys) in, 137
  DB's post-tour thoughts on, 297
  Development Zone in, 75
  Garmsir in, *see main entry*
  Gereshk in, 111, 194
  Helmand Province of, *see main entry*
  Helmand River in, 86, 101, 110, 111, 175, 202, 224, 235, 255
  Hindu Kush in, 80
  Incident Response Team (IRT) in, 165, 173, 273
  International Security and Assistance Force (ISAF) in, 7, 74, 79, 159, 170, 177, 194, 219, 251, 271
  JTAC Hill in, 112, 131, 134, 140, 163, 170, 193, 217, 220, 224–5, 232, 235, 243, 270, 272, 275, 277, 281, 287
  Jugroom in, 159, 212, 225, 232–3, 249, 256, 263, 277
  Kabul in, 74, 224
  Kajaki in, 75, 163
  Kandahar airfield (KAF), 74–5, 79, 140, 164, 179, 195, 197, 202–3, 218, 250–2, 273, 284

Afghanistan – *continued*
Kandahar in, 71, 74
Lashkar Gah in, *see main entry*
Musa Qala in, 163, 259
National Army (ANA) in, *see* Afghan National Army
National Directorate of Security (NDS) in, 7, 9, 165*n*
National Police (ANP) in, *see* Afghan National Police
nations contributing manpower to, 74
Now Zad in, 75, 163, 194
Operational Mentoring and Liaison Team (OMLT) in, 79, 84, 88, 112, 136, 141, 145, 160, 162–3, 164, 168, 171, 179, 180, 195, 197, 216–19 *passim*, 222, 226, 274–5, 277–80 *passim*, 284, 287
Poppy Eradication Programme (PEP) in, 8
Provincial Reconstruction Team (PRT) in, 6, 8, 11, 70, 75, 168
Provincial Security and Co-ordination Centre (PSCC) in, 75, 77, 226
Psychological Operations team in, 176
Sangin in, 75, 194, 233
Soviet Invasion of, 71, 230
Taliban in, *see main entry*
Al Medina, 55, 66, 67
Alexander the Great, 111
al-Qaeda, 71, 83
Atkinson, Rowan, 299

Beattie, Donna (sister), 26–7
Beattie, Doug:
in Afghanistan, 1–16, 69–73, 74–197, 199–233, 235–92
Afghanistan left by, 293
air-strike decision of, 202–3
army joined by, 19, 28–9
attitude towards subordinates of, 221
battalion joined by, 35–6
in Berlin, 35–41
birth of, 20
body armour of, described, 167–8
at Buckingham Palace, 298–300
casualty evacuation of, 291–2
commission of, 73, 74
decision to leave army taken by, 227, 300
dislocated fingers of, 290
early life of, 20–9
experiences recorded by, 296–7
first army award of, 35
first kill of, 98–9
friend shot by, 18, 295
Garmsir departure of, 286–7
Garmsir operation and, 85–197, 199–220
in Garmsir post OMLT pull-out, 221–33, 235–86
Garmsir return of, 287–92
Hess guarded by, 39–41
initial army training of, 31–5
in Iraq, 55, 56–68
Langan interviews, 182
manpower worries of, 202
Military Cross awarded to, 12–13, 299–300
Military Cross citation of, 303–5
McGovern offers training role to, 301
mines fear of, 230
in North America, 47
nose injury to, 290
passing-out of, 35
return attack led by, 289
promotion ladder of, 47, 73
Queen's Commendation for Bravery awarded to, 59*n*
recruitment post of, 51–3
relief mission to ANA southern outpost led by, 230–3, 235–43, 260–70, 275–7
rogue bomb and, 253–5
Sandhurst post offered to, 50
Shahrukh's death's effects on, 291–2, 295, 296
on southern crossing mission, 289–90
Taliban ambush, 236–43
training instructor's post of, 56, 73
wall collapse and, 289–90
Beattie, Edwina (sister), 25
Beattie, Eve (mother), 20–1, 24
terminal illness and death of, 25–7
Beattie, Leigh (daughter), 45–6, 227
DB's sense of duty towards, 188
Beattie, Luke (son), 47, 227
DB's sense of duty towards, 188
Beattie, Margaret (wife), 13, 45–9, 142, 227, 296
at Buckingham Palace, 298

DB's return to, 293–4
DB's sense of duty towards, 188
Queen's questions about, 299
Beattie, Rab (brother), 20, 25, 27
at DB's passing-out parade, 35
platoon of, 37
Beattie, Steve (brother), 20, 25, 27, 36
platoon of, 37
Beattie, Tanya (sister), 25
Beattie, William (father), 19, 20–1, 24–9, 34
absence of, from DB's passing-out parade, 35
DB's sense of duty towards, 188
drinking of, 27–8
in Ulster Defence Regiment (UDR), 17, 25
Bennett, Charles, 7
Berlin, 35–6
Wall, 36
Wavell Barracks in, 36
Best, Raymond, 15, 17–19
DB shoots, 18, 295
Bin Laden, Osama, 71
Black, Ranger, 44
body armour:
described, 167–8
unpopularity of, 168
British Helmand Task Force, 74, 194
Butler, Brigadier Ed, 12

Camp Bastion, 14, 74, 76, 165*n*, 274, 288
'chai boys' (rent boys), 137
Chambers, Steve:
ammunition shortage of, 207, 208
departures of, 222, 256
Garmsir operation and, 88, 100, 118, 128, 146–7, 168, 184, 186, 187, 190, 191, 195, 210, 213
in Garmsir post OMLT pull-out, 228–9
Garmsir return of, 228–9
Charles, Prince, 298
Checkpoint Charlie, 36
Chilli, 2, 5, 10
DB's sense of paternalism towards, 6
Claus (Estonian captain), 163, 178, 179, 250–2, 257
Cold War, 35, 36, 89
Collins, Colonel Tim, 49–50, 65, 67–8, 83*n*, 175
'American Tourist' sobriquet of, 66–7, 83*n*
eve-of-war address of, 59–63
OBE awarded to, 298
recruitment policy of, 51–3
Cowley, Corporal Tony, 93–4, 104, 140, 154, 162, 164, 165, 173, 175, 216
Cummings, Sergeant-Major Joe, 69, 79, 81–2, 295
Garmsir recapture and, 88, 89, 100, 111, 112, 118, 119, 125, 128, 136, 172
injury to, 153–4, 160, 165, 190

Daoud, Mohammed, 77, 79
Darveshan, *see* Garmsir: Darveshan name of
Davidson, Sergeant-Major Chipper:
ammunition shortage of, 207, 208
departure of, 222
Garmsir recapture and, 88, 89, 93, 94, 96, 97, 100, 109, 112, 116, 118, 121, 125, 128, 134, 136, 144, 146, 156, 157, 162–3, 180–1, 184, 187, 189, 191, 192, 195, 204, 210
Dispatches: 'Fighting the Taliban' (Langan), 227*n*
Draiva, Ranger Anare, 14
Durani, General, 69, 82–3, 87, 93, 102–9 passim, 111, 119–20, 125–6, 132, 133, 135, 137, 138, 157, 159, 176–7, 196
Gulzar's complaints against, 229
ruthlessness reputation of, 275

Elgie, Michael ('Geordie'):
departure of, 222
Garmsir recapture and, 88, 125, 128, 156, 162, 180, 183–7 *passim*, 193, 195
Elizabeth II, Queen, 298–300
Entebbe, 52
Exercise Rocking Horse, 37–8

firefly strobe, 280
Foreign and Commonwealth Office (FCO), 8–9
Frost, Lieutenant Jay, 229, 235–7, 239–42 *passim*, 244

Garmsir, 12–13, 15, 71, 78–81, 82
Afghan TV coverage of recapture of, 224
agricultural college in, 179
bakery in, 178
Danes arrive in, 256, 258
Darveshan name of, 115
DB awarded Military Cross for operation in, 12–13
DB's group leaves, 286–7
disparate nature of British troops in, 200
42 northing in, 112, 131, 136, 149, 159, 192, 193, 195, 201, 209, 211, 244
Illingworth awarded Conspicuous Gallantry Cross for operation in, 161*n*
liberation operation in, 85–197, 199–220
mission's primary aim achieved in, 194
mosque in, 170
new OMLT relief arrives in, 280–2
north-eastern fringes of, 86
post OMLT pull-out defence of, 221–33, 235–87, 288–92
OMLT pull-out order and, 218–21
shabby, ramshackle nature of, 110
Taliban's gateway, 13
Taliban overrun, 71
Taliban take southern crossing in, 282–3
see also Afghan National Army (ANA); Afghan National Police (ANP); Taliban
Gereshk, 111, 194
Glorious Twelfth, 22
Gulzar, Colonel, 87, 90, 92, 103, 104, 107, 108, 120, 125–6, 127, 132, 133, 135, 137, 138, 148, 157, 159, 164, 174, 176–7, 186, 188–9, 191, 192, 196–7, 201, 205–6, 210, 211, 212–15, 227–8, 243, 245–6, 250, 256, 282, 285, 291
ANP casualties and, 216–17, 230
complaints by, 229–30
Danish medical equipment admired by, 259
DB's dislike of, 230
OMLT's distrust of, 288
pull-out order and, 218–19, 220
Taliban intelligence of, 205
vehicle request to, 272–3
withdrawal threat of, 287

Hamilton, Duke of, 40
Helmand Province, 1, 6, 13–14, 72, 137, 101, 194
DB leaves, 293
memorial in, 14
Poppy Eradication Programme (PEP) in, 8
provincial tribal council in, 79
tourist department in, 111
Helmand River, 86, 101, 110, 111, 175, 202, 224, 235, 255
HESCOs, 178, 180, 224
Hess, Rudolph, 39–41
Hindu Kush, 80
Hitler, Adolf, 40
Household Cavalry, 66, 83, 279
Howes, Corporal Derek, 56

Illingworth, Lieutenant/Acting Captain Tim, 71
Conspicuous Gallantry Cross awarded to, 161*n*
departure of, 222
Garmsir recapture and, 79, 87, 88, 94, 97, 102–5 *passim*, 112, 149, 152, 155–7, 160–2, 163–4, 193, 195, 197, 202, 214, 217
improvised explosive devices (IEDs), 134, 135–6, 250–1
Incident Response Team (IRT), 165, 173, 273
Infantry Training Centre (ITC), 300
Intelligence Corps, 172
International Security and Assistance Force (ISAF), 7, 74, 79, 159, 170, 177, 194, 219, 251, 271
Iraq:
Al Medina in, 55, 66, 67
Basra in, 66
gas and oil separation plants (GOSPs) in, 63, 65
Op Telic in, 174
Royal Irish Regiment, 1st Battalion, in, 55, 56–68
War, 55, 59–68
see also Beattie, Doug: in Iraq

Irish Guards, 51, 75
Irish Republican Army (IRA), 24, 43, 56

James II, King, 22
John (teenage friend), 17
Johnstone, Sergeant-Major Tommy, 98, 134, 201, 205, 206–8, 209–11 *passim*, 212, 213
  mentioned in dispatches, 286*n*
Joint Helicopter Command (JHC), 51
Joint Tactical Air Controllers (JTACs), 90, 102, 277
  short supply of, 226
JTAC Hill, 112, 131, 134, 140, 163, 170, 193, 217, 220, 224–5, 232, 235, 243, 270, 272, 275, 277, 281, 287
Junior Leaders Battalion, 25
Junior Soldiers Battalion (JSB), 31
  award given by, 35

Kabul, 74, 224
Kajaki, 75, 163
Kandahar airfield (KAF), 74–5, 79, 140, 164, 179, 195, 197, 202–3, 218, 250–2, 273, 284
Kandahar, 71, 74
Karzai, Hamid, 72, 297
King's Own Scottish Borderers, 43
Knaggs, Colonel Charlie, 70, 72, 75, 79, 168, 287

Langan, Sean, 70, 101, 140, 173, 181–2, 209, 213, 216, 219, 227*n*
  DB interviewed by, 182
Lashkar Gah, 1, 7, 79, 168, 179, 226, 229, 287
  DB chooses to work in, 75
  British fatalities in, 9
Londonderry Air Show, 52–3

McConnell, 'Legs', 36
McCulloch, Lance-Corporal Luke, 14
McGovern, Lieutenant-Colonel Mike, 300–1
McNair, Sergeant Jim ('Swayze'), 58
McWilliams, Lance-Corporal Scone, 35–6
Mail on Sunday, 60
Maureen (Portadown neighbour), 26
Mein Kampf (Hitler), 40
Middleton, Captain Dave, 52
Millar, Regimental Sergeant-Major John, 300–1
Muirhead, Lance Corporal Paul, 14
Musa Qala, 163, 259

Namir (interpreter), 5, 77, 111
  DB's sense of paternalism towards, 6
National Directorate of Security (NDS), 7, 9, 165*n*
Neill, Joseph, 22
New, Bombardier Sam, 69
  ANA outpost relief operation and, 260, 261, 263–4, 266–9, 275–7
  Garmsir operation and, 79, 85, 89–90, 92–4 *passim*, 96, 100, 106, 108, 111, 112, 113, 114–17, 119, 120–1, 126, 127, 128, 132–4, 135, 136, 144, 147–56 *passim*, 158–9, 163, 179, 181, 186–7, 189–92, 201–10 *passim*, 212, 213, 219
  in Garmsir post OMLT pull-out, 221, 223, 225–6, 228, 232, 238, 240, 242, 249, 254–8 *passim*, 277–9, 280, 282, 283, 286, 288–90 *passim*
  hornets attack, 268–9
  imminent end of tour of, 226
  rogue bomb and, 254–5
  on southern crossing mission, 289, 290
  unrecognised for Garmsir conduct, 286*n*
Nick (KAF contact), 179
Niven, Air Vice-Marshall, 51
Northern Ireland Training Wing, 56
Norton Manor Camp, 31
Now Zad, 75, 163, 194

Oliver, Sarah, 60, 61
Omar, Mullah, 71
'Op Deny' strategy, 239
Operational Mentoring and Liaison Team (OMLT), 79, 84, 88, 112, 136, 141, 145, 160, 162–3, 164, 168, 171, 179, 180, 195, 197, 216–19 *passim*, 222, 226, 274–5, 277–80 *passim*, 284, 287
Orange Order, 22

Pakistan, 71
Parachute Regiment, 84

Pashtuns, 71
Pathfinders, 86, 89, 179, 219
Patten, Captain David, 14
phosphorous grenades, 105
Poppy Eradication Programme (PEP), 8
Portadown, 21–9
  Burke's Bar in, 23–4
  explosion in, 23
'Potter, Harry', 258, 260, 274, 286
Pritchard, RSM Jim, 50
Provincial Security and Co-ordination Centre (PSCC), 75, 77, 226

Quick Reaction Force (QRF), 5, 292

Rachel (in FCO) group, 8–9
recoilless rifle (RCL), 248–9
regimental wives' club, 48–9
Reid, John, 100
Relief in Place (RIP), 274
Royal Irish Rangers, 2nd Battalion of, 35
Royal Irish Regiment, 1st Battalion ('1 R IRISH') of:
  Collins joins, 49
  Collins's eve-of-war address to, 59–63
  further Afghanistan tour for, 300
  in Iraq, 55, 56–68
  Mike Company of, 58, 66
  prisoner-holding pen organised by, 63
  recruitment for, 51
Royal Logistics Corps, 121, 229
Russell, Major Robin, 43, 44

Saddam Hussein, 55
Sam (uncle), 24
Sangin, 75, 194, 233
Shahrukh, Major, 111, 114, 117, 120, 122–3, 125–6, 136, 137, 138–9, 145, 148, 151, 154, 157, 158, 185, 192, 196–7, 201, 204, 209, 213–14, 269–70, 285
  background of, 196
  DB's trust in and admiration for, 233, 285, 291
  death of, 291, 295, 296
  injured bodyguard of, 291, 292
  on southern crossing mission, 289–90
  Taliban alliance of, 196
  TV crew and, 223–4
Sharia law, 72, 138
Simon (battery commander), 228–30, 233, 244, 245–6, 256
16 Air Assault Brigade 12, 229, 274
  in Afghanistan, 14, 69–73, 74–197, 199–233, 235–92
  Garmsir liberation and defence operations by members of, 85–197, 199–220, 221–33, 235–87, 288–92
  Helmand-wide presence of, 194
  3 PARA battlegroup in Helmand as part of, 79, 230*n*, 292, 293, 297
  town-centre bases manned by men of, 163, 194
Spandau Prison, 39, 40–1
Special Air Service (SAS), 84
Stocker, Major Al, 70, 179
Susan (mother-in-law), 45, 46

TacSat, 90, 119, 156, 191, 201
Taliban, 8, 13, 70, 71–2, 77, 78, 80, 82–4, 87–135 *passim*, 138–9, 144–59 *passim*, 163–4, 168, 173, 176–8, 182, 183–97 *passim*, 202–19, 224, 225, 230–2 *passim*, 244–57, 263–71, 275–6, 278, 281–4
  ambush by, 236–43
  Jugroom stronghold of, 159, 212, 225, 232–3, 249, 256, 263, 277
  killing of local commanders of, 106, 138, 256
  plan to take southern crossing from, 289–90
  recoilless technology acquired by, 248–9
  reinforcements to, 159, 164, 205, 250
  southern crossing taken by, 282–3
Territorial Army (TA), 121, 172, 200
Thatcher, Margaret, 43–5
3 Commando Brigade 12, 274
Tommy (uncle), 24
21 Air Defence Battery, Royal Artillery, 7, 219, 222–3, 226, 227, 228–30, 256–7, 277
Twin Towers, New York, 83

Ulster Defence Regiment (UDR), 8, 17

Vashir District, 10
Vietnam War, 150

Wavell Barracks, 36
Weapons Mount Installation Kit Land Rovers (WMIKs), 69, 81, 89, 93, 96, 152, 181, 195, 200, 285–6
William of Orange, 22
Williams, Captain Paddy, 69, 70, 79, 287
  Afghanistan tenure of, 226
  background and appearance of, 83
  Garmsir base moved by, 159–60
  Garmsir departure of, 286–7
  Garmsir operation and, 86–9 *passim*, 92, 93–7, 100, 102–3, 108, 109, 111–12, 114, 115, 120, 125–7 *passim*, 131, 133, 134, 135, 141, 145, 149, 152, 154, 163–5, 168, 170–3 *passim*, 176–9, 180–1, 186, 193, 194–5, 197, 202, 208, 212
  in Garmsir post OMLT pull-out, 221, 225, 228, 229, 238, 239, 244, 245–6, 249–51, 256–60 *passim*, 270, 272–3, 274–5, 277–8, 279–82 *passim*, 284
  Military Cross awarded to, 286*n*
  OMLT pull-out order relayed by, 218, 219
  rogue bomb and, 254
  support worries of, 195
  wounded Taliban fighter and, 140
Wood, Corporal David, 56
Wright, Royal Marine Gary, 9
Wright, Corporal Mark, 230*n*

Yasir (interpreter), 81–2, 90–1, 92, 100, 102, 111, 122, 145, 153, 158, 188–9, 206, 213, 217, 224, 228, 231
  ammunition duties of, 249
  departure of, 256, 257
  effects of carnage on, 216

Zemar (interpreter), 229, 258, 260–2 *passim*, 269, 275, 279, 282, 285, 286